High-Stakes Reform

Titles in the Series

High-Stakes Reform

The Politics of Educational Accountability

Kathryn A. McDermott

Georgetown University Press/Washington, DC

Library of Congress Cataloging-in-Publication Data

McDermott, Kathryn A., 1969–
   High-stakes reform : the politics of educational accountability / Kathryn A.
McDermott.
      p. cm. — (Public management and change series)
   Includes bibliographical references and index.
   ISBN 978-1-58901-767-2 (pbk. : alk. paper)
   1. Educational accountability—United States—States—Case studies.
2. School improvement programs—United States—States—Evaluation—
Case studies. 3. Educational accountability—Connecticut. 4. Educational
accountability—Massachusetts. 5. Educational accountability—New Jersey.
6. Education—Standards—Connecticut. 7. Education—Standards—
Massachusetts. 8. Education—Standards—New Jersey. I. Title.
LB2806.22.M38 2011
379.1'58973—dc22

                                                                    2010043162

18 17 16 15 14 13 12 11   9 8 7 6 5 4 3 2
First printing

Printed in the United States of America

For Mark, Charlotte, and James

Contents

List of Illustrations

Figures

Tables

Acknowledgments

This book and my third-grade son are approximately the same age, since James was born shortly after I sent my research proposal and application materials to the Advanced Studies Fellowship Program at Brown University. The program's faculty and staff and the group of fellows all helped shape this project and provided a wonderful source of moral support. Thanks to Marguerite Clarke, Elizabeth DeBray, Kim Freeman, David Gamson, Nora Gordon, Chris Lubienski, Adam Nelson, Doug Reed, Beth Rose, John Modell, and Wendy Schiller, and especially to Mimi Coughlin, Alyssa Lodewick, and Carl Kaestle for bringing us all together. Beth Rose and two anonymous reviewers for Georgetown University Press deserve special thanks for reading and commenting on a draft of the entire manuscript, a task whose difficulty I appreciated only after I reread it myself. Peg Goertz, Craig Thomas, and my father, John McDermott, read parts of the manuscript. [Patrick McGuinn helped me get up to date in New Jersey.] I particularly appreciate Dad's willingness to write marginal comments like "huh?" where they were most needed. Beryl Radin has been a wonderful editor, generous with both encouragement and constructive criticism, and patient when other commitments kept me from writing as fast as we both wanted me to. Thanks also to Don Jacobs at Georgetown University Press for bearing with me through several changes of deadline.

My colleagues and students in both the School of Education and the Center for Public Policy and Administration have been a constant source of intellectual stimulation and friendship. Discussions with students in various sections of "Education and Public Policy" and "Theories of Educational Equity" sharpened my thinking in ways that improved this book. Staff members at the University of Massachusetts' W. E. B. DuBois Library, the Massachusetts State Library, the Suffolk University Law Library, the New England School of Law Library, and numerous other states' libraries and education departments assisted in tracking down documents and locating enactment dates and texts of policies. Karen Addesso, Bernice Clark, Mike Hamel,

Lisa Hilt, Kathy Naito, Alanna Nelson, and Michelle Sagan Gonçalves provided research assistance. Josh Geyer and Clare Marks get special thanks for appearing at the very end of the process and helping turn a large pile of paper and electronic references into an actual bibliography. Sue Overstreet and Robbie Calliham cheerfully coped with my requests for clerical help. I'm especially grateful to the friendly people of Rao's in downtown Amherst, who make magic coffee that dissolves writers' block, and who don't mind when people use their café as an office. On a different note, there is no good time to confront a serious illness in one's family, but when a frightening diagnosis collides with the last month of work on a book, the challenges are compounded. Words cannot express my gratitude to everybody who made the summer of 2010 less awful by providing food, distracting the kids, and being there for us.

I gratefully acknowledge financial support for this project, through the Advanced Fellowship Studies Program, from The Spencer Foundation and the William and Flora Hewlett Foundation. The data presented, the statements made, and the views expressed (especially any that are in error) are solely my responsibility. I also received support from a University of Massachusetts Faculty Research Grant and from the Center for Public Policy and Administration at the University of Massachusetts, Amherst. Portions of this research were presented at meetings of the Advanced Studies Fellowship Program at Brown University, the 2005 and 2006 annual meetings of the American Educational Research Association, the 2006 annual meeting of the American Political Science Association, the 2006 Policy History Conference, and the *Clio at the Table* conference at Brown University. I first developed the argument that evolved into this book in "'Expanding the Moral Community' or 'Blaming the Victim?' The Politics of State Accountability Policy," *American Educational Research Journal* 44, no. 1 (2007). An earlier version of the analysis of state legislation presented in chapter 4 was published in *Clio at the Table*, edited by Kenneth Wong and Robert Rothman (Peter Lang Publishing, 2009). Earlier versions of the Connecticut and Massachusetts case studies appeared as a chapter in *To Educate a Nation*, edited by Carl F. Kaestle and Alyssa E. Lodewick (University Press of Kansas, 2007).

Finally, and most importantly, although this book would have happened faster without them, I am deeply grateful to my family for their love and tolerance.

Abbreviations

CBEC	Connecticut Business for Education Coalition
CEEC	Commission on Educational Excellence for Connecticut
CMT	Connecticut Mastery Tests
CSDE	Connecticut State Department of Education
CT-SOS	Connecticut-Save Our Schools
DOE	Department of Education
DUE	Division of Urban Education
EEA	Education Enhancement Act
EIP	Education Improvement Panel
ELC	Education Law Center
GPRA	Government Performance and Results Act
GTB	guaranteed tax base
IASA	Improving America's Schools Act
IQ	intelligence quotient
MBAE	Massachusetts Business Alliance for Education
MCAS	Massachusetts Comprehensive Assessment System
MERA	Massachusetts Education Reform Act of 1993
MTA	Massachusetts Teachers' Association
NAEP	National Assessment of Educational Progress
NCLB	No Child Left Behind Act
NGA	National Governors' Association
NPM	new public management
OBE	outcomes-based education
OCR	Office of Civil Rights
QEA	Quality Education Act
RIL	Racial Imbalance Law
SAT	Scholastic Aptitude Test
SBR	standards-based reform
SJC	Supreme Judicial Court
TANF	Temporary Assistance for Needy Families
T&E	thorough and efficient
TIERS	Title I Evaluation and Reporting System

CHAPTER ONE

Scrutinizing Educational Performance

The author and cartoonist Dr. Seuss, best known for creating the Cat in the Hat, once produced a commentary on public-sector accountability. In *Did I Ever Tell You How Lucky You Are?*, he introduced readers to the predicament of the people of Hawtch-Hawtch:

> Oh, the jobs people work at! Out west, near Hawtch-Hawtch, there's a Hawtch-Hawtcher Bee-Watcher. His job is to watch—is to keep both his eyes on the lazy town bee. A bee that is watched will work harder, you see.
>
> Well, he watched and he watched. But, in spite of his watch, that bee didn't work any harder. Not mawtch.
>
> So then somebody said, "Our old bee-watching man just isn't bee-watching as hard as he can. He ought to be watched by another Hawtch-Hawtcher. The thing that we need is a Bee-Watcher-Watcher."
>
> Well, the Bee-Watcher Watcher watched the Bee-Watcher. He didn't watch well. So another Hawtch-Hawtcher had to come in as a Watch-Watcher-Watcher. And today all the Hawtchers who live in Hawtch-Hawtch are watching on Watch-Watcher-Watchering-Watch, Watch-Watching the Watcher who's watching that bee. You're not a Hawtch-Hawtcher. You're lucky, you see. (Geisel 1973, 26–27)

Were Dr. Seuss still alive, he might want to revise the last line. We are all Hawtch-Hawtchers now, especially in public education. People who work in schools most likely identify with the bee. The rest of us, whether we are policymakers, state and federal agency employees, parents, or voters, fit into the system either as Bee-Watchers or perhaps as Bee-Watcher-Watchers.

Although the press toward measuring the results of public activity, reporting the results, and attaching consequences to results has affected public education more than just about any area of government activity, public education has not been alone in experiencing increased performance scrutiny. Throughout the public sector, accountability for performance has been growing since the advent of the "New Public Management" and has survived even into the "middle age" (Hood and Peters 2004) and senescence of the "new public management" label. Public agencies and government contractors now routinely identify measurable performance targets, report on their performance, and possibly earn rewards or face penalties for performance. These expectations have added onto existing systems of accountability. As Barbara Romzek and Melvin Dubnick point out in their analysis of how changes at NASA contributed to the *Challenger* accident, agencies face a range of accountability demands that vary according to whether control is being exercised inside or outside the agency along with the extent to which the agency's work is subject to control. Performance accountability could be part of any of the four kinds of accountability they identify but is likeliest to be part of political accountability, in which people outside an agency set expectations for the work of front-line staff they do not directly control. Performance accountability also raises fundamental questions about equity and intergovernmental relations, which have not received the attention they deserve from scholars of performance accountability. Studying the enactment of performance-accountability policies in education, and specifically the sanctions associated with performance, provides an opportunity to consider both of these issues. In education, equity has been the primary justification for performance accountability. Education is also one of the most intergovernmental policy areas in the United States, with local, state, and federal governments sharing and often contesting authority.

It is common for analysts of education policy to talk in terms of an "accountability movement," implying that accountability systems developed where none had previously been. However, schools and teachers have always been accountable to somebody for something. A century and a half ago in the rural United States, parents judged teachers according to their ability to keep order in the classroom and they scrutinized teachers' private lives to an extent that would be both impossible and illegal today (Grant and Murray 1999). Local taxpayers have long kept a close eye on their schools' fiscal responsibility and adherence to community values, and have voted out boards of education that fell short in either area (Iannaccone and Lutz 1970). Beginning in the early twentieth century, larger school systems built extensive bureaucratic control systems (Tyack 1974); later, as teachers gained the right to collective bargaining, contracts and work rules generated more layers of standard operating procedures. States regulated public schools' compliance with health and safety regulations. Later, state and federal regulations protected the educational rights of vulnerable populations such as students of color, students with disabilities, and students without academic proficiency in English (Nelson

2005; and Cohen and Moffitt 2009). All of these local, state, and federal policies and practices constituted forms of accountability.

The idea of "organizational report cards" caught on first in public education
(Gormley and Weimer 1999). Since the last quarter of the twentieth century,
policymakers have added requirements for performance measurement and
sanctions to educational accountability. Students in U.S. public schools now
routinely take tests to measure their progress, and if aggregate scores do not
reach benchmarks, the schools and districts are subject to sanctions. In about
half of the states, students themselves are accountable for their performance
because they cannot earn a high school diploma without passing a state test,
regardless of their course grades. All of the major federal education programs
require states to have subject standards in place and to test students on their
progress toward meeting those standards. Scholars of education policy have
published a large and growing literature on the positive and negative effects
of this shift, with the most attention to how emphasis on test results has distorted curricula and why performance accountability systems have perverse effects (Smith 1995; Hatry 1999; Grizzle 2002; DeBruijn 2002; Dahler-Larsen
2007; Ebrahim 2007). This book takes a different approach to the study of
performance-based accountability in education by situating it in the broader
context of public administration research. Educational accountability is a valuable area for public administration scholars to consider not just because it is
the most visible form of public performance accountability (Radin 2006, 2)
but primarily because of the ways in which equity and intergovernmental
relations interact with educational accountability.

Beginning with a national overview and moving into three state-level
case studies, this book provides an account of how shifts in policymakers'
and educational advocates' definitions of educational equity led them to
the conclusion that efforts to hold schools accountable should focus on
performance—specifically, what students actually learn and what they can
do. This account contributes to scholarship in public administration because
education shows how changing ideas about equity influence performance
management and how performance management interacts with intergovernmental relations. Performance accountability has emphasized efficiency over
equity in some other policy areas. In contrast, in public education, equity has
been the main justification for the move to judge performance. The emphasis
on equity has also strengthened the tendency of performance accountability
to lead to centralization of authority over public education, continuing a centralizing trend that predates performance accountability in education. Before
performance accountability, states intervened to keep local authorities from
violating students' state constitutional rights to public education, and the

federal government has enforced mandates for desegregation and equal treatment of students. In its 1994 reauthorization of the main federal education grant program, and again in the better-known 2001 No Child Left Behind Act, the federal government has pressured states to adopt educational performance accountability systems that include tests, performance standards, and interventions targeting low-performing schools and districts.

High-Stakes Reform, Equity, and Intergovernmental Relations in Education

Education was a natural field for the expansion of performance accountability because, unlike in other policy areas, a way of measuring results was in place before anybody thought of basing an accountability system on it. Many public and private schools used tests such as the Iowa Test of Basic Skills and IQ measurements to identify students' academic strengths and weaknesses. These earlier tests attempted to measure students' innate levels of intellectual talent aside from what schools had done for them, and they were designed to be independent of any specific curriculum. The crucial shift for purposes of accountability was toward designing tests intended to measure the extent to which students had learned a particular body of academic material (Koretz 2008, ch. 4).

Tests designed to measure what students have learned are at the core of performance-based accountability in education or, as people in education most commonly call it, standards-based reform. The "standards" are state-level statements about what students should know and be able to do at each stage of their schooling. The central tenet of standards-based reform is that all state education policies, including funding, evaluation of performance, and training for teachers, should be reorganized around the goal of ensuring that students learn what state authorities (generally in conjunction with teacher and educational-administrator representatives) have identified as important (Smith and O'Day 1991).

To make performance, as measured by tests, the first priority of educators and students, states often attach consequences to test performance. Students might be denied a diploma if they score low, or get special recognition if they score high. Schools and districts could be rewarded for good performance, or subject to penalties and state intervention if their students perform poorly. These sanctions are what make standards-based reform and testing "high stakes." This book focuses on the enactment of the most stringent forms of performance-based sanctions: high school graduation tests, state powers to close schools or replace school staff, and state powers to take control of school districts.

Probably the best-known current example of policy based on high-stakes testing is the federal No Child Left Behind Act (NCLB), passed by Congress in 2001 and signed by President George W. Bush in the first days of 2002. NCLB requires states to have performance standards for schools and districts, to set "adequate yearly progress" targets according to federal guidelines, and to have an escalating sequence of sanctions in place for poor performance. Some of these sanctions, such as requirements that students be allowed to transfer out of underperforming schools and that districts provide students in under-performing schools with a choice of "supplemental education services" that can be provided by private contractors, are specified in the law, and the details of others are left to the states. Although NCLB looms largest in the public mind and is a source of many requirements that educators find frustrating, the state performance-accountability policies that preceded NCLB are important in their own right and provided the models for federal performance-account-ability policies in education.

The focus on performance as the goal of education policy followed logically from shifting definitions of educational equity. The best-known landmark in this evolution is the U.S. Supreme Court's 1954 *Brown v. Board of Education* decision, which declared that state laws requiring racial segregation in public education violated the U.S. Constitution. Later federal policies extended analogous civil rights guarantees to students with disabilities and students who do not speak English, and banned gender discrimination in education. In all these policies, equity was defined in terms of access to the same schools for all children. Around the same time as the federal government expanded the meaning of equal protection in education, activists also began to push for greater equality in education spending across communities and students. This activity was in the state courts. All fifty states' constitutions guarantee public education for their residents, and even where those guarantees do not specifically include the word "equity," courts have interpreted these guaran-tees to mean that public schooling must be provided to all students in a way that meets some definition of equality (Reed 2001). Toward the end of the twentieth century, educators and policymakers became disenchanted with both the equal-access and the equal-funding understandings of educational equity. Racial integration of schools had often proved politically difficult. In the fragmented education systems of the North and Midwest, racial integra-tion was often logistically impossible after the U.S. Supreme Court ruled out mandatory transfers of students across school district lines (Orfield and Eaton

1996). At the same time, legislators and taxpayers were demanding evidence that schools were doing something constructive with increased state funding. Some lawyers working on school-finance cases sought to go beyond pushing for equal spending by making claims that disadvantaged students actually required more education funding to be able to succeed in college and on the job market (Rebell 2009). A new definition of educational equity in terms of students' attainment of a threshold level of knowledge and skills responded to these political challenges and, like the standards-based reform movement, promised to focus equity efforts on what was most important for students.

The final important characteristic of performance accountability in education is that it attempts to achieve this performance-threshold definition of educational equity by centralizing authority in the intergovernmental system. The most important shift has been the increased state power over curriculum and assessment of performance, but as the NCLB shows, the federal government has also expanded its powers in these areas. Performance accountability was not the first instance of centralization in education policy. In the early twentieth century, states began requiring tiny one-school districts to consolidate (Strang 1987) and extending regulations related to minimum school programs and mandatory attendance (Tyack and Hansot 1982; Kaestle 1983; Tyack, James, and Benavot 1987, ch. 3). In both federal desegregation enforcement and state-level financial equalization, larger government entities increased their power and their roles in the system. All of these shifts illustrated E. E. Schattschneider's claim that expanding the scope of a political conflict (or, in this case, of policymaking) advantages different participants (1960).

Why Study States' Performance-Based Sanctions in Education?

This book analyzes the history of accountability in U.S. education policy and compares three states' "high stakes" uses of testing: the various kinds of sanctions against students, schools, and school districts with low test scores enacted prior to the No Child Left Behind Act. One of the three states, Massachusetts, enacted all three kinds of sanctions in the Education Reform Act of 1993. Massachusetts students cannot earn a high school diploma without passing state tests or securing a state waiver of the requirement. The Education Reform Act of 1993 gave the state the power to declare a school or a district to be "chronically underperforming." With this designation, the state board of education could remove the principal of a school and place a district in receivership. The policies of Connecticut, Massachusetts' neighbor to the south, are quite different. Connecticut developed a set of tests with a national reputation for quality and rigor but chose not to attach many sanctions to poor performance. Connecticut students, before and after the No Child Left Behind Act, do not have to pass a state test to graduate from high school. The state identifies underperforming schools based on test scores but leaves the question of how to intervene up to school districts. It did take over the Hartford Public Schools in 1997 but with the understanding that this was an exceptional situation rather than a precedent to follow elsewhere. The third state in the study, New Jersey, was one of the first states to require students to pass a graduation test. It also was the first to enact legislation empowering the state to take control of local school districts, and it has used this power in three cities. Along with these fairly standard, if early adopted, performance sanctions, New Jersey's supreme court and state department of education have also required districts receiving extra funds in response to a lawsuit to spend the new money on specific kinds of programs, thus combining procedural accountability with performance-based accountability.

Neither Massachusetts nor New Jersey has used its takeover powers frequently. Nevertheless, these states stand out for having used their takeover powers at all. Nationally as of 2004, only fifty-four school districts out of approximately fifteen thousand had been taken over by a state, and only eighteen of those takeovers were for primarily academic reasons (Ziebarth 2004). Only five states have ever taken over a school (Steiner 2005). Even though these powers are not used frequently, it is still worth studying the processes by which they were enacted and the arguments mustered for and against them. First, even in the absence of sanctions, performance targets influence schools and districts by setting out goals. Failure to meet these goals may require explanation, even if there are no penalties (McDonnell 2004). Second, where sanctions do exist, they provide a sense of urgency and pressure on schools and districts. No matter how small the actual likelihood of a takeover might be, no principal or superintendent ever wants to read in a newspaper that his or her school or district is performing below state expectations. In themselves, the heightened scrutiny and additional requirements on schools that have begun to miss performance targets feel like a form of punishment (Mintrop 2004; Therriault 2005).

Although most people outside of public schools became aware of the press for performance accountability in education only after President George W. Bush signed the No Child Left Behind Act in 2002, much of the important action on educational accountability took place in the states prior to NCLB. As chapter 4 of this book will show, the performance accountability (or standards-based reform) movement in public education began in the states in the 1970s. The 1994 addition of performance accountability to the federal Elementary and Secondary Act came after many states had already moved in that direction, and was intended not just to press more states to do the same but also to make federal requirements more consistent with those of the more innovative states (Cohen and Moffitt 2009). Many states' quarrel with NCLB was not that they were being forced to enact performance accountability policies for education but instead that they were being pressed to change their existing performance accountability policies, which they believed were better tailored to state conditions.

Overview of the Book

Chapter 2 outlines performance-based accountability. Two ideas in particular are central. First, new forms of accountability generally do not replace older ones; rather, accountability demands on agencies multiply and accrete over time. Second, the performance accountability model in general does not emphasize issues of equity and intergovernmental relations, even though it has clear implications for both. Performance-based educational accountability is an exception to this general pattern, since a results-based understanding of equity and a more centralized version of intergovernmental relations are both explicitly at the center of recent educational accountability policies.

Chapter 3 traces the history of the forms of educational accountability that preceded the recent shift to performance-based accountability. Three interconnected trends characterize the evolution of educational accountability up to the 1980s. First, although equity was always a central policy goal, the dominant understanding of educational equity changed, from access to common schooling, to scientific placement of students in different but appropriate academic programs, to equal funding, and finally to common educational outcomes for all students. This shift in the definition of equity meant a shift in the goals for which schools were being held accountable. Second, authority in the intergovernmental system of education policy became steadily more centralized, with growing state and then federal involvement in what had previously been a highly localized system. Third, the public understanding of who ought to control public education shifted. Initially, an officially depoliticized system of bureaucratic professionalism displaced lay control as schooling became less locally controlled. Then, in part as a response to the shortcomings of professional control and the evident impossibility of separating schooling from political questions, a wide variety of participants challenged the educators' authority. This shift was not just a reassertion of lay authority against professionals but also a broadening of which laypeople were involved, to include historically disenfranchised groups whose voices had not been heard in the early history of public education or in the period of bureaucratic professionalism.

Chapter 4 provides an overview of the development and spread of state-level performance-based educational accountability policies. This development occurred in three stages. During the 1970s states began administering "minimum-competency" tests to students, sometimes attaching consequences to student performance on these tests. Unlike many other policy innovations, the emphasis on educational performance began in the southern states where governors were pushing hard to overcome decades of neglect of public education. In the 1980s, especially after the release of the *A Nation at Risk* report in 1983, state policy began to shift from "minimum competency" as a goal to "high" or "world-class" standards. In the third stage of the development of performance-based educational accountability, the federal government joined the movement, enacting policies that imposed a common framework on states' policies.

Chapters 5, 6, 7, and 8 present the three case studies of states' enactment of performance-based sanctions in public education. Chapter 5 provides overviews of the states' policies and explains methodology and data sources. Chapter 6 analyzes the Massachusetts Education Reform Act of 1993. Chapter 7 surveys key moments in the development of New Jersey's unique hybrid of performance accountability and process accountability. Chapter 8 explains how Connecticut policymakers arrived at a set of standards-based policies that emphasize sanctions far less than those of many other states.

Chapter 9 connects conclusions from the case studies to the national trends in educational accountability and summarizes the implications of my analysis for education policy, with particular attention to the political consequences of performance accountability in education. Chapter 10 reviews the implications of performance accountability in education for the general movement toward performance measurement and accountability. Experience thus far with education raises several challenges that any performance-accountability system needs to confront. These challenges include the interaction between performance goals and other forms of accountability, the tension between realism and aspiration in goal setting, the paradoxical role of experts, and the tendency of performance-accountability policies to ignore the need to build agency capacity.

Many contributions to the public debate on performance accountability in education present it as a general cure for the problems with U.S. public education or, at the very least, as the necessary final stage in the movement for educational civil rights. An equal if not even larger body of work criticizes testing and accountability as a destructive mistake or even an attack on public education. In this book I strive to walk a middle course, asking why these policies became popular, how the assumptions behind them shaped their results, and what public administration scholars can learn from the education example.

CHAPTER TWO

Performance-Based Accountability

Throughout the public sector in many countries, administrators and front-line workers have been under increasing pressure to demonstrate that their agencies are performing effectively. A vast academic literature analyzes the myriad forms of public-sector accountability and the reasons why these forms change and accumulate over time. A "new public management" has emphasized the results of government activity and has attempted to replace the many competing accountability demands with one unified system based on performance. In public education the focus on results has taken the form of policies that hold schools and school districts accountable for their students' performance on standardized tests.

Critics of the performance-accountability movement have tended to focus on the ways in which attempts to measure and evaluate agency performance have generated unintended, even perverse, results. There has been less attention to two general and enduring concerns of public administration. The first is equity. The second is the dispersal of authority throughout federal, state, and local governments. Although a full review of the academic literature on performance measurement and accountability is beyond the scope of this study, I will highlight in this chapter the ways in which scholars explain the tendency of accountability demands to multiply, and the ways in which accountability for performance is theoretically different from other forms of accountability. I conclude by identifying general challenges of equity and intergovernmental relations before turning back to the specific analysis of educational accountability in chapter 3.

Multiple Accountability Demands in Public Organizations

Like public schools, other public-sector agencies need to respond to pressures from various constituencies. Beryl A. Radin (2002) has characterized federal administrators as "accountable jugglers," and the metaphor applies well to public managers at all levels. In addition to the primary goals of their activities, such as repairing roads, retraining laid-off steelworkers, or preventing crime, public agencies also have what James Q. Wilson has labeled "contextual" goals: the "descriptions of desired states of affairs other than the one the agency was brought into being to create," which limit how the primary goals can be pursued (1989, 129). For example, a police department not only must try to prevent crime and catch criminals, it must also protect the rights of the accused, safeguard the confidentiality of its records, and provide necessary health services to arrestees. Public schools teach children, but they also comply with civil rights laws, respect the terms of employee labor contracts, and follow local procedures for putting building maintenance out to bid. Public-sector organizations and their managers might be held accountable for achieving any, or all, of their primary and contextual goals. As Wilson points out, every contextual goal imposed on an agency is "the written affirmation of the claim of some external constituency" (1989, 131). Or, as Donald Savoie has said, "one person's red tape is another's due process" (1995, 116). Politics matters for public managers as a source of new goals and of pressure to set particular priorities among goals. By "politics" I mean not partisanship or patronage but the process of establishing these priorities. It is unrealistic to expect that politics in this sense could really be eliminated from public activity.

In an influential 1987 article, Barbara S. Romzek and Melvin A. Dubnick used the history that led to the explosion of the space shuttle *Challenger* as an example of how the accountability demands on an agency shift over time. In their "institutional" analysis of accountability, Romzek and Dubnick consider both NASA's internal norms of who is accountable to whom for what and the external pressures for accountability from the larger social and political system (1987, 228). The Rogers Commission, which reported on the reasons why one of *Challenger*'s solid rocket boosters exploded shortly after launch, blamed the extremely cold weather and the shuttle program managers' failure to take engineers' warnings seriously enough. For Romzek and Dubnick, this explanation is too simple. A full account of the reasons for the accident must also include the increased emphasis on political accountability at NASA. In the 1980s congressional oversight of NASA increased the pressure to maintain tight launch schedules at the expense of the agency's historic culture of internal professional accountability and managerial deference to engineers. This increased responsiveness to outside pressures created the circumstances within which a decision to launch could be made despite opposition from engineers.

Romzek and Dubnick's analysis adds ongoing political dynamics to the layering of primary and contextual goals identified by Wilson. For Romzek and Dubnick, agency accountability is about management of a "diversity of legitimate and occasionally conflicting expectations" (1987, 228). They propose

Table 2.1   Romzek and Dubnick's Accountability Typology

Degree of Control over Agency	Source of Control over Agency	
	Internal	*External*
High	Bureaucratic accountability	Legal accountability
Low	Professional accountability	Political accountability

a fourfold typology of accountability, with the categories based on whether the ability to define and control expectations is internal or external to the agency, and on whether the extent to which the agency's activities can be controlled is high or low.

Where managers internal to an agency are able to exercise a high degree of control over line workers, accountability is bureaucratic. Where generalist managers within an agency do not or cannot tightly control the work of specialists on the front lines of a program, accountability is professional. Tight control from outside an agency characterizes legal accountability, and loose oversight from outsiders such as elected officials constitutes political accountability. Romzek and Dubnick do not describe these four options as mutually exclusive. At any given time, an agency may be experiencing several different kinds of accountability pressure. Multiple agency goals mean that at any given time, an agency is subject to multiple forms of accountability, although some may be "underutilized" or "dormant" (Romzek and Dubnick 1987, 62). In Wilson's terms, an agency's managers will simultaneously be held accountable for achieving both primary and contextual goals.

Why Do Accountability Policies Change?

Because accountability demands are generally related to particular goals, it follows that one source of change in accountability policies is the addition of new goals to an agency's agenda. New policy enactments may add new primary goals. For example, after the 1996 federal welfare reform law converted the legal entitlement of "families with dependent children" to financial assistance without time limits into a program of "temporary assistance to needy families" with strict time limits, the federal government began to hold states accountable for the rate at which they were able to move welfare clients into nonwelfare employment. New goals may also add to the contextual goals that agencies experience as legal or political constraints. It is easy to assume that procedural "red tape" is trivial; however, some contextual goals have profound importance. For example, the Civil Rights Act of 1964 forbids the distribution of federal funds to a racially segregated entity and thus requires government agencies and their private-sector partners to be able to demonstrate that they are operating in a racially nondiscriminatory way.

With or without the addition of new goals, agencies may also experience a shift in the priority they need to place on various goals. According to Romzek and Dubnick, new or previously less important forms of accountability for an agency can be "triggered" by crises or scandals (1987, 62). During NASA's heyday, although the agency was in principle answerable to Congress for meeting goals set through the political process, in practice the politicians and nonspecialist administrators deferred to the scientists' and engineers' notions of professionalism. After the moon missions ended and the United States went into economic recession, political accountability became more important at NASA. Fiscal constraints shifted the agency's priorities, making it more important that they keep their political masters happy. The result was an environment in which managers could push engineers to launch *Challenger* and keep the overall shuttle program on schedule, despite the likely dangers of a cold-weather launch.

As at NASA, where political pressures to launch *Challenger* on that cold January morning overrode engineering reasons not to launch, there is no reason to expect that layered goals and sanctions will be consistent with each other. In fact, as a rule we should expect this sort of conflict among goals, and thus among accountability pressures as well. For example, unless policy-makers believed that an agency might overlook certain interests in the process of achieving its primary goals, they would not bother enacting procedural requirements with accountability sanctions attached to them. In the late twentieth century, however, the profusion of forms of accountability throughout the public sector led to a sense that contextual goal-setting had gone too far, and that the managers and clients of government programs would all be better served if agencies reemphasized their primary goals—the intended results of government activity.

The Theory of Performance-Based Accountability

The focus on results over procedures is one of the core tenets of "new public management," which in the United States has included state and local efforts to "reinvent government" along with the federal National Performance Review, Government Performance and Results Act (GPRA), and Performance Accountability Rating Tool. Some versions of new public management (NPM) include competition among potential providers of public service, which will weed out poor performers either through the market choices of citizen-consumers or through the terms of contracts to provide government services. Other lower-stakes versions of NPM emphasize the ways in which managers can use performance data to lead an organizational learning process within their agencies without the immediate pressure of loss of funding. Overall, both advocates and critics of NPM agree that the focus on measuring results is at the core of the enterprise (Hatry 1999; Grizzle 2002; DeBruijn 2002; Stark 2002; Hood and Peters 2004; Kettl 2005; Frederickson and Frederickson 2006; Radin 2006; Riccucci and Thompson 2008; Diefenbach 2009; Taylor 2009; Bumgardner and Newswander 2009; Meier and O'Toole 2009). Although Christopher Hood and Guy Peters have declared that NPM is "middle aging" and the term is falling out of favor, the performance-measurement emphasis that NPM advocated remains a major influence on public policy and administration.

Components of Performance-Based Accountability

Evaluators frequently characterize policies and programs in terms of their theories of action. A theory of action is simply the way in which the designers of a policy or program expect that its various parts will interact to produce its intended result. To take a very simple example, when parents pay their children an allowance and reduce the amount if their children neglect their household chores, their theory of action is that the children's desire to maximize their allowance payments will make them likelier to complete their chores. Breaking down this theory to its individual assumptions, the parents assume that their children prefer more money to less, and that the children value the money more highly than the additional leisure time they would get from ignoring their chores. If the children slack off, and the parents happen to be program evaluators, the parents might conclude that their theory of action was invalid. Perhaps, for example, the children view the lost money as a fair price to pay for the privilege of not taking out the trash or folding laundry.

Most public policies are more complicated than paying children's allowance, but it is still possible to identify the assumptions behind the theory of action that links interventions to results. Consider public-sector accountability policies. In all of them, one entity is "accountable for" something "to" somebody (Bardach and Lesser 1996, 200). Behn (2001) identifies as "holdees" those who must account for achieving something, and "holders" are those to whom the holdees are accountable. The theory of action of an accountability policy or program is the set of ideas that explains how the interaction between holders and holdees will lead to a goal. For example, when my university requires our department assistant to fill out a purchase order before it will authorize an expense, the goal is honest spending of university funds, the holdee is the assistant (as well as those who supervise her work), and the holder is a campus-level administrator. The theory of action is that requiring staff members to follow procedures and document expenditures will make it impossible (or at least very difficult) for those staff members to divert funds to their private use or to devise kickback schemes with suppliers.

Moving back to performance-based accountability, the core of its theory of action is that managers and front-line workers should concentrate on their primary goals rather than becoming bogged down in the contextual ones, such as mastering the intricacies of purchase orders. Thus, the first component of a system of performance-based accountability is a *performance measurement*, such as parts per million of pollutants in the air, number of crimes reported, or hospital morbidity and mortality rates. The second component of performance-based accountability is a *benchmark*, or a set of benchmarks, which are the targets to which performance will be compared (Blalock and Barnow 2001, 490). Benchmarking is supposed to lead accountability holdees to examine the effectiveness of how they work, and thus to improve their performance when it falls short of the targets. Agency workers' response to the news that their performance has fallen short of particular benchmarks might produce any of several kinds of reaction, including not only the intended efforts to improve performance but also a shrug of indifference or an effort to discredit the measurements or the benchmarks. Policymakers who design performance accountability systems know this, and in response, they use *sanctions*, the third key component of performance-based accountability, to ensure that agency workers will take the benchmarks seriously.

Some sanctions operate from the "bottom" via pressure from consumers, citizens or other users of a system. Organizational report cards, which are third-party compilations of performance information on a set of organizations such as hospitals, nursing homes, or schools, are intended to generate bottom-up pressure (Gormley and Weimer 1999). If a university, hospital, or nursing home in a competitive market posts poor results, people may choose to take their business elsewhere (Gormley 1998; Mukamel et al. 2007). In a policy area in which citizens are not choosing among service providers, such as the federal Empowerment Zone/Empowerment Community program, the information on report cards may inspire political pressure for improvement (Fung, Graham, and Weil 2007; Ingraham and Moynihan 2001; Wright 2001). "May" is the operative word here; consumers and voters do not necessarily use performance information (Kettl 2005; Gormley and Weimer 1999).

The uncertainty over whether citizens and customers can, or will, actually act on performance information leads policymakers to impose several different kinds of top-down sanctions for poor performance. Some of these use funding to influence agency behavior. The "reinventing government" approach described earlier emphasizes the importance of tightly connecting funding to performance. This has been done in two general ways: performance budgeting, in which measurements of agency and program results are incorporated into annual budgets; and contracting, in which the government, rather than directly providing a service, invites private and public providers to compete for the right to do so. Recent examples of contracting for services can be found in the implementation of welfare reform (DeParle 2004) and in prisons (Trebilcock 1995) as well as in support areas such as building maintenance. Even if performance information is not part of the general budgeting process, supplementary prizes can be used as positive sanctions for performance. Gormley and Weimer present competition for financial rewards as an alternative to market pressure as an incentive in areas of activity in which there is little or no actual market competition among providers (1999, 223). Wisconsin and Florida, for example, both offered bonuses to high-performing contractors implementing the state Temporary Assistance for Needy Families (TANF) programs (Boyer, Lawrence, and Wilson 2001, 192–93).

Actual performance budgeting, although important in theory, remains rare in practice. At the federal level, factors other than performance ratings affect budget decisions (Gilmour and Lewis 2006). Even in public education, where the public tends to assume that the main consequence of a school's test scores is whether its budget will increase or decrease, administrative sanctions such as state takeovers or replacement of school staff loom far larger in performance accountability than do any financial consequences for low test scores.

The Performance-Based Accountability Theory of Action

Policymakers enact performance-based accountability because they expect that the collection and reporting of performance data, evaluated against benchmarks and coupled with some sort of consequences for performance, will induce agencies to improve their actual performance. In terms of Romzek and Dubnick's typology, performance-based accountability constitutes a challenge to professional accountability because external overseers generally set the benchmarks. Although performance-based accountability does not fit neatly into any of Romzek and Dubnick's other three categories, its emphasis on control is similar to that of bureaucratic accountability, and its generally external origins could provide connections to political or even legal accountability. In effect, performance-based accountability uses benchmarking and sanctions as incentives for behavior that cannot easily be compelled or monitored through a bureaucratic hierarchy. Performance data could also be used to enhance political accountability or to replace some of the procedures at the heart of legal accountability. The extent to which performance accountability leads to improvement depends on the extent to which the key assumptions in its theory of action are a valid reflection of reality. These key assumptions concern measurements, incentives, and the potential for improved performance.

Measurements

Most obviously, performance-based accountability assumes that important results of an agency's activities can be observed and measured so they can be tracked instead of monitoring only program inputs, such as the amount of money spent or the number of staff hours devoted to serving clients. Ideally the performance measurements would capture the actual consequences of the agency's activity or, in the terminology of policy evaluation, its "outcomes" (Hatry 1999), such as family stability, career success, or better child health. However, outcomes of this type are generally difficult to measure and difficult to attribute to a particular agency, so performance measurement and accountability generally focus on "outputs" of identifiable agencies' activity, such as the length of time children stay in foster care before being returned to their parents or adopted, the scores students achieve on tests, or the change in the percentage of babies who have low birth weights.

Incentives

Equally important, the theory of action in performance-based accountability assumes that the people who work in the targeted agencies will respond to the pressure to improve their *measured* performance in ways that improve their *actual* performance. For example, the theory assumes that pressure on agencies being held accountable for results will mean that children who spend less time in foster care will actually be in more stable and positive families, that children who score better on the test will also perform well when they have to apply what they have learned in some other setting, and that the hospital's decreased rate of low-birth-weight babies will result from improved prenatal care rather than successful efforts to attract healthier women to its obstetrics department.

The Potential for Improvement

For performance pressure to lead to improved performance, it must first be true that the targeted agency or system is not already performing as well as it might in the targeted area and is capable of doing better. Performance-based accountability implicitly assumes that unsatisfactory performance is primarily due to a lack of will or of focus, rather than of capacity to perform. Perhaps staff members have not noticed that a performance problem exists, but once it is brought to light through measurement, they will be able to address it. Or perhaps they are shirking their responsibilities and choosing not to address a performance problem they already know about, in which case the threat of being sanctioned for poor performance will shock them out of their complacency. In either case, no additional resources or adjustments in workload will be needed. There is theoretically no reason why ambitious performance targets could not be combined with increased resources; as we will see later in the book, performance-based accountability in education often does accompany increased funding for at least some school districts.

Perverse Effects

Where the assumptions of performance-based accountability do not reflect reality, perverse incentives are possible. There is a body of research on the perverse effects of performance measurement and accountability, which is at least as large as the body of writing that explains why accountability for performance is a good idea and how it ought to work. I will not attempt a full summary of this research here except to identify some of the basic ways in which flaws in assumptions about measurements, incentives, and capacity for response contribute to unintended consequences. In the first place, measurement itself is not always straightforward. Radin has criticized what she calls the "naïve approach" to information, which assumes that neutral information (including baseline data) is available, that goals are clear and easily defined, that causal relationships can be easily identified, and that activities can actually be measured and quantified (2006, 207–9). With respect to this last point, some of what any agency does can probably be quantified; the important question is whether what is quantifiable actually captures the essence of what matters. As James Q. Wilson pointed out in his influential study of bureaucracies, some agency activities are unobservable, such as what teachers do all day in their classrooms when no other adults are present. Some of the results of agency activities are also unobservable. In terms of Wilson's typology of agencies, performance accountability implicitly assumes that all agencies can be treated to some extent as if they were "craft" or "production" organizations whose activities have observable results, rather than "procedural" or "coping" organizations whose activities do not.

If what is measured is consistent with what is not measurable, this gap need not be problematic (Kelman and Friedman 2009). However, there are many examples of agencies whose performance has been distorted rather than improved by attention to the measurable or measured indicators (Smith 1995; DeBruijn 2002; Dahler-Larsen 2007; Ebrahim 2007). Some of the less measurable goals may be as important as the measurable ones that crowd them out. A related risk is that agencies may game the measurement system by changing their behavior in ways that produce improvement in the measured indicators without necessarily improving underlying performance. For example, when the British National Health Service set a target for the maximum amount of time a patient in an emergency room would have to wait before his or her treatment began, some hospitals managed to improve their measured but not actual performance by creating the role of the "hello nurse." These nurses would make initial contact with the patient, at which point the hospital would record that "treatment" had begun, even if the patient still had a long time to wait before actually receiving medical care. Later, the National Health Service did manage to reduce emergency room waiting times when it shifted from targeting the wait before treatment began to targeting the total elapsed time between a patient's arrival and the *completion* of his or her emergency treatment. The "hello nurse" gambit did not help with this indicator, and hospitals developed new organizational practices that permitted actual medical treatment to begin and end sooner (Kelman and Friedman 2009).

Advocates and critics of performance-based accountability agree that the likelihood of system gaming tends to rise as the measurements are linked to more stringent and significant sanctions (Hatry 1999; Grizzle 2002; DeBruijn 2002). They disagree on the potential for avoiding perverse outcomes. Dahler-Larsen, a critic of performance-based accountability, argues that negative unintended consequences are, ironically, likeliest when accountability systems include a set of incentives that are "an optimal mix" from the standpoint of creating pressure for reform, as in New Public Management theory (2007, 31).

The assumptions about the potential for improved performance also can be problematic. Intuitively, it seems true that organizations generally have room to improve their performance. However, particular improvement benchmarks may be unrealistic given existing levels of skill and expertise. Assuming that poor performance is primarily a problem of will, not capacity, implies that the people who work in organizations tolerate shoddy work, and that outside scrutiny is needed to shake them out of their complacency. However, it is at least equally likely that staff members are already well aware of their suboptimal performance, and that what looks like shirking is actually a response to a mismatch between the load on an agency and its resources. Michael Lipsky's work on "street-level bureaucrats," such as teachers, social workers, and police officers, makes the point that people in these jobs rarely have resources commensurate with the demands placed on their agencies. In response, they cope in a variety of ways that have implications for agency performance. According to Lipsky, the core problem for street-level bureaucrats is that they have an ideal—a professional standard—of how their jobs ought to be done, but they work in situations where their jobs cannot be done according to these ideals. For example, a social worker may believe that she ought to provide her clients with individualized support services, but she also knows that, with a caseload in the hundreds, she will not be able to do so. Faced with this tension, street-level bureaucrats "manifestly attempt to do a good job *in some way*" instead of achieving the professional ideal (Lipsky 1980, 81, emphasis in original). Lipsky's book describes the resulting patterns of practice, which include treating some clients better than others and lowering or narrowing of objectives to make them attainable. Although the performance of an agency whose staff is behaving in these ways will probably fall short of ideal, putting more pressure on staff to meet particular targets will not solve the underlying problems that led them to tolerate suboptimal performance in the first place. Performance-based accountability wrongly assumes away capacity issues (McDermott 2006).

Two Enduring Administrative Issues

In addition to the unintended consequences that may result when the performance-accountability model's theory of action does not fit real conditions, public administration scholars have noted that the model does not deal adequately with two broad concerns. One is equity and the other is relations among federal, state, and local governments. Public education is an ideal policy area in which to examine these issues because equity is actually central to the argument for performance-based accountability in education and because governance of the U.S. public education system spans federal, state, and local governments, which places intergovernmental relations at the core of the enterprise.

Equity

Many critics of performance-based accountability have pointed out that its focus on improving performance and efficiency can crowd out attention to equity. According to Frederickson (1996), the "reinventing government" movement attempts to use data-based analytic techniques to skirt difficult but important choices among competing values. Radin charges that the federal government's forays into performance accountability have not paid sufficient attention to equity. The definitions of equity are contested, and equity is difficult to measure

(2006, 97). A further conceptual challenge is that equity has important dimensions that actually are processes, not outcomes. Thus, for some agencies, due process is not just a contextual goal but also a primary one. Citizens and voters (and noncitizens, nonvoters) want to know whether their police forces and their welfare systems are using nondiscriminatory processes and applying them without race, socioeconomic, or gender bias (Radin 1998, 314).

One place where performance-based assessment models can address equity concerns is in how they attempt to compare the performance of organizations that serve different populations. For example, hospitals that serve low-income or particularly unhealthy populations are likely to have higher levels of patient mortality and other bad outcomes than hospitals whose patient intake tends to be higher income and healthier. So that hospitals with harder-to-serve patients are not inaccurately identified as doing a bad job, hospital performance indicators are often risk-adjusted (Gormley 1998). The goal of risk adjustment is to avoid wrongly identifying agencies with easy caseloads as more effective than agencies with difficult caseloads, when it is actually possible that the apparently lower-performing agency is doing a better job of serving its higher-need clients. Risk adjustment also may reduce incentives for agencies to "game" performance-accountability systems by seeking easier clients (a practice sometimes called "cream-skimming"). Nevertheless, risk adjustment remains uncommon because it requires the use of statistical techniques that are hard for elected officials and the public to understand (Barnow and Heinrich 2010, 63). A major challenge here is that risk adjustment may treat organizations more fairly while seeming to legitimize the idea that not all individual citizens can expect the same quality of experience.

Intergovernmental Relations

Simplistic versions of "federalism" in contemporary political debate suggest that federal, state, and local governments all have clearly defined spheres of influence. For example, during the 1996 presidential campaign, Senator Robert Dole liked to pull a copy of the Tenth Amendment (which reserves to the states or the people "the powers not delegated to the United States by the Constitution, nor prohibited by it to the states") out of his pocket and read it at campaign events, promising to rein in federal power to its constitutional limits (Pear 1995). Liberals sometimes adopt a similar rhetorical strategy. For example, the National Education Association, which was instrumental in pushing for the creation of the U.S. Department of Education in 1979, later attacked the federal No Child Left Behind Act for improperly expanding federal authority over education and violating "states' rights" (McDermott and Jensen 2005). In contrast to these popular, arguably naïve, views of how federalism works, scholarly accounts of U.S. political development agree that the boundaries among the various levels of government have blurred, beginning in the 1930s with federal New Deal programs and continuing through various forms of "cooperative federalism" and attempts to devolve authority back to the states. The result of these developments is a complicated set of policy networks linking the three levels of government, with frequent tussles over who is really in charge. Academics thus prefer the term "intergovernmental relations" to "federalism" because it is more consistent with the real messiness of the system. Each of the three levels of government has sources of political legitimacy independent of the others, and policymakers at each level are answerable to different political constituencies (Stoker 1991).

The reality of intergovernmental relations is problematic for performance-based accountability. On one hand, focusing on performance improvement may be a means of encouraging agencies to collaborate with each other where there are not clear lines of authority linking them (Kettl 2007). On the other hand, performance accountability in an intergovernmental system may lead to agencies being held accountable for the performance of entities that they do not fully control or even fund. For example, half of the funds for Medicaid come from state governments, and the states actually administer the program. State Medicaid directors may find that federal data reporting priorities conflict with state program priorities (Radin 2006, 154). The design of GPRA assumes agencies with stable histories and "manageable" levels of conflict among external actors, but state agencies involved in intergovernmental programs "do not have agreement on data categories or indeed on the legitimacy of the federal government's requests for information" (Radin 1998, 310). When state and local officials perceive accountability mandates from "above" as efforts to limit their autonomy, they are generally perceiving the situation accurately. Electorally independent state and local officials are often "reluctant partners," as Robert Stoker titled his book on federal policy implementation (Stoker 1991). Resolving tensions among government bodies with overlapping but different constituencies and claims to legitimacy is a political problem, not a managerial one (Frederickson and Frederickson 2006).

Links between Intergovernmental Relations and Equity

In the United States, intergovernmental relations and equity have often been linked. Federal laws such as the Civil Rights Act of 1964 and the Voting Rights Act of 1965 empower federal authorities to impose nondiscrimination conditions on state and local (or private) actors, and to determine whether changes to state and local elections procedures are acceptable. The federal civil rights role supports the assumption that expanding the scope of conflict (Schattschneider 1960) by requiring a larger governmental entity to supervise a smaller one is a move in the direction of greater equity, since the larger entity can shift the smaller jurisdiction's balance of power to favor groups that are outnumbered or overpowered. As I will detail in chapter 3, U.S. education policy since the 1950s provides numerous examples of centralizing authority in pursuit of equity, including federal pressure for school desegregation, federal and state requirements for special programs for students with disabilities or students without proficiency in English, and the ban on federal funds going to educational institutions that discriminate on the basis of gender. The expanded state role in funding public education, following lawsuits challenging inequalities among school districts' ability to finance their schools with local property taxes, also fits in this general category.

None of these equity-promoting, centralizing shifts in intergovernmental relations has come without controversy. U.S. public schooling began as an intensely local activity, and even after a century and a half of centralization, the local role in education remains much larger than the local role in other areas of public policy. Despite growth in state and federal education funding, local governments still provide 44.4 percent of funds for K–12 public education (NCES 2009). Local education authorities also inspire a level of public support in principle that few other governmental entities can match. When a Gallup poll asked "who should have the greatest influence on deciding what is taught in the public schools," a plurality of respondents (46 percent) chose the local school board over state or federal government (Bushaw and Gallup 2008). The federal government is a relatively late addition to the education policy system, and an even later participant in accountability for educational performance.

In public education, unlike other policy areas in which pressure for performance seems to compete with equity as a policy goal, advocates of performance accountability have insisted that educational equity should be defined in terms of a common set of outcomes for public schooling, as measured by standardized tests. Making the outcomes "common," rather than specific to particular schools or communities, has implied centralizing authority over student assessment, intensifying the centralization of educational authority that was already under way due to desegregation and financial equalization. Along with the centralization of intergovernmental relations, there has been an expansion of the population of officials and institutions involved in making education policy. Formerly the domain of specialist governments such as local and state boards of education, education policy is now a major concern of general-government institutions such as mayors' offices, state legislatures, governors, and even presidents (Henig 2009; Fusarelli 2005; DeBray-Pelot 2007; Kaestle 2007). I will address all these shifts in detail in subsequent chapters.

The broadening of what Carl Kaestle (2007) has labeled the "education polity" has come with increased expression of skepticism about teachers' and administrators' ability or willingness to do their jobs well, and about the priorities of the network of education interest groups sometimes derided as "the blob." In the area of accountability, this meant that schools have not experienced the same sort of deference as hospitals and other health care organizations. Unlike in health care, where performance indicators like hospital morbidity and mortality rates are often adjusted for risk, the fact that educational performance benchmarks or indicators are *not* adjusted for risk has become an article of faith, as expressed in the slogan "no child left behind." Accountability advocates insist that measuring and reporting student performance and holding schools and districts accountable for shortfalls will compel greater uniformity of outcomes. Chapter 3 begins the story of how that idea evolved, and how it shaped educational accountability policy.

The Evolution of Educational Accountability

The forms that accountability policies take—who is accountable to whom for what—depend on the larger political context in which the policies are situated. This context generates the "institutional conditions" and "expectations" identified by Romzek and Dubnick as the forces that shape accountability (1987). To get a sense of the institutional conditions and expectations that shape educational accountability, consider Ms. Carlisle, the principal of a public elementary school. If Ms. Carlisle had her way, she would spend most of her day observing teachers and students, helping her less-experienced teachers learn the tricks of the trade, gently but firmly disciplining the students who end up in her office, and performing other tasks that improve the experiences of her staff and their students.

To Ms. Carlisle's frustration, this is not how most of her days actually go. Although she was out late last night at a school board meeting (an unwritten requirement of the job), she has arrived at school today at seven o'clock so she can get a head start on her e-mail. Four messages are from parents of children in Ms. White's fifth grade class, complaining that Ms. White yells too much, disciplines boys more harshly than girls, assigns too much homework, and makes grammatical errors in her class newsletters. All four parents call on Ms. Carlisle to "get Ms. White out of the classroom," or at least out of *their children's* classroom. Ms. Carlisle privately agrees that Ms. White ought to make a career change, but under the terms of the teachers' contract Ms. White cannot be fired until Ms. Carlisle has evaluated her performance, documented her shortcomings, given her a chance to do better, and then further documented that Ms. White cannot or will not change.

Ms. Carlisle's inbox also includes three e-mails relating to an upcoming routine audit of the school district's compliance with state and federal regulations. Today's messages remind her that she will need to provide evidence that requests from parents for evaluations of their children's possible learning disabilities receive a response within statutory time limits, and that the school's parent council members have been elected by other parents rather than hand-picked by administrators. She will also need to get rid of the art display cases because their windows are made of Plexiglas, which can burn and thus violates the fire code. Speaking of state regulations, the third graders will be taking the state reading test today, so Ms. Carlisle will need to remove the test booklets and answer sheets from their secure storage location and distribute them, then collect and package them for shipment to the test contractor, according to an extraordinarily detailed set of official procedures.

Ms. Carlisle glances at the clock and realizes that she is running late for the eight o'clock meeting to finalize the individualized education program for a kindergartner who was recently diagnosed with autism. Federal and state laws require not only that this child receive appropriate educational services but also that the school and district make their decisions about these services according to standard procedures, which include mandatory parental partici-pation. As Ms. Carlisle races out of her office, her cell phone rings. This call distracts her from saying hello to the middle-aged couple who are sitting in the waiting area of the office. They are probably parents, and it occurs to Ms. Carlisle that for all she knows, one of them is the person who recently complained, on a "school climate" survey (required by the local board of edu-cation to be done annually in all schools), that she is aloof and unwelcoming. All the more reason for Ms. Carlisle to make sure that she is there to give an enthusiastic welcome to the audience at tonight's school concert, even though by doing so she will miss the first fifteen minutes of her own children's school art fair.

All of these pressures are examples of accountability. As a professional, Ms. Carlisle holds herself to certain standards of educational leadership, and she interacts with a community of other school administrators who informally keep track of each other's reputations. As a person in charge of implement-ing local board of education policy, Ms. Carlisle needs to be responsive to the board that sets these policies; the board is in turn held politically account-able by the community's voters at election time. Maintaining good public relations—as with the parents waiting in the outer office and those who will be at the concert tonight—is part of being politically aware. In addition to professional and political considerations, Ms. Carlisle fits into a bureaucratic hierarchy within the school district, subordinate to the superintendent and other central-office administrators but outranking the teachers in her school. If Ms. Carlisle develops an improvement plan for Ms. White and Ms. White ignores it, the result could be a firing for insubordination. Finally, there are the miscellaneous legal and procedural requirements related to what Ms. Carlisle does on the job. This chapter traces the evolution of the system, or systems, of accountability within which Ms. Carlisle and other educators work. The analysis begins with the earliest U.S. public schools and ends in the late twentieth century, at the point when the movement for greater performance accountability began.

Overview

The history of public schooling in the United States is a story that has been told many times, with many shifts in emphasis. To set the stage for analysis of the national- and state-level movements for performance-based accountability in education, this chapter emphasizes three shifts that took place between the early years of public "common schools" and the beginning of the push for testing and performance accountability in the late 1970s. First, the prevailing definition of educational equity shifted. When New England communities first founded public schools, the predominant understanding of equity was that all children should have access to the same schools. As public schools became professionalized and bureaucratized, educators increasingly embraced differentiation of curriculum as the essence of equity. In the 1970s participants in education policy began to contest both the equal-access and differentiated views of equity. Eventually educational outcomes became the dominant metric for assessing equity.

Second, the balance among local, state, and federal elements of the inter-governmental system shifted toward greater centralization. From the middle of the twentieth century on, states began to enact statutes that built upon their constitutional power over public education, both in support of local educators and when local educators did not want them to. The federal government intervened on the side of vulnerable populations such as students of color, students who were not proficient in English, and students with disabilities. Newly assertive states and the federal government reinforced each other, pushing in the direction of a more centralized intergovernmental system.

Third, and most significantly for the development of educational accountability, a governance system that emphasized bureaucracy and professional autonomy (of administrators, more so than teachers) opened to a great deal more lay influence and political dispute about goals. New participants entered the education subsystem. Some of this new participation came from the bottom up, such as when urban communities of color demanded greater control over their children's schooling. Some came from the top down, as governors, mayors, state legislators, and members of the U.S. Congress expanded their roles in school governance.

I have organized this chapter in terms of three periods. The earliest is the common-school period, from the beginnings of local public schools in the oldest colonies through, approximately, the 1870s. The middle is the years of professional bureaucratization, beginning with the rise of "administrative progressivism" in the last quarter of the nineteenth century, and ending approximately in the middle of the twentieth. The last is a period of inclusion and conflict, beginning with the 1954 *Brown v. Board of Education* Supreme Court decision and continuing to the present, even though this chapter's analysis concludes in the 1970s.

During the first half of the twentieth century an "administrative progressive" worldview became the dominant model of public education (Tyack 1974). Consolidation of small schools and districts, plus state-level standardization of school requirements, enabled the development of bureaucratic systems through which educational administrators could exercise professional control with minimal political interference. Later, collective-bargaining agreements imposed other bureaucratic controls to protect teachers against administrative caprice. Political accountability was attenuated both by institutions that put control of public education under parallel systems separate from general state and local government and by a general belief that education should be outside of politics.

By the 1970s U.S. public schools were open to a far broader range of influences than had been the case for the public schools of the 1870s. The public was losing faith in public education—and, indeed, in government overall (Patterson 2005, 89). Historians of education criticized the assumptions behind administrative progressivism and traced the contemporary inequities of the system back to their roots in the progressives' "universal, tax-supported, free, compulsory, bureaucratically arranged, class-biased, and racist" system (Katz 1975, 106). In a similar spirit, urban activists insisted on greater "community control" of their children's schools, claiming that black and Latino leadership would do a better job of serving black and Latino children. Within schools and districts, organized teachers insisted on more power with respect to administration, and students pushed the limits of free expression and discipline. Formerly excluded groups, especially students with disabilities and students of color, were successfully advancing greater legal claims on the system for access and equal treatment. States were also under pressure to equalize spending among communities with different levels of wealth. On the whole, authority shifted more toward the state and federal levels of the intergovernmental system, although there was much tension among state, federal, and local governing bodies. New political demands added to, rather than replaced, earlier accountability developments such as professionalized bureaucracy and legal sanctions. Eventually, the standards-based reform movement would claim that the accumulated forms of accountability made it harder for educators to do their jobs. At the same time, the most important part of the schools' work continued to take place in thousands of individual classrooms, largely beyond the reach of political or administrative intervention due to the "loose coupling" of schools (Weick 1976).

Several caveats are in order before I move into the more detailed account. First, this chapter is an attempt to identify the origins of the various forms of accountability at work in the U.S. public education system by the end of the twentieth century. It is not intended as a synthesis of the entire history of U.S. public education. Second, the beginning and end dates of the three periods are imprecise, and there are undoubtedly several different ways in which I could have identified key periods. Finally, it is important to keep in mind that the various forms of accountability generally did not replace each other but rather accumulated into an ungainly collection of requirements, some of which are at cross-purposes. This is not a story of triumphant progress toward an ideal, but neither is it a story of decline from a prior golden age. Recall from chapter 2 the idea that one person's red tape is another's due-process guarantee; although the accumulation of accountability policies produced a tangle of demands, each strand in the tangle was important to somebody at the time it was added. The goal of this chapter is to explain the origins of the context in which performance-based educational accountability appealed to policy makers beginning in the 1970s.

The Common-School Era

During most of the nineteenth century, as Carl Kaestle said in his influential book on the period, the United States had schools but not school systems (Kaestle 1983, 62). Attendance at these one-room, one-teacher "common schools" was widespread but not universal or mandatory. Educational leaders such as Horace Mann crusaded to create more schools so more children would be able to have access to the basic education they needed to participate in civic life as adults. The dominant conception of educational equity emphasized common educational experiences. Accountability of public schools was direct and political because district school boards employed their teachers without other intermediaries, and there was little sense that teaching was a profession. Local institutions were by far the most important; to the extent that state government mattered, it was as a source of regulations that provided leverage for ensuring that local districts spent enough money to make their schoolhouses physically safe and adequate.

Access and Democratic Equality

In contrast to other industrialized countries where development of public school systems was a nationally led, top-down component of state building, U.S. public schooling began in its towns and villages (Katznelson and Weir 1985). Particularly in the Northeast, localities began running their own common schools before there were national, or even state, governments. Even after state governments came into being, local control was a practical way of providing schooling for a geographically dispersed, mostly rural population (Fischel 2009). It also probably led to more schools than would have been provided by a state government, since a community that valued schooling could tax itself and found a school without waiting for the rest of the state's population to agree to do the same (Goldin and Katz 2008, 338). The motives of the common-school founders were a combination of religion and civic morality. Members of some Protestant denominations believed that the ability to read scripture was crucial to religious salvation. In the secular realm, there was a broadly shared fear that the nation's republican experiment might collapse if its people lacked education and a sense of public virtue. Thus, despite their general fear of "despotism" and government power, Americans of the colonial and early national period supported the expansion of schools funded by a mixture of public funds and private payments (Kaestle 1983; Goldin and Katz 2008).

Educators and laypeople alike believed that the point of schooling was to prepare children to be political participants who had internalized a particular set of civic ideals and public morality. Horace Mann, one of the leading crusaders for common schools, saw lay control as a strength because it would ensure public influence over the philosophy being taught to their children (Cremin 1980). Schooling was not the source of job skills or social mobility that it would become after the nation industrialized because most adult occupations did not require much formal education. As of 1870, 53 percent of the U.S. labor force worked in agriculture, 10 percent as domestic servants, and 13 percent as laborers and manufacturing operatives (Goldin and Katz 2008, 167). Teaching was not a profession but rather was something that young men did between terms in seminary, or in addition to other work, or that a young woman of good character might do for a time in between the end of her own schooling and her marriage (Lortie 2002; Kaestle 1983). In general, school districts had only one school, and schools had only one teacher, so there was little if any need for administrators.

The academic curriculum consisted primarily of reading, spelling, and basic arithmetic. Typically, children brought to school whatever books they had at home, so a given school might have several textbooks in use (Kaestle 1983, 17). In the colonial period and into the nineteenth century, schoolbooks combined lessons about letters and sounds with lessons in Christianity and civic virtue (Johnson 1963). One widely used nineteenth-century series, *McGuffey's Eclectic Readers*, remains available for purchase. The website ChristianBook.com includes the series in its offerings for homeschooling families, describing the *Readers* as "renowned for their teaching of reading through the integration of faith with learning."

State Government as Professional Ally

Historians of the common-school period tell a story in which educators began a social movement and then enlisted state government to reinforce their efforts (Tyack and Hansot 1982, 5–6; Tyack, James, and Benavot 1987, ch. 3; Kaestle 1983). Kaestle notes, however, that despite the reputations of historic figures such as Horace Mann and Henry Barnard, the state education superintendency was an office "not conducive to heroism" (1983, 114), and activist state leaders such as Mann and Barnard were "more like preachers than bureaucrats" (1983, 115). The state role was limited to regulations and exhortations, since there was at most a rudimentary state administrative apparatus. Mann, the first Massachusetts secretary of education, toured the state's schools on horseback and issued reports on what he found. Often these reports revealed that local schools were in deplorable condition, with inadequate facilities and other resources. Mann pressed for improvements, using the prestige of his position to help his fellow educators win political arguments with local taxpayers who did not want to support their schools further. State governments did not have much practical ability to force local schools to do things against their will, or even to compel individual behavior. For example, historians note that states did not enact compulsory education laws until after school attendance had already expanded (Tyack, James, and Benavot 1987, 97; Cremin 1964). By the middle of the nineteenth century, the states required localities to provide free schools, and set some basic parameters for their operation, but the state role remained minimal (Kaestle 1983, 95–96; Cremin 1980).

Local Political Accountability

At a time when most school districts included only a single, one-room school and all families lived within walking distance of that school, political accountability was typically done at first hand. Kaestle identified the "chief goal" of district schools as to "provide children with rudimentary education at low cost under firm community control" (Kaestle 1983, 21). A district's voters elected a school board, which in turn directly hired the teacher. Board members might drop by to monitor what was going on at school. Under a 1789 Massachusetts law, a district's school committee was to visit and inspect its school at least once every six months (Johnson 1963, 101). A Connecticut statute from the 1820s empowered school visitors to "examine the instructors" in common schools "and to displace such as may be found deficient in any requisite qualification, or who will not conform to the regulations by them adopted; to superintend and direct the general instruction of scholars." (Conn. General Statutes 1824–26, Title 86, Ch. 1, Sec. 9, as quoted in Flaharty 1969, 194n5). In the early nineteenth century, the schoolbooks in use were often those that children had brought from home, so parents would have known exactly what their children were learning. Students also performed at public exhibitions, which made the school's curriculum quite visible (Kaestle 1983, 23). In terms of the goals for which teachers were held accountable, a teacher's ability to keep order, especially among the older boys, was at least as important as his or her ability to teach (Johnson 1963, 121). Indeed, because schools of the period included children ranging in age from four or five years old through adolescence, gathered in a small space and required to work their way through textbooks while the teacher heard recitations, the emphasis on keeping order was probably not misplaced.

Despite the continued availability of *McGuffey's Readers* and the powerful ideal of local democracy, it is important not to idealize the common schools of the eighteenth and nineteenth centuries. School governance may have entailed more local participation than it later would, but the franchise was

Table 3.1   Educational Accountability in the Common-School Era

Type of Accountability	Means of Accountability
Bureaucratic	Not yet relevant; most schools had single teacher
	Teachers responsible for own daily activities
Professional	Education not yet a profession; most teachers taught only a few years
	Broadly accepted ideas about how to teach (schoolroom order and memorization)
Legal	Minimal state regulations, supported by educators as means of securing increased local funding
Political	Direct inspection of schools by school board/examiners
	Locally elected school boards

Source: Categories from Romzek and Dubnick 1987.

limited (Reese 1986). The emphasis on rote learning presumably failed to engage some number of students, and most young people discontinued their schooling early. The teachers were barely more educated than their students. Moreover, they worked under a level of public scrutiny that most contemporary American adults would find intolerable. In addition to expecting visits from the Board of Education, teachers had to behave according to community norms outside of school time. Eyebrows would be raised if the teacher did not regularly attend church or otherwise deviated from community norms (Lortie 2002). Teachers who did not already live in the district boarded with their pupils' families in circumstances that permitted little if any privacy.

Overall, the dominant form of accountability in the eighteenth and nineteenth centuries was political and local. Bureaucracy was nonexistent and state regulations were minimal. Teachers generally shared a common set of ideas about what and how to teach but did not think of themselves as members of a profession.

Bureaucratic Professionalism

The second period considered in this chapter began with the professionalization and administrative innovations of the Progressive Era (roughly 1870–1920), but its priorities and its characteristic forms of educational accountability persisted at least into the 1950s and 1960s. Where their predecessors had worked to provide free elementary schools for all children, in which the curriculum would be the same for everybody, the Progressives initiated an understanding of educational equity that was grounded in social efficiency: matching children with the school experiences most suited to their intellectual abilities and adult destinies. State education departments grew, and the professional community of school-level, district, and state educational administrators became more tightly knit by common training and experience. They expressed their professionalism via bureaucracy and increasing centralization of local school systems.

Social Efficiency as Equity

In the late nineteenth and early twentieth century, educators came to understand equity in terms of whether different curricula were suited to students' different needs, rather than in terms of access to a common school experience. By the start of the Progressive Era in the late nineteenth century, at least some attendance in elementary school had become commonplace. Instead of worrying about how to expand education to more children, educational leaders now focused on how to achieve efficiency in serving large numbers of students, many of them immigrants, and with many students of different ages crowded into the lower grades because they did not meet criteria for promotion. More students were also attending at least some secondary school, and states eventually enacted attendance laws that extended compulsory schooling into the teenage years. This further expansion of schooling led to an additional question about efficiency: what would be the best way to serve high school students who did not aspire to attend college or to work in the professions, unlike most of their predecessors? The society and economy of the United States were becoming more complex and industrial, with more occupational niches that young people might fill. School systems were becoming larger, and their leaders were seeking ways of enhancing their status in a time when Americans revered science and expertise.

The ideal of "social efficiency" emerged as the solution to these problems. Social efficiency meant making schools "a mechanism for adapting students to the requirements of a hierarchical social structure and the demands of the occupational marketplace" (Labaree 1997, 22). Educators saw their job as measuring each student's talents and intellectual capacities, identifying his or her likely adult role, and then providing schooling experiences that would be appropriate for fitting students to their station in life. The following statement about the "basic functions" of education from the New Jersey Education Commissioner's 1949–50 annual report exemplifies "social efficiency" applied to educational goals: "provid[ing], for the individual, growth opportunities appropriate to his particular abilities, needs, interests, and aspirations." The report also praised this sort of education as the one that would make the state's residents "freer from the frustrations which warp personalities and impair the pursuit of happiness" (Palmer 1969, 826). In this context, equity came to mean not that all students would be taught the same material and prepared to be equal participants in civic life but rather that they would learn what educators judged that they each needed to learn (Gamson 2007). Willard Waller's influential account of the sociology of teaching, first published in the 1930s, noted that "schools tend to bring children at least up to an intellectual level which will enable them to function in the same economic and social stratum as their parents" (Waller 1965, 20). In Waller's words, "the sorting process of the schools produces results which roughly conform to the (cultural or inherent) qualities of the individuals sorted" (ibid., 21).

The emerging science of mental testing inspired the pursuit of social efficiency and made it possible. Alfred Binet, whose work led to the concept of "intelligence quotient" or IQ, believed that "natural intelligence" could and should be distinguished from the results of schooling. The U.S. Army developed tests to assess recruits' abilities and assign them to appropriate jobs, again emphasizing the idea that intelligence was innate, rather than a malleable consequence of education and training (Gould 1981, ch. 5). When the Ivy League colleges decided that they ought to draw their students from a larger pool than the East Coast's elite boarding school graduates, they replaced the written College Board exams with the standardized Scholastic Aptitude Test (SAT), designed to be able to identify the most able students regardless of what curriculum they had followed in high school (Karabel 2005). Although IQ tests and the SAT would both later be attacked as biased against low-income students and students from racial and ethnic minority groups, educators of the early twentieth century saw them as potentially egalitarian because they could help identify promising young people regardless of economic or educational disadvantage. Educational leaders also believed that "tracking" students into college-preparatory, vocational, and general curricula based on their test scores expressed the true meaning of equal educational opportunity (Gamson 2007, 180–81). Not incidentally, educational administrators also enhanced their occupational prestige by positioning themselves as the people who had the necessary expertise to determine who belonged where and to sort them appropriately (Callahan 1962).

State Education Agencies and the "Interlocking Directorate"

During the Progressive Era, two different reform visions dominated education. The first variant of progressive education is the one generally associated with John Dewey. Dewey, and those who claimed to be following his vision, emphasized the need for new pedagogical techniques to replace the rote memorization that prevailed in most schools. For Dewey, broad participation in democratic decision making was also a form of education and thus was something public officials ought to embrace. The second version of progressive education took a far dimmer view of the average person's ability to participate in making important decisions. These "administrative progressives" (Tyack 1974, 196–97) instead put their trust in expertise, to be exercised via bureaucracies and sheltered from the influence of ignorant politicos, urban patronage machines, and the voters who supported them (Tyack and Hansot 1982, 106–7). Much of the administrative-progressive worldview can be found in the textbooks written by Ellwood Patterson Cubberley, which were so widely used in the early twentieth century that one historian has said that they "gave a generation of American schoolmen their way of looking at the world" (Cremin 1965, 2).

As the profession of educational leadership developed, state and local education bureaucrats were generally men who had come through similar training and socialization experiences, and who tended to band together against lay-people who did not share their outlook. During the last decades of the nine-teenth century and the first half of the twentieth, the professional ties between state-level education leaders and their local counterparts strengthened, and the states' ability to exert pressure on local school districts increased somewhat. Thomas Timar described the development of U.S. state departments of education as having first entailed strengthening the professional claim to control education and later "integrating state administrative authority with professional hierarchies" so that "state education bureaucracies became dominated by professional interests" (Timar 1997, 241). The result was a situation in which local educational administrators and their state-level counterparts sometimes acted together to advance a professional agenda despite local resistance. Critics sometimes labeled this alliance as an "interlocking directorate" of state and local professionals, and the label is not inaccurate.

For example, one of the great bureaucratic-professional causes was the consolidation of local school districts (Strang 1987). At the time, municipalities generally encompassed multiple school districts corresponding to neighborhoods or wards. For example, when Lowell, Massachusetts, was incorporated as a city in 1826, it encompassed five school districts (Cremin 1980, 417). Lest the prevalence of small districts in a large city like Lowell be seen as a result of urban population density, it should be noted that even a rural town like Middlebury, Vermont, showed thirteen school districts on its 1871 map (Fischel 2009, 37). Tiny school districts were anathema to administrative progressives because their fiscal capacity did not permit them to raise sufficient funds to support modern school systems—in particular large, comprehensive high schools.

Administrative reformers also disliked small, local districts because they forced school administrators to engage with a broad cross section of the public on school boards. According to the views embodied in Ellwood Patterson Cubberley's textbooks, school board members should be drawn from the elite of society because relatively few people had the appropriate outlook and skills for board service. If a state contained hundreds of small school districts, it would certainly run out of elites well before it ran out of school board seats to fill. In his textbook *Public School Administration*, Cubberley charged that "district-school authorities are usually short-sighted," that "the district unit is entirely too small an area in which to provide modern educational facilities," and that the proliferation of district-level governing boards, which required "an army of thirty to forty-five thousand [trustees] in an average well-settled State—in itself almost precludes the possibility of securing any large proportion of competent and efficient men" to hold office (1916, 52). In

Cubberley's understanding, merging school districts would not only increase the availability of resources but also decrease the necessary number of board members until it more closely matched the number of people who were fit to serve. State governments strengthened the hand of administrative-progressive reformers by making consolidation a condition for receipt of state education funds. Consolidation facilitated bureaucratization and professionalization of local educational administration (Tyack, James, and Benavot 1987, 120; and Strang 1987), and it was a favored cause of good-government progressives who wanted to put more distance between the public schools and ward politics (Tyack 1974). Consolidation of districts in turn helped state education authorities exercise their own power by making the entire education system more bureaucratically rational (Strang 1987).

"Depoliticizing" Public Education

The intent and effect of administrative progressivism was to build up bureaucratic accountability at the expense of political accountability. In the administrative-progressive vision, resisting the public's participation was a crucial part of educational administrators' work, since the public often wanted the wrong things. Under these circumstances, the experts' duty was to override majority opinion, particularly the opinions of people the experts believed to be intellectually or culturally inferior. Ellwood Patterson Cubberley's textbook *Public School Administration* made his biases about public participation clear. The chapter on "Organization of School Boards" includes a map of a city with nine wards, in which three "best residence wards" "always select good members for the Board of Education," but three others labeled "red-light district," "saloons and tenements," and "Negro ward shacks" "always select poor members" (Cubberley 1916, 94). Based on this example, he asserts that school boards should always be elected from the city at large rather than from wards so "the inevitable representation from 'poor wards' is eliminated, and the board as a whole comes to partake of the best characteristics of the city as a whole" (ibid., 95). Reformers wanted state legislatures to "standardize schools according to the plans of the professional educators" (Tyack, James, and Benavot 1987, 115). Boards of education were to make basic policy decisions but then delegate implementation of those decisions to school superintendents and other members of the growing profession of educational administration. Enforcement of compulsory education also contributed to growth of bureaucracy by adding new kinds of employees such as census takers, social workers, and special teachers (Tyack and Hansot 1982, 155).

Administrators controlled the newly consolidated school districts through a variety of bureaucratic means, such as "printed outlines, seating plans, recitation cards, attendance sheets, and other 'labor saving devices'" (Callahan 1962, 58). The large, urban school districts that were at the time the showplaces of educational quality and innovation displayed the most elaborate administrative control systems. For example, in the early twentieth century, the Washington, DC, school district distributed a weekly schedule to its teachers outlining how much time they were to spend on each subject. Historical evidence suggests that teachers tended to satisfy the letter of these requirements without actually being as lockstep in their practice as their supervisors might have preferred, but the norm of standardization remained (Cuban 1993).

Although all this bureaucracy may strike contemporary readers as anti-professional, at the time when reformers built the bureaucratic systems they viewed themselves as making education more professional and increasing the field's prestige. The early twentieth century was a period of great faith in scientific expertise, including the use of time and motion studies to ensure efficiency in business and manufacturing. Bureaucratized systems and standard operating procedures in schools were crucial to school administrators' (or "schoolmen's," to use their term) positioning of themselves as experts and professionals equal to scientists and captains of industry (Callahan 1962). Raymond Callahan's influential history of this period shows how the influence of business methods in public education came from "the vulnerability of schools and schoolmen and the great strength of the business community and the business philosophy in an age of efficiency" (179). Callahan quotes an efficiency expert as saying that increased attention to standards and efficiency is a way of taking on the problem of "creating a new kind of confidence on the part of the public in the work of public schools" (111).

Educational administrators clearly viewed themselves as members of an emerging profession, but they did not fully extend this view to the teachers. In Cubberley's *Public School Administration*, the chapters on selecting, training, and managing teachers frequently refer to the "professional" attributes of teachers, and how administrators can ensure that their district's teachers are well trained and efficient. However, in the same book, Cubberley also cites the deficiencies of the "home girls" who school boards often insisted on appointing to teaching positions (1916, 201) and notes that because the American teaching force includes "so many women teachers who possess but the required minimum of professional training and who expect or hope to remain in the service but a short time," supervision has "an importance which it does not have in countries where teaching represents more of a life-career"

(240). In effect, administrators' professional status came at the expense of that of the teachers because administrators' professionalism rested on the extent to which they used modern bureaucratic methods to control subordinates. Tyack and Hansot make a connection between the feminization of teaching and its bureaucratization: "When women first replaced men as teachers in urban public schools, they were valued not only because they were cheaper and supposedly more nurturing and skillful instructors of young children, but also because they were presumed to be more compliant with the direction of male superintendents than were the old schoolmasters" (1982, 183). Teaching was at the time a high-turnover occupation (Lortie 2002, ch. 2). Rather than try to enhance the retention of teachers, education reformers tended to take the opposite tack and build systems in which teachers were interchangeable operators carrying out well-specified tasks (ibid., 74).

Collective bargaining for school employees was another source of bureaucratic proliferation and persistence. Teachers turned to collective bargaining as a way of asserting their professional status and resisting arbitrary control by administrators or boards of education (Murphy 1990). One of the first education labor-management conflicts took place in Chicago in the early 1900s, when the city's school administrators were centralizing the system along the lines favored by Cubberleyan progressives. Labor activists among the teachers resisted having to shift their loyalty from the neighborhoods where they worked to the city's central office (ibid., 23). Ironically, however, unions protected teachers by putting in place highly centralized systems of seniority and work rules, which added to bureaucratization (Urban 1982, 175–76). Over the course of the twentieth century, progressive educators' claims to scientific expertise lost legitimacy, but the bureaucracies they built persisted. Educational paperwork and red tape were notorious. Memoirs of the New York City public schools often mention the Delaney cards for attendance-taking as well as the requirement that teachers write the "aim" of each lesson on the blackboard. The Brooklyn street address of the New York City Public Schools' headquarters was so well known that it became the title of *110 Livingston Street*, a book on the system's hidebound, sluggish, and incompetent management (Rogers 1968).

Part of the progressives' faith in science was a fascination with measurement. Although the administrative progressives' characteristic form of accountability was bureaucracy, they also employed "school surveys" as a means of professional accountability. In a school survey, an outside group of education professionals would visit a school district and study the extent to which its resources and practices reflected professional ideas about exemplary practices

(Tyack and Hansot 1982, 160–67). Tyack and Hansot's description of the results of surveys foreshadows the goals of standardized testing policies that would follow at the end of the century: "It [the school survey] helped muck-rakers to expose evils, foundation officials to gain leverage to change society, and federal or state educational bureaucrats to enlarge governmental power to regulate and standardize" (ibid., 161). Lawrence Cremin's history of the Progressive movement in U.S. education quotes an influential educational researcher of the time who remembered his graduate training as "one long orgy of tabulation" (Cremin 1964, 181).

The main difference between the progressive-era school surveys and the performance measurement efforts of the future was that the administrators whose districts were being surveyed generally endorsed the surveys' measurement priorities and the standards to which they were being held. As Tyack, James, and Benavot note, "the surveys were fairly predictable" because of the common socialization and outlook of the small group of experts who conducted them (1987, 113). A reformist superintendent might even call for a survey to help make the case for change to a recalcitrant school board or electorate. Although the surveys came from outside school districts, they were still internal to the educational profession. Overall, as Callahan notes, the effect of the surveys was to enhance the professional status of school administrators (1962, 113).

Bureaucracy was the characteristic form of educational accountability in the system that the administrative progressives built. Rather than being an alternative to professional accountability, bureaucracy during this period was at the core of educational administrators' claims to being a profession. By deploying the same kinds of managerial control techniques as their counterparts in industry, with a similarly scientific grounding, "schoolmen" demonstrated that they were equally worthy of being taken seriously. State regulation was increasing but generally with the support of local administrators; during this period, the state regulators and the local administrators tended to agree on what needed to be regulated and how. As for political accountability, the central idea of the period was that politics should be kept away from the schools by having school boards elected (or appointed) separately from the rest of municipal government. These boards would set broad outlines of policy and leave the rest to professional administration. It is easy to caricature early twentieth-century administrators, particularly their faith that administration and politics could be clearly separated and their ideas about intelligence and academic capability. Nevertheless, it is important to keep in mind that they were acting in the public interest as they understood it, and that some of what they did actually

Table 3.2 Educational Accountability and Administrative Progressivism

Type of Accountability	*Means of Accountability*
Bureaucratic	Local administrative control of teachers Bureaucracy used to bolster administrators' claims of professionalism
Professional	Administrators aware of developing professional consensus Teachers not yet seen as professionals
Legal	Increasing state regulations, still generally supported by educators and coming from within "interlocking directorate"
Political	Whenever possible, administrators tried to limit power of locally elected school boards

Source: Categories from Romzek and Dubnick 1987.

was in the public interest—for example, expanding public schools to serve larger numbers of students in an industrializing and urbanizing country, and institutionalizing the idea that teachers and principals ought to be selected for their expertise rather than their political connections.

Inclusion and Conflict

Much of the progressives' received wisdom had been turned on its head by the last quarter of the twentieth century. Casual elitism like that expressed in Cubberley's books may still have existed, but the explicit goals of public schooling shifted to include combating racial prejudice. Testing and tracking students, formerly understood as the fairest way of serving a diverse population, were attacked as inherently discriminatory. The centralization of educational authority continued but now was generally undertaken in the interests of equalizing access or funding. At the same time, the kinds of people that Cubberley would have dismissed as unfit to participate in education governance demanded decentralization of school governance so that they could have more power over their children's schools. Despite this attack on some assumptions behind administrative progressivism, bureaucracy continued to proliferate. In its late-century form, educational bureaucracy often was linked to new legal mandates for schools to serve, and demonstrate that they were fairly serving, all students. By the 1970s U.S. public schools faced demands from multiple constituencies for all four of Romzek and Dubnick's forms of accountability.

Questioning Expertise

The idea of social efficiency backed by educational expertise began to lose its luster in the 1950s. One line of criticism came from people who believed that the system produced mediocrity for all. Once primary and secondary education became nearly universal, the public began to demand evidence that something of high quality was being taught (Grant and Murray 1999, 221). Arthur Bestor's book *Educational Wastelands*, first published in 1953, gave voice to the mainstream of these criticisms. Bestor criticized what he saw as the silliest excesses of progressive education and charged that educators who "assert that the ideal of rigorous intellectual training throughout the public schools is a false or unattainable ideal" were taking "precisely the position that was occupied a century ago by the *opponents* of public education" (Bestor 1985, 28). In arguing for the National Defense Education Act of 1957, which provided some federal funds to enhance teaching of science and foreign languages, advocates of federal funding for primary and secondary education used popular fears that the United States would lose the "space race" to the USSR (Davies 2007, 13–16).

Another line of criticism emerged in the 1970s on behalf of students who were likeliest to score low on tests and to be sorted into less intellectually demanding tracks. Educational researchers began to question whether tracking students by ability was actually as beneficial as its midcentury advocates had assumed (Oakes 1985). People who were skeptical of tracking pointed out that separating students into ability groups was often a way of perpetuating racial segregation within ostensibly integrated schools (Meier, Stewart, and England 1989). The very notion of measuring "intelligence" came under critical scrutiny (Gould 1981). The Progressive Era faith in the results of intelligence testing and in the ability of educators to slot students into curricula that would suit their eventual place in the social system was nearly unthinkable by the end of the century. By then, it was still often the case, as Waller had found in the 1930s, that public schools tended to prepare their students to take the same places in society as their parents; however, what had been the goal of an earlier generation of public schools was now seen as a problem. Increasing numbers of educators and parents wanted the schools to emphasize social mobility over social efficiency.

The goals of social efficiency and social mobility were partially in tension with each other. Although people might agree in principle that it makes sense for schools to spend money efficiently by giving students exactly the training they need for their likely future adult roles, they also tend to disagree with social efficiency when it means that their own children are the ones who are going to be pointed toward lower-status occupations. According to Labaree's historical analysis, "adults in their taxpayer role tend to apply more stringent criteria to the support of education as a public good than they do in their role as consumers thinking of education as a private good" (1997, 39). In the second half of the twentieth century, however, it became increasingly clear that people with more schooling, including college, were coming out ahead in the contest for well-paying jobs (Goldin and Katz 2008). Thinking as taxpayers, the public might concede that social efficiency made sense as a general principle, but thinking as parents of individual children, citizens wanted to be sure that their children had access to the educational experiences that would make it possible for them to succeed in the contest for social mobility (Labaree 1997; Reese 2005). Increasingly, "good enough" was not good enough.

Desegregation and Financial Equalization

The common-school advocates had defined educational equity as a place in school for all children, and the administrative progressives had defined it as an appropriate schooling experience for each child, considering his or her talents and likely adult role. From roughly the middle of the twentieth century on, two more definitions emerged from federal and state courts. The first such definition linked equity with desegregation. Initially desegregation lawsuits in federal courts targeted the states whose laws required racially separate schools. The U.S. Supreme Court had upheld segregation, so long as the separate facilities were equal, in its 1896 *Plessy v. Ferguson* decision. Attacking segregation, the NAACP Legal Defense Fund took a long-term strategy of first arguing that the separate facilities were not, in fact, equal, and then moving on from there to target segregation per se (Kluger 1975). In its 1954 *Brown v. Board of Education* decision, the U.S. Supreme Court acknowledged that the states whose laws were under challenge had essentially equalized the resources available to white and black schools but concluded that segregation implicitly taught children that whites were superior to blacks, and thus that racially segregated schools were inherently unequal. Later rulings in two more southern cases, *Green v. New Kent County* and *Swann v. Charlotte-Mecklenburg Public Schools*, required formerly segregated districts not just to declare their schools open to students of all races but actually to achieve racial balance in their schools by busing students outside their home neighborhoods if necessary. The *Brown* decision and its progeny led to increased racial integration in the states that had formerly had legally mandated segregation. Indeed, by 1970 the South had the most racially integrated schools of any region in the United States (Frankenberg, Lee, and Orfield 2003).

The de facto segregation of the North and West presented a more difficult target. Segregation had complex origins in housing markets, which themselves had been shaped by explicitly racist federal loan guarantee and public-housing policies (Jackson 1985) as well as by school board decisions on where to site schools and how to draw attendance boundaries. Sometimes these local decisions were racially discriminatory on their face (Sugrue 2008), but often they appeared racially neutral. During an eighteen-month period in the mid-1970s, the U.S. Supreme Court issued a series of decisions on northern school desegregation, bilingual education, and education finance, which complicated the relatively simple *Brown* "separate is inherently unequal" principle (Nelson 2007). The ruling in *Brown* had implied that education was one of the rights protected by the Fourteenth Amendment to the U.S. Constitution. However, in the March 1973 *San Antonio Independent School District v. Rodriguez* decision, the court stated that education is not a right protected under the Fourteenth Amendment, and thus that federal courts could not order states to provide equal school funding to all communities. Despite its restraint in *Rodriguez*, three months later, in *Keyes v. School District #1*, the court extended the *Green* and *Swann* requirement for racial balance, via busing if necessary, to states that had not practiced de jure segregation, and defined educational equality as "a system of desegregation and integration which provides compensatory education in an integrated environment" (quoted in Nelson 2007, 203). The court's next education ruling, in *Lau v. Nichols* (1974), found that the 1964 Civil Rights Act's prohibition of discrimination required school districts to provide bilingual education, which in practice often meant clustering Latino or Asian students in particular schools rather than integrating them across a school district. Finally, the court seemed to back away from the *Brown* doctrine that separate schools are intrinsically unequal, even if funded equally, in its 1974 and 1977 *Milliken v. Bradley* decisions. In the two *Milliken* decisions, the court ruled that a desegregation plan for the city of Detroit could not extend beyond the city boundaries in order to produce greater racial integration, and that the state of Michigan could be required to increase Detroit's state aid in order to fund special compensatory programs for its largely African American student population.

Taken together, the two *Milliken* rulings suggest that—contra *Brown*—increased funding could be substituted for racial integration (Nelson 2007). Equality of funding was at the core of the second definition of educational equity that came out of court rulings, mostly at the state level. After the federal *Rodriguez* decision, it was clear that future funding litigation would take place in the states. The Ford Foundation provided funding and a national network for state-level efforts, funding both research on school finance and lawsuits that made use of the information uncovered in the research (McDermott 2009). Plaintiffs based their cases on state equal-protection guarantees and argued that equal protection required equal funding (Verstegan and Whitney 1997).

When the National Commission on Excellence in Education released its 1983 *A Nation at Risk* report, critics of the public schools claimed that excessive attention to equity had crowded out sufficient concern for excellence (Ravitch 1983; Toch 1991). However, what was really going on was a redefinition of equity, and thus of the goal of public schooling. By the late 1970s many paths converged on defining educational equity in terms of academic results, and on claiming that the schools ought to produce better academic outcomes for all students. This principle was implicit in criticisms of IQ testing, tracking, and second-generation segregation as well as in the new generation of education finance lawsuits based on state adequacy guarantees.

The Expanding State and Federal Legal Role

State educational authorities increased their power in the middle of the twentieth century, sometimes pursuing different priorities from local school boards. Increased state power was consistent with the states' constitutional and statutory powers. In their legal history of U.S. public education, Tyack, James, and Benavot suggest that the mandatory attendance laws, even though their practical effect was minor, were an important philosophical turning point. By requiring that children attend school up to a certain age, state governments were introducing the assumption that children have educational rights of which the state is ultimately the protector. Protecting children's educational rights could extend even to the point of intervening in family relationships by forbidding parents to keep children home from school (1987, 97). (Some states went even further than this, requiring attendance at public rather than private schools, but the U.S. Supreme Court invalidated such laws in the 1925 *Pierce v. Society of Sisters* decision.) State and federal governments also began to intervene to protect students' individual rights to an education from encroachment by lower levels of government. Like the rest of the federal role in public education, federal-level legal accountability grew dramatically during the second half of the twentieth century. The chief examples are desegregation, as discussed earlier, as well as criteria that must be met in programs for children with limited English proficiency and children with disabilities.

Because the federal government does not have direct power over education, the main instrument of legal accountability used by the federal government was (and still is) to attach conditions to grant programs so that the states or localities that wanted the funds must adhere to federal policy (McDermott and Jensen 2005). The principal such vehicle has been the compensatory education grants included in the Elementary and Secondary Education Act of 1965 (ESEA) and its successors (Cohen and Moffitt 2009). Under Title VI of the Civil Rights Act of 1964, no segregated entity may receive federal funding. Thus, immediately after its enactment, ESEA's large Title I compensatory-grant program provided leverage for desegregation of southern school systems that had spent the previous decade ignoring or resisting *Brown v. Board of Education* (Rosenberg 1991; Davies 2007; Orfield 1969). Title I also facilitated the spread of pressure for integration into school districts that had patterns of segregation in their schools even though their states had not mandated racially separate schools (Davies 2007; Sugrue 2008). Later, Congress responded to two landmark lawsuits by enacting the Education for All Handicapped Children Act of 1975, which created a legal entitlement to a "free and appropriate public education" in the "least restrictive environment" for students with disabilities. The Office of Civil Rights (OCR) within the U.S. Office of Education also promulgated regulations intended to eliminate discrimination based on gender, disability, and native language. To enable enforcement, OCR's budget increased sixfold between 1970 and 1977 (Davies 2007, 142).

State and federal grant programs have generated procedures to be followed and offices staffed by people whose job it is to enforce those procedures. If a grant is categorical, then schools and districts need to be able to document that the funds from it were spent on the right kind of student (disabled, disadvantaged, limited English proficient, etc.). If a grant is of the type that requires districts to submit a proposal for how the funds will be used, then, in addition to the proposals, there will be follow-up documentation that the money was spent as proposed. The goal of preventing targeted funds—often targeted toward politically vulnerable constituencies—from being swallowed up in general operating expenses is a reasonable one. The result often seems unreasonable: program staff working in "silos" where they concentrate on one element of the schools' activities rather than on the system as a whole (Cohen and Moffitt 2009).

Unlike their predecessors, who welcomed state requirements that gave them legal cover for doing things they believed were right, educational administrators of the middle and late twentieth century often felt besieged by legal mandates. The legal route was a strategy especially favored by "dispossessed" groups such as women, African Americans, Latinos, and Native Americans (Tyack 1986) using the law to pursue social justice they had been unable to gain otherwise (Tyack, James, and Benavot 1987, 194). These were the very groups that the administrative progressives had tended to slot into low-status curriculum tracks and had attempted to block from participation in governing the schools. Those administrators' successors did not necessarily appreciate now being compelled to follow new procedures on their behalf.

Even if administrators were sympathetic to these demands, the collective burden of court mandates could be overwhelming. In 1980 Boston school superintendent Robert Wood, facing a severe fiscal crisis, noted that his control of the school department budget was hemmed in by more than two hundred court orders, which not only limited where he could make cuts but also obscured overall accountability in the system (Nelson 2005, 202). In addition to antidiscrimination rulings, school administrators also needed to comply with rulings related to student and employee free speech and due process. The U.S. Supreme Court ruled in *Tinker v. Des Moines* (1969) that both students and teachers retained some free-speech rights within schools, even if administrators did not agree with what they were saying (Fischer, Schimmel, and Stellman 2007). Administrators' power to expel students was subject to following appropriate procedures. Union contracts protected teachers from arbitrary dismissal and reassignment, via due-process requirements.

New Participants with New Demands

One of the clearest trends of the late twentieth century was a loss of faith in expertise and an increase in demands for public participation. In local governance, this trend manifested itself as calls for "community control" of schools and as greater scrutiny of administrators' decisions by lay people. At the state and federal level, legislators, governors, presidents, and members of Congress responded to increased public concern about educational issues by becoming engaged in the sort of decisions that were once left up to specialists in state departments and boards of education.

To a great extent, the increased demand for public participation and rejection of administrative-progressive forms of governance expressed the ideals of Deweyan educational progressivism. Dewey believed that participation in public debate and decision making was in itself an educative process, and thus that informing the uninformed was a key part of democratic politics (Morris and Shapiro 1993, ix–xix). Clearly, this was a different view of participation than that enshrined in Cubberley's textbooks for administrators. Educational administrators educated in the Cubberleyan tradition, or at most a generation removed from it, were in positions of authority all over the United States when the African American civil rights movement and the other movements it inspired confronted the schools. Many administrators had a hard time accepting community activists' claims because they believed themselves to be neutral experts, not political actors (Tyack and Hansot 1982, 238–39). From urban communities of color demanding "community control" of their schools to suburban and rural communities divided over cultural issues such as the teaching of evolution and the content of textbooks, administrators found themselves politically accountable to mobilized constituents in a way for which most were completely unprepared.

In the 1960s the push for community control of urban schools by people of color exemplified the collision between new demands for political accountability and older conceptions of professionalism and bureaucratic procedure. The best-known episode pitted a "demonstration" school board in New York City's black and Latino Ocean Hill–Brownsville neighborhood, where the Ford Foundation was sponsoring an experiment with community control, against mostly white teachers who had only recently won the right to citywide collective bargaining. When the Ocean Hill–Brownsville administrators reassigned a group of teachers, insisting that they needed to have authority over personnel for community control to be real, the citywide United Federation of Teachers went on strike to protect the hard-won principle that teacher assignments had to be done centrally, according to seniority. Charges of racism flew in both directions. By many accounts, the Ocean Hill–Brownsville conflict split the original civil rights coalition and created a lasting rift between black and Jewish communities in New York City, since Jews were among the largest demographic groups in the city's teacher population (Kahlenberg 2007; Murphy 1990). In terms of accountability, the community control movement insisted that what mattered most was that a community's schools be run by people from that community so they would be responsive to their constituency. The community-control activists also questioned parts of the legal-accountability

Table 3.3   Educational Accountability in the Era of Inclusion and Conflict

Type of Accountability	*Means of Accountability*
Bureaucratic	Earlier bureaucracy persists
	New legislation and rights claims generate more bureaucracy
Professional	Administrators have strong professional identity
	Teachers increasingly asserting a professional identity
Legal	Civil rights claims
	Emphasis on due process or students and teachers
Political	Increasing demands for local participation
	Challenges to politics/administration dichotomy

Source: Categories from Romzek and Dubnick 1987.

agenda, since they rejected the idea that racial integration was necessary for their children's schools to improve.

The main characteristic of educational accountability in the late twentieth century was profusion of all four of Romzek and Dubnick's types of accountability. Within school districts and schools, the bureaucracy built in earlier years stayed in place. Teachers asserted themselves as professionals; through collective bargaining, they also secured legal rights to due process in hiring, placement, and firing. Schools and districts were increasingly accountable through the legal system for upholding teachers' and students' rights to procedural due process and meeting federal and state standards concerning desegregation and other civil rights issues. An increasingly organized and restive public (especially in cities) made it difficult if not impossible for school administrators to maintain the idea that their work should (or could) be kept separate from politics.

Conclusion

As Romzek and Dubnick (1987) would predict, shifts in prevailing public expectations and understandings of equity have produced shifts in what public officials want to hold schools accountable for achieving. The pursuit of educational accountability led to conflict between definition and control of expectations by people internal to the schools (bureaucratic and professional accountability) and by people outside of them (legal and political accountability).

Equality of educational opportunity has long been one of the central goals of U.S. public education. Since the origins of U.S. public schools, the definition of this goal has shifted. For most of the nineteenth century, the goal of the public education system was to provide access to primary schooling for an expanding number of children (except for enslaved children in the South). Most school districts operated only a single school, so accountability was prebureaucratic. Local taxpayers and school directors could directly scrutinize the school and its teacher; the characteristic form of accountability was local and political. State regulation was minimal but tended to emphasize the goals of increasing access (via mandatory attendance laws) and to use state requirements for length of school term or quality of facilities as a counterweight to local desires to keep education spending low. In the intergovernmental system—such as it was—the state tended to act as an ally of education experts.

Beginning in the Progressive Era and continuing until approximately the middle of the twentieth century, equity continued to be defined in terms of access. However, now the goal was to get more young people to enroll in and complete secondary school. As secondary-school populations grew larger and

Table 3.4 Evolving Ideas about Equity, Intergovernmental Relations, and Accountability

	Equity	Accountability	Intergovernmental Relations
Common-School Era (until 1870s)	Access to primary school Common curriculum	Prebureaucratic organizations Political (to district boards of education) Minimal state regulation Direct community scrutiny	District-based schooling State as occasional ally of pro-fessional educators
Administrative Pro-gressivism (high point in early 1900s; persisted until 1950s)	Access to secondary school Different but appropriate curricula	Emphasis on keeping politics out of the schools Professional, enabled by bureaucracy	Centralization at municipal level "Interlocking Directorate" of state education departments and pro-fessional educators
Inclusion and Conflict (1960s–1970s)	Desegregation Equal funding Critique of tracking and differentiation	Proliferation of bureaucratic, political, and legal accountability Less deference to professional educators	Growing federal role in civil rights enforcement Growing state role in funding equity

more diverse, education experts added ideas about appropriate curriculum to their understanding of equity. They assumed that not all students could master the academic high school curriculum and thus broadened high schools to include vocational or general curricula. Administrators used the emerging science of mental testing to decide which alternative would be appropriate for each student. One-school districts remained quite common during this period, but in the larger city systems bureaucratic accountability became a key tool for educational professionals. Educators and laypeople both assumed that politics could, and should, be kept out of schools, and educational decisions should be left to the experts. Authority over public education became more centralized during this period. State laws forced consolidation of small school districts. State regulators typically emerged from the same professional community as the local administrators they regulated, which led some critics to label the education system an "interlocking directorate."

Throughout this history the trend in intergovernmental relations has been toward greater centralization, although the boundaries between local, state, and federal authority remain contested. When state education authorities actually began taking the expansive governance role implied by their constitutional powers, they were in effect activating a latent fiduciary or principal–agent relationship with local authorities. In this new understanding of state power in education governance, the state was acting as if it had delegated its power over education to the localities, subject to their carrying out their responsibilities, rather than continuing to act as if the state's job was to back up local educators. In Romzek and Dubnick's terms, this was a strengthening of legal accountability. Gareth Davies' history of the expanding federal role in education notes that federal agency staff, especially in the Office of Civil Rights, came to assume that local administrators and boards of education were prejudiced and untrustworthy (2007, 156). This assumption had a solid grounding in the reality of OCR's experiences with desegregation. Federal education policy since the 1960s has positioned federal authorities as the protectors of other vulnerable student populations, such as girls, students with disabilities, and students who do not speak English well, from local authorities who must be held to strict compliance with regulations.

Multiple levels of authority have led to a complex set of accountability relationships. As will be seen in the next chapter, although the push for standards and performance accountability in education began with the notion of exchanging deregulation of process for closer scrutiny of results, there was actually not much room to remove bureaucratic accountability measures when state and federal governments began to emphasize results. Doing so would have required greater trust between administrators and teachers than often existed. Teachers were increasingly likely to see themselves as professionals and to resent bureaucratic control. Legal accountability also strengthened. Requirements for documenting individualized education programs for students with disabilities, complying with Section 504 of the Rehabilitation Act, and preventing gender discrimination did not wither away just because the priorities of Title I had changed. As Eugene Bardach points out, educational paperwork serves a political purpose. Requirements for which characteristics of students must be recorded, or how money must be tracked, "is a constant reminder that these are matters one is supposed to care about" (1986, 130).

In this new, more complicated world, professional, bureaucratic, legal, and political accountability demands pulled school administrators and teachers in many directions at once. Many policymakers and members of the public sought a return to "basics" and reassurance that, amidst the turmoil, students were still learning to read, write, and do arithmetic. Some educators and researchers reached the conclusion that the system pulled schools in too many inconsistent directions; they sought a means of making education policy more coherent and organized around core teaching goals. The result was a nationwide trend toward accountability based on the results of standardized tests. These tests, as part of a new model of standards-based education reform, promised to extend policymaker influence into the classrooms themselves, where it had hitherto not been able to reach. Chapter 4 tells the story of how this national movement spread around the states.

CHAPTER FOUR

Education Standards and Performance Accountability, 1970–2001

By the 1970s U.S. public schools and the people who worked in them were enmeshed in multiple systems of accountability. However, discontent with the schools' performance was mounting. Critics charged that excessive pressure for equity had crowded out attention to excellence in education. Economic dislocation inspired elected officials to link educational improvement with economic development strategies and to seek greater control over education policy. Emphasizing schools' performance seemed like the answer to these problems, and new kinds of tests provided a means of measuring performance. Increasingly, state policies used test scores as the basis for accountability sanctions: withholding diplomas from students who had not passed tests; intervening in schools with low scores, including replacement of some or all staff members; and even instituting state control over entire school districts.

The chapter is divided into three roughly chronological sections. The first covers the beginnings of performance-based educational accountability in the 1970s. The second analyzes the surge of education reform activity in the 1980s, much of it inspired by the 1983 *A Nation at Risk* report. A new conception of educational equity, based on the idea that all students should master a common body of knowledge and skills, was at the foundation of these reform efforts. Many of the states enacted performance-accountability policies in education, including sanctions for underperforming schools and school districts.[1] The final section follows the intensification of federal accountability policy, influenced by what the states were doing, during Bill Clinton's two terms as president and George W. Bush's first term.

Origins

By the 1970s standardized tests had become a familiar feature of U.S. public schools, which could be turned to the purpose of evaluating schools and districts, not just students. The earliest states to base performance-accountability policies on test scores tended to be in the South. However, by the 1980s test-based accountability policies, including sanctions, existed outside the South as well.

The Evolution of Educational Measurement

The IQ and SAT tests mentioned in chapter 3 were landmarks in the history of educational measurement. Crucially, both were designed to measure people's innate level of educational ability so they could be sorted into the right school programs leading them to appropriate occupations. By the 1970s several popular standardized tests for students in grades kindergarten through twelve had been in use for several decades (Koretz 2008). These tests were designed to compare individual students' learning and ability to national norms of performance for particular grade levels.

Two changes in the design and use of standardized tests accompanied standards-based reform in education. The first shift in testing concerned its purpose. Beginning in the 1960s with the National Assessment of Educational Progress (NAEP) and the testing requirements in the Title I Evaluation and Reporting System (TIERS), policymakers began using tests to assess the performance of education programs and even the nation as a whole, rather than just to measure the achievement or ability of individual students. The second shift was in the design of the tests. During the 1970s and 1980s testing companies began to produce "criterion-referenced" tests designed to measure whether a particular test-taker's performance met a particular absolute threshold level of performance, rather than to compare test-takers to population norms.

The Reformist South

During the 1970s governors and other policymakers in the southern states took an increased interest in education reform. The southern state-level reforms often included student testing, attention to teacher qualifications, and accountability measures that would later become models for other states. Southern reformism presents a puzzle because research on the spread of policy ideas among the states has typically concluded that the wealthiest, most industrialized states are the most frequent innovators, but most of the southern states were neither wealthy nor heavily industrialized in the late 1970s (see Gray 1973; Walker 1969). What, then, explains why the press for state-level education reform began there?

One part of the explanation is that the development of public education in the South was well behind that of other regions. In the antebellum South, white children had attended private school, if they attended school at all. It was illegal to educate slaves, although there was some resistance to these laws. During Reconstruction, the reconstituted state governments included departments of education, and some northern educators came south to teach the freedmen. However, the Jim Crow laws enacted in the South after Reconstruction reversed these gains and entrenched segregation more deeply (Woodward 1974). In some cases, the states compounded their educational disadvantages by disinvesting in public schooling during conflicts over school desegregation. For example, Mississippi, the last state in the United States to have made schooling mandatory, went so far as to repeal its mandatory-attendance law in 1956 and did not reinstate it until 1977 (Jenkins and Person 1991).

By the 1970s many Southerners—particularly elected officials concerned about economic development—were tired of being ranked at the bottom of the country in terms of educational indicators (Vold and DeVitis 1991). Reformist governors in Alabama, Florida, and South Carolina hoped to use education to make their states more competitive in efforts to attract skilled, high-paying jobs from other parts of the United States and from abroad, particularly West Germany (as it then was) and Japan (Harvey 2002). The next generation of southern "education governors," including Lamar Alexander of Tennessee, James Hunt of North Carolina, Chuck Robb of Virginia, Bill Clinton of Arkansas, William Winter of Mississippi, and Richard Riley of South Carolina (Toch 1991, 19), pursued this strategy even more energetically. Alexander's reform agenda in Tennessee was cited as one reason why General Motors chose to locate its new Saturn plant there (ibid., 18). David E. Osborne, one of the coauthors of the influential book *Reinventing Government*, featured Gov. Bill Clinton's reform agenda in Arkansas in another book, *Laboratories of Democracy*. According to Osborne, Clinton explicitly made the connection between education reform and economic competitiveness. Clinton began with increased education spending, higher teacher salaries, a requirement that teachers pass the National Teacher Examination to be certified, and a residential summer school for gifted students. After he lost office—partially because he had angered the state's business community—and then regained it, Clinton emphasized standards and graduation requirements (Osborne 1988, ch. 3).

Education reform also fit with the electoral interests of officials who needed to be able to win elections after the southern electorate expanded to include black voters. In many places, school desegregation had exacerbated racial tensions. Some politicians exploited these tensions for political advantage. Others sought to build biracial reform coalitions as the post–Voting Rights Act electorate came to look more like the states' overall populations. In contrast to desegregation, school reform promised to be an issue that would move politics beyond "massive resistance" and speak to shared interests (Harvey 2002). For example, Alabama governor Albert Brewer proposed in 1968 to increase the state's funding of public education. He combined this proposal with calls for more accountability, including reorganizing state authority over education, merit pay for teachers, and teacher tenure reform (ibid., 48–51). In 1970, Brewer proclaimed, "the question is not one of integration or segregation. We crossed that bridge several years ago. The question is about what kind of education we are going to give our children" (quoted in ibid., 41). Florida governor Reubin Askew criticized busing but also campaigned against a state antibusing referendum (ibid., 83). Reform of education finance and governance was central to Askew's efforts to build a biracial coalition and position Florida as a model of peaceful race relations (ibid., 92–95).

High School Graduation Tests

During the 1970s many states—including nearly all of the South—enacted testing programs designed to certify that students had met minimum standards of academic competency. Ten of these states made passing the minimum-competency test a requirement for earning a high-school diploma. Of these ten, six were southern.[2] One was New Jersey, which will be discussed in more detail later in this book. Other states, including Connecticut, enacted minimum-competency tests but did not make passing them a graduation prerequisite.

Advocates of graduation tests often said (and still say) that their goal is to "restore the meaning of the high-school diploma." Like any educational credential, a high school diploma might have either or both of two kinds of value: as evidence that a person actually has learned a particular body of material, and as a source of "competitive advantage in the struggle for desirable social positions" (Labaree 1997, 18). An effort to restore the meaning of the high school diploma could thus emphasize either connecting it to a particular body of knowledge or making it scarcer and thereby increasing its competitive value. These two kinds of value are not mutually exclusive; a diploma from an elite, selective high school such as the Boston Latin School both signals that a graduate has completed a rigorous curriculum and gives that student an advantage in college admissions over students from less prestigious high schools.

The shift to mass secondary education in comprehensive high schools and the "social efficiency" movement discussed in chapter 3 blurred the educational meaning of the high school diploma while also reducing its competitive value. As more students enrolled in high school and states raised the legal school-leaving age, the schools had to serve a more diverse student population than when most teenagers went into farming, homemaking, or factory jobs instead of staying in school. Rather than trying to get a less academically inclined population through the existing college preparatory and business-oriented curricula, schools added vocational and "general" tracks and redefined their goal as facilitating the "adjustment" of teenagers to various adult destinies. A high school diploma came to mean that a student had completed a particular number of courses and spent a certain number of years in school, rather than that she or he had mastered any particular body of knowledge.

Critiques of this approach came from two sides. Some critics, like Arthur Bestor, focused on high schools' lack of academic rigor; the Soviet Union's apparent head start in the "space race" provided them with backing for their claims that American schools were not producing well-educated students. Other critics emphasized the racial, ethnic, and socioeconomic biases of the differentiated curriculum. Sorting students according to their future roles in life also tended to mean sorting them according to their race, ethnicity, and family background, thus making high schools the site of self-fulfilling prophecies about their destinies (Oakes 1985). The "meaning" that policymakers wanted to restore to the U.S. high school diploma beginning in the 1970s was chiefly defined in terms of academic content, and in terms of signaling to employers and colleges that a graduate had mastered a body of knowledge, or at least of basic skills. As we will see in this book's case studies of the Massachusetts and New Jersey graduation tests, advocates of the tests tended to claim that restoring the diploma's meaning would allow graduates from different communities to compete on a more level playing field.

Intergovernmental Relations

State graduation tests were part of the overall centralization of intergovernmental relations in education, discussed in chapter 3. The states enacting sanctions in the 1970s also started out with somewhat more centralized education systems. In the ten states with graduation tests, state funds accounted for 49 percent of education spending between 1972 and 1980, compared with 43 percent in the other states. The ten graduation-test states also had fewer school districts relative to their population, indicating that even the local level of their intergovernmental system was more centralized than in other states. One of them, Hawaii, has no local school districts. The other nine had an average of 11,186 students per district during the period from 1972 to 1980, compared with 2,992 in the states without graduation tests.

The federal government had almost no role in the minimum-competency testing movement or in the enactment of the first test-based sanctions. In 1978 Rep. Ronald Mottl (D-OH) introduced legislation that would have required states to have secondary education standards and graduation tests as a condition for receiving federal elementary and secondary education aid, but Congress did not approve the bills. The Education Amendments of 1978 did include technical assistance for states developing minimum-competency tests, but Congress never appropriated funds for this program (Vlanderen 1980). Thus, despite the beginnings of increased centralization, not much shift in intergovernmental relations had yet taken place in the area of performance accountability by the end of the 1970s.

Commissions, Business, and Education Governors, 1980–94

By the end of the 1970s concern about the performance of U.S. public schools was becoming widespread as college-bound students' scores on the Scholastic Achievement Test dropped. Motivated by this concern and by the desire to show President Ronald Reagan that there was a benefit in having a federal-level department of education, U.S. education secretary Terrel Bell convened a commission that released its report in 1983. This report, titled *A Nation at Risk*, was a crucial moment in the creation of state and national pressure for education reform. Also during the 1980s, educators and education researchers developed a new, systemic, "standards-based" model of education reform with clear connections to the performance-measurement models of accountability taking hold in public and business management. The politics of education reform changed, with governors and state legislators claiming authority that they had previously been content to leave in the hands of state boards of education and state superintendents. States enacted more performance-based accountability policies and took on a larger role in the intergovernmental system of education policy. Some participants in policy debates claimed that schools focused too much attention on equity and needed to renew their push for excellence; the result was a different understanding of equity that incorporated performance.

A Nation at Risk and Its Predecessors

The standards movement in education is often assumed to have begun with the 1983 release of *A Nation at Risk*, but state-level concern about the performance of public schools actually intensified earlier. Although most of the actual tests would later be replaced in the name of raising standards, the minimum-competency-test movement of the 1970s shows that state-level concern over student performance predated 1983. *Time* magazine had devoted a 1980 cover story to Americans' sense that their schools were in trouble. Before *A Nation at Risk*, the Southern Regional Education Board had published *The Need for Quality* in 1981. In 1982 Californians elected Bill Honig as chief state school officer after he campaigned on a "traditional" platform including more homework and higher academic standards. In addition to *A Nation at Risk*, 1983 saw the publication of education-reform reports by the Education Commission of the States, the 20th Century Fund, and the College Board (Toch 1991, ch. 1).

President Ronald Reagan, elected in 1980, came into office with the stated goal of eliminating the U.S. Department of Education. It is thus quite ironic that his secretary of education, Terrel Bell, convened the commission whose report marked the beginning of a national movement for school improvement. Bell, rather than overseeing the promised dismantling of the department, instead sought ways of strengthening its position (Davies 2007, 270–71). *A Nation at Risk* was written as an "open letter to the American people" and as such did not show much grounding in data or research. However, its political impact was immense, probably because of its dramatic tone and accessible language. Perhaps the most-quoted passage of the report lamented the "rising tide of mediocrity" in U.S. schools. The report placed the failings of U.S. schools in a global context, saying that if a foreign power had imposed such bad schools on America, we would regard it as an act of war, and asserting that without improved schools, the United States would lose ground in the military and economic realms.

The Standards-Based Reform Model

A Nation at Risk and the attendant public discussion of the country's apparent education crisis reinforced existing efforts to make schools work better. As the political prospects for both racial integration and financial equalization had become increasingly unclear during the 1970s, some researchers had begun to investigate the characteristics of "effective schools" in hopes that these schools were doing something that could be replicated elsewhere, even in the absence of racial integration or increased levels of resources. This research emphasized the goal of improved outcomes for all children and laid the groundwork for what would later become the standards-based reform movement. What would later be the model of standards-based reform was clear in the identified set of "effective school" characteristics: high staff expectations of students; a high degree of staff control over instructional and training decisions; strong leadership from principals and other leaders; school-wide staff training; and clear, easily understood goals for the school, including an emphasis on academic excellence (Purkey and Smith 1982). Purkey and Smith reasoned that because schools are such loosely coupled systems, top-down reform efforts could not succeed. Rather, reformers should target school culture and staff development. The other person who figured largely in the development of a model of effective schools was Ron Edmonds, who emphasized "strong administrative leadership, high expectations for children's achievement, an orderly atmosphere conducive to learning, an emphasis on basic-skill acquisition, and frequent monitoring of pupil progress" (Purkey and Smith 1983, 429).

The standards-based reform (SBR) model grew out of the "effective schools" research. The core idea of SBR is to replace the tangle of often-conflicting educational policies with a single idea: all students should master a common core of academic material, and if they do not, then the state should hold teachers, administrators, and sometimes the students themselves accountable. Instead of regulating "inputs" such as class sizes or time spent on certain subjects, the state should concentrate on setting standards and maintaining accountability through a system of rewards and punishments (see, e.g., Smith and O'Day 1991). This model is clearly related to the theory of performance measurement that was also gaining popularity in business and public administration. An essay by Marshall Smith (later U.S. undersecretary of education) and Jennifer O'Day summarized the theory of SBR. Although it was not published until 1991, the ideas in Smith and O'Day's paper were already in wide circulation in the 1980s among academics and practitioners concerned with school improvement. Smith and O'Day began by identifying the existing administrative, governance, resource, and policy barriers to successful schools. Overall, they argued, the system lacks coherence and imposes too many unrelated goals on schools. To go from the status quo to a system in which all students attend successful schools, Smith and O'Day called for states to create "coherent system[s] of instructional guidance" (ibid., 247), including curriculum frameworks "which set out the best thinking from the field about the knowledge, processes, and skills students from K-12 need to know." Smith and O'Day explicitly distinguished the kind of frameworks they had in mind from the more common emphasis on minimum competency:

"The frameworks must provide a viable and compelling alternative to the 'basic skills' fact-based orientation that is the norm in US schooling today" (ibid., 248). Teachers and other school staff would receive improved preservice training and in-service professional development aligned with the frameworks. The progress of the whole system would be monitored through "completely overhauled" state tests (ibid., 249, 252). As we will see, the model outlined by Smith and O'Day was considerably more complex than what generally found its way into policy. Some versions of SBR included "opportunity to learn" standards that addressed school funding, but other reformers criticized the idea of "opportunity to learn" for being too much like the earlier input-based definitions of equity that they were trying to replace (Jennings 1998, 57–59).

Equity in Standards-Based Reform

Standards-based reform implied a new way of understanding equity in education in terms of what students learned rather than in terms of earlier criteria such as access to school, desegregation, compliance with legal procedures, time spent in school, or equal spending. In standards-based reform, test scores constituted the measurement of student learning. The next question to answer was whether everybody needed to learn the same things.

For most people, the word "equity" implies equality, and "equality" further implies sameness. Mandating equality of learning (or even of test scores) suggests two equally unlikely possibilities: either that the dim will somehow be forced to reach the same level as the bright, or that the brightest students will be forced down to a level that all can achieve. However, "equity" need not entail strict equality (Stone 2002). People who define educational accountability in terms of measured learning generally employ a threshold principle rather than a principle of strict equality: educational equity means a system in which all students reach at least a level of knowledge and skills that equips them for later participation in society, even though some may go far beyond this level. Arguments for a threshold definition of educational equity do not specify the details of what the threshold ought to be other than to make clear that it should be higher than a minimal standard. By defining equity in terms of a specific threshold of educational achievement, advocates of standards-based reform resolved the apparent tension between "equity" and "excellence." If the definition of equity is based on students' achievement of the level of academic skills and knowledge they need for later success, with the proviso that some students may choose to go further, then excellence can become part of the equity agenda.

The States Respond

The expansion of the education policy subsystem to include elected officials in general government, not just professionals and their allies in state education departments, continued during the 1980s. This expansion continued both the reform wave that had begun in the South in the 1970s and the critique of the "education establishment" that traced back to the 1950s and Arthur Bestor. When officeholders such as governors and legislators made education a priority, they opened themselves to political accountability for educational performance. Anticipating greater political accountability pressure on themselves, they increased accountability pressure on schools and school districts.

Business leaders and governors were a key part of the pressure for educational accountability. Even before *A Nation at Risk*, the U.S. Chamber of Commerce issued a report of its own titled *American Education: An Economic Issue*. The *Nation at Risk* report itself used language that appealed to business leaders (Ray and Mickelson 1990), especially in its invocation of the need to improve schools so that U.S. companies would remain competitive with firms in West Germany and Japan. Governors were particularly high-profile entrants to education policymaking. In 1985 Tennessee's "education governor," Lamar Alexander, became chair of the National Governors' Association (NGA) and decided to make education the organization's main priority. The NGA became the major clearinghouse and distributor of SBR ideas. NGA outlined its reform agenda in *Time for Results*, a five-year reform agenda released in 1986, and tracked progress toward reform in an annual series of reports titled *Results in Education*.

State Reform Priorities

Shortly after the inauguration of President George H. W. Bush in January 1989, the executive director of the NGA wrote to President Bush's communications director to request a meeting between Bush and the governors on education with the goal of "announc[ing] priority areas in which they intend to establish goals and targets" (Vinovskis 1999, 28), such as high school dropout and completion rates, "reading, language, and literacy skills," math competence, international education and languages, kindergarten readiness, and teaching force quality and composition (ibid., 27–29). The outcome of this process was the Charlottesville "education summit" of May 1989 and the announcement of joint "national education goals" by the president and the governors. The identification of goals was clearly part of a performance-accountability approach to reform. The joint communiqué from the president and the governors stated, "as elected chief executives, we expect to be held accountable for progress in meeting the new national goals, and we expect to hold others accountable as well" (ibid., 40).

Following the Charlottesville summit, the Business Roundtable convened an education task force (Sipple et al. 1997). Its members formed state-level education reform groups consisting of the governor, corporate CEOs, and other leaders. The roundtable, the U.S. Chamber of Commerce, and the National Association of Manufacturers formed a business coalition for education reform, which lobbied for national education standards, "improvements in the teaching profession," and more fair ways of funding education (Borman, Castenell, and Gallagher 1993, 78).

By 1994 forty-two states had developed, or were developing, content standards in academic subjects, and thirty had developed, or were developing, student performance standards based on those content standards (Jennings 1998, 8). They were also developing policies related to the other NGA priorities, such as professionalizing teaching, enhancing parental involvement and choice, improving the use of technology, using resources more effectively, and making higher education institutions more mission-driven and effective (Vinovskis 1999, 17). The Carnegie Foundation had made teacher issues a priority, particularly in a 1987 task force report that recommended improving training and professional development for teachers while also restructuring schools so teachers would have a greater voice in determining curriculum and school policies (Schwartz 2003).

State Performance Sanctions

During the 1980s some states enacted sanctions for low-performing schools and districts. For example, Arkansas required a school or district where less than 85 percent of students met a "mastery" level score on state tests "to participate in a school improvement program administered by the State Department of Education," after which it would lose its accreditation if scores did not rise.[3] Texas required all school districts to be accredited by its Central Education Agency according to standards that included test scores.[4] In Texas, loss of accreditation could lead to state appointment of a "master to oversee the operations of the district," and in Arkansas, it could lead to a district's being dissolved and annexed by another district.[5]

From the late 1980s through the early 1990s, more states enacted accountability policies with sanctions, but they often combined accountability policy with other policy ideas. The most lasting development during the late 1980s was the enactment of omnibus reform laws intended to reorganize a state's entire education system around performance standards. Although earlier laws sometimes targeted only districts or only schools, the new reform laws included both in a common accountability system. States upgraded their testing programs to focus on higher-level material rather than "basic skills." This shift affected graduation tests. States that first enacted graduation test requirements during the 1980s did not frame them as guarantees of minimal competency but rather as tests intended to push students to match their international competitors.

Despite the new emphasis on student performance, inputs and processes remained prominent in states' reviews of schools and districts. Indiana, for example, enacted a new "performance based accreditation system" section of the state code in 1987, but the system was not exclusively performance-based.[6] In addition to stipulating that schools and districts must attain their expected performance levels to earn full accreditation, Indiana's statute also required review of "minimum time requirements for school activity," staff-to-student ratios, staff evaluation plans, and internship programs for beginning teachers. West Virginia's "performance-based" accreditation system also included evaluation of school districts' "average class size; pupil-teacher ratio; number of exceptions to pupil-teacher ratio requested by the county board and the number of exceptions granted; the number of split-grade classrooms; pupil-administrator ratio; and the operating expenditure per pupil."[7] A 1991 California law required the state Superintendent of Public Instruction to review county education budgets, a process that could culminate in the state's developing a fiscal plan for a county, rescinding its spending decisions, and monitoring the county office of education.

States did not want to intervene in large numbers of schools or districts. Even in the states with more clearly standards-based systems, in which low test scores alone could put a district or school on a warning list or identify it for further scrutiny, intervention was to happen only after a review of resources or management practices, and, in practice, it was rare. During this period several states enacted laws that specifically targeted a single school district for intervention rather than creating more generally applicable intervention powers. For example, the California legislature passed a law that approved a state loan to the Compton public schools while also requiring the school district to take corrective actions that included improvement of services for Latino students and others with limited proficiency in English.[8] New state laws also instituted greater mayoral control of urban schools, undoing the administrative-progressive separation of schools from general government.

School and district sanctions enacted during this period were mostly variations on the theme of replacement of staff, or of limits or changes to local powers. Illinois and Kansas both could declare a district "nonrecognized," which would lead to its being dissolved, and districts in Oklahoma and Texas could be annexed by another district. New Jersey could (and did) place districts within state control, and other states could place districts in various types of receivership. In Massachusetts, the state could remove the principal of a chronically underperforming school and grant broad personnel powers to the new principal.[9] It could also place a chronically underperforming district into receivership.[10] Kentucky and Michigan both gave students the right to transfer out of a school with poor performance, a way of bringing market pressures to bear. There was clearly a common theme in the accountability policies of the late 1980s and 1990s in that they were all grounded at least partially in student performance on statewide tests, and all threatened many of the same sanctions against schools and districts.

Equity and Intergovernmental Relations

The idea that equity means "high standards for all" began to take hold during the 1980s. On the "high standards" front, states began to identify something beyond just "basic skills" as the focus of their reform efforts. Of twenty state graduation tests enacted after 1989, only three were labeled as "minimum-competency tests." Most of the standards-based graduation tests enacted during this period replaced older minimum-competency tests. Graduation tests remained more common in the South than in the rest of the country. Of the thirteen states that participated in both the minimum-competency and standards-based waves of graduation tests, only four (New Jersey, Nevada, New York, and Ohio) were nonsouthern. Increasing the difficulty of graduation tests could be an inegalitarian change because low-income students, African Americans, Latinos, Native Americans, and some Asian Americans generally score lower on standardized tests than their higher-income and white counterparts. However, as will be seen in chapters 6–8, state policymakers seem to have believed that "raising the bar" in this way would lead mainly to improved performance across the board, rather than just to fewer students earning diplomas.

All performance accountability systems must somehow answer the question of whether to adjust performance targets according to how difficult a particular agency's task is. In the case of schools, the question is whether schools with higher proportions of low-income students and students whose first language is not English should be held to the same performance standards as schools with more advantaged students. This question is analogous to the idea of risk adjustment of hospital performance data. Some school and district accountability policies from the 1980s include some sort of risk adjustment. For example, Georgia law required schools and districts to compare themselves to others that were "comparable in terms of demographic characteristics," and reserved the "nonstandard" designation for those who were unsuccessful "relative to comparable units," which suggests that the state accepted different standards of performance for institutions serving different populations of students. [These differences contrast with the federal government's later insistence that all students should reach the same "proficient" level.] Under a law passed in 1987 Indiana's state education agency was to determine "the level of performance expected for each school in light of the socioeconomic factors of and resources available to the school," which was to serve as the minimum level for the school to attain.[11] A 1989 Texas law stipulated that the state's performance indicators for school districts were to include "a comparison of the district's performance to a projection of the district's expected performance."[12]

Linking Standards-Based Reform with Finance Equalization

By the late 1980s supporters of equalizing education spending were having difficulty making their case. State-level finance litigation had an uneven record, and even when courts ruled on behalf of the plaintiffs, the task of getting a more egalitarian funding system through the legislature remained huge (Reed 2001). However, standards-based reform and funding reform often occurred together. Legislators' support for performance-based accountability and sanctio 'n education was often the result of their skepticism that the schools and districts receiving increased state aid were spending it effectively. As will be seen more clearly in chapters 6–8, advocates framed educational accountability policies as a way of protecting the interests of state taxpayers against certain localities' malfeasance or incompetence.

However, once states began setting educational standards and using them as a basis for measuring student and school performance, they also inspired a new round of education-finance lawsuits. After the *Rodriguez* decision relegated education finance to state, rather than federal, courts, attorneys and plaintiffs had a choice. They could emphasize state-level equal-protection guarantees, or they could base their claims on the states' constitutional guarantees of public education for all, which generally promised either explicitly or implicitly that the level of education provided would be "adequate." Initially, it was not clear how to specify what "adequate" might mean, but once the states began setting educational standards, they provided the outlines of a definition. It makes logical sense that if a state's policymakers have identified a body of academic knowledge that all students should master, then an "adequate" level of education spending is one that enables students to reach that level of mastery. Plaintiffs began using this logic in the 1980s, and beginning with the Kentucky Supreme Court's landmark *Rose* decision in 1989, they won their cases at a higher rate than before (Verstegan and Whitney 1997). By the time Bill Clinton took office as president in 1993, the basics of the SBR model were in place in state policy. More states were enacting powers to intervene in underperforming schools and districts, and state graduation tests were increasingly linked to "world-class" standards rather than to "minimum competency." SBR was backed by a national network but was not yet part of federal policy. That change would come in the 1990s, beginning with Clinton's first-term education agenda.

Intergovernmental Relations

On their face, state laws that require students to pass a test to earn a diploma, or that sanction schools and districts for underperformance, indicate that states are taking on more power at the expense of school districts. What is less visible is that the earliest states to enact performance-based sanctions, such as the first states with graduation tests, tended to be states that already had relatively more centralized governance system. For example, one indicator of centralized state authority is the state-level power to approve textbooks for local use. The southern states that led the performance-accountability movement in education were much likelier than states in other regions to have textbook-approval power. Of the fifteen southern states, thirteen have the power to approve public school textbooks, compared with only nine out of the thirty-five nonsouthern states (Manzo 2003). Three of the first four states to enact strong accountability sanctions against school districts were states that also approved textbooks. Performance sanctions eventually came to many states that had previously been less centralized, including this book's three case-study states.

From the 1980s through the presidency of George H. W. Bush, the federal role tended to follow the states' lead. Even *A Nation at Risk* came after several state-level commissions on education reform. One federal change that would later be quite important was the revision of the NAEP testing program so it would provide state-level results (Vinovskis 1999, 14). These results became an important source of evidence in debates over the effects of accountability policies. Although George H. W. Bush had announced his intention to be the "education president," when he left office in 1993 he had not produced much of an education record beyond his role at the Charlottesville education summit. After Charlottesville he introduced a bill called "America 2000," which would have committed Congress to the goals agreed on at the summit. However, for various reasons, including Education Secretary Lauro Cavazos's

lack of legislative advocacy skills, congressional Democrats' anger at not having been involved in the summit, and partisan tensions leading into the 1992
election, Congress did not pass the bill. Bush's main contribution to the SBR
agenda was to appoint the National Commission on Educational Standards
and Tests, which recommended voluntary national standards and a "system of
tests" related to them (Jennings 1998, 23). The U.S. Department of Education,
the National Science Foundation, the National Endowment for the Arts, and
the National Endowment for the Humanities also funded and began work on
the national subject standards (ibid., 32).

The failure to pass the America 2000 bill left the states as the main actors
in educational accountability policy. The SBR movement had begun at the
state level, so it could readily continue with leadership coming primarily from
states. Reform advocates were working from the same general set of principles,
but the details of state policy reflected the states' distinctive political traditions
and political cultures (Fuhrman 1989; McDermott 2009, 756–58). Ultimately,
the states' SBR policies of the 1980s influenced federal policy more than they
were influenced by federal policy. Indeed, some scholars have argued that the
federal role could not have expanded as it did, beginning in the 1990s, without the ability to piggyback on the expanded state role (McDonnell 2005;
Manna 2006).

Intensified Federal Involvement, 1994–2001

In 1994, well into the national movement for state-level standards-based
reform, only nineteen states had the strongest forms of sanctions in place for
schools, and only fourteen had them for districts. SBR advocates found this
situation frustrating. And as more states enacted results-based accountability
through SBR, they found that their new policies sometimes conflicted with the
more procedural, legal forms of accountability embodied in the requirements
for compliance with federal grant requirements. Although the states were trying to achieve high standards for all students, federal policy still permitted tests
of basic skills to be used in evaluating compensatory education programs and
required that school districts be able to document that federal compensatory
program funds had been targeted only to the particular group of students who
were eligible for services. State officials, especially governors, began to push for
federal policy to be more consistent with state-level SBR and more focused on
outcomes, rather than inputs and procedures. After former Arkansas "education governor" Bill Clinton became president in 1993, SBR advocates began
working through the federal government.

The Clinton Administration and Educational Accountability

Very early in President Bill Clinton's first term, the administration sent two key bills to Congress. The first, called Goals 2000, was essentially a repeat of the Bush America 2000 bill with two additional goals. It provided grants for states and districts to use in implementing standards-based reform and created the National Education Standards and Improvement Council to lead these efforts. Goals 2000 survived a highly partisan debate in Congress, during which Republicans accused Democrats of trying to create a "national school board" and seize control of public education (Jennings 1998). The second Clinton education bill was the 1994 ESEA reauthorization, titled the Improving America's Schools Act (IASA), which was designed to bring compensatory education programs into better alignment with state SBR policies and with the national education goals. Although Congress spent more time and energy on Goals 2000 than on IASA (Jennings 1998), IASA had the greater impact on states and localities. Goals 2000 made new federal funds available to support SBR policies if states and localities had undertaken them. IASA was more coercive. It attached new SBR-inspired conditions to continued receipt of the federal compensatory-education funds on which states and localities had come to depend (McDermott and Jensen 2005).

IASA's roots in the standards-based reform movement were clear. The law's "Statement of Policy" explicitly endorsed the theory of standards-based reform in a set of propositions labeled "what has been learned since 1988" (the previous ESEA reauthorization year). This section outlined the inadequacy of basic skills tests, as opposed to tests based on challenging academic standards. It also declared that the purpose of Title I programs was "to enable schools to provide opportunities for children served to acquire the knowledge and skills contained in the challenging State content standards and to meet the challenging State performance standards developed for all children."[13] Toward this end, IASA required that assessment of Title I students be integrated with the assessments the states were using for the mainstream student population. Subsequently, the idea of a unitary assessment system was extended to students in special education programs by the Individuals with Disabilities Education Act of 1997 and to students participating in vocational education by the Perkins Vocational-Technical Act of 1998. IASA also required states to assess whether districts and schools' aggregate scores on the assessments were showing "adequate yearly progress," and to impose sanctions if a school or district repeatedly failed to make such progress.

IASA marked a significant departure from earlier versions of ESEA, but it still left the states with many options. Although IASA required that states had to set standards, test students on those standards in at least three grade levels, and administer the same tests to Title I and non-Title I students, it also placed standard-setting authority in the states. The federal law required states to monitor whether schools and districts were making "adequate yearly progress," defined "primarily" in terms of student performance on the state tests, but left the rest of the definition of "adequate" progress up to the states.[14] IASA required states to sanction schools and districts that did not make adequate yearly progress but did not require "corrective action" until the fourth year without adequate yearly progress and even then left the precise set of sanctions to the states to determine.[15] NCLB would later use much of the same terminology but with less discretion for the states (McDermott and Jensen 2005; McDermott and DeBray-Pelot 2009).

New State Sanctions

IASA's flexibility meant that many states did not need to make major changes to their existing SBR laws in order to comply with it. Several states, including Alabama, Texas, North Carolina, Vermont, South Carolina, and California, enacted omnibus SBR laws between 1995 and 2001. Some of these laws revised existing accountability policies. For example, the new Texas Education Code enacted in 1995 made the state's accreditation policies more clearly performance-based than they had previously been.[16] States such as Vermont, Rhode Island, and Pennsylvania, all with strong traditions of local control, enacted accountability laws for the first time. Vermont's Act 60 of 1997 built accountability into an unusually redistributive revision of its education finance system following the Vermont Supreme Court's decision that its education finance system was unconstitutional.[17]

In accordance with IASA, state laws enacted during this period call for progressively more aggressive interventions as schools and districts spend more time classified as low performing.[18] Still, despite the new federal requirements and the flurry of state legislative activity, by 2001 only about half of the states had the power to replace school staff, close schools, place districts in receivership, eliminate districts, or directly operate districts. About half of these state laws actually predated the 1994 IASA, as figure 4.1 shows. Further evidence that state-level political considerations were more important influences on accountability policy than federal requirements is that about half of the states had graduation-test laws by 2001, even though they were never required or encouraged under federal law.

Changes in Equity and Intergovernmental Relations, 1989–2001

The most important shift in the relationship between equity and intergovernmental relations during the Clinton presidency was the reinforcement of the

Figure 4.1   Ultimate State-Level Sanctions for Schools and Districts

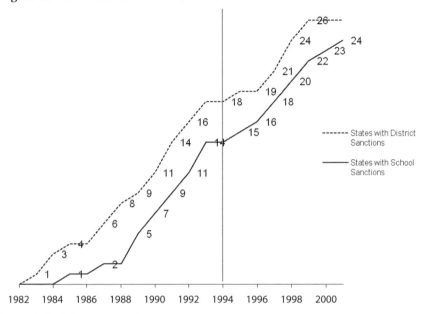

Source: Author's data on state policy enactments.

shift toward defining equity in terms of test results. As discussed in chapter 3, by the middle of the 1970s the federal stance on educational equity was a confusing mixture of definitions based on desegregation, special programming, and compensatory funding (Nelson 2007). During the Clinton administration performance thresholds became an important part of the definition of equity that drove federal policy.

From Desegregation to Performance Accountability

In retrospect, the shift from desegregation to performance accountability seems to have begun during the Nixon administration, which ironically was also the time when federal court orders for integration were the most far-reaching. Even as the courts required the elimination of racially identifiable schools (*Green v. New Kent County*), permitted citywide busing as a remedy in the South (*Swann v. Charlotte-Mecklenburg*), and extended busing to the North (*Keyes v. School District #1*, as well as the *Morgan v. Hennigan* District Court decision that required busing in Boston), Congress and the executive branch were retreating. The Nixon administration emphasized increasing federal aid to education while opposing busing, to show that low-income students could succeed without desegregation. Paul Cook of MIT said in 1972, "the threat of [court-ordered desegregation] has produced friends for educational equality in hardcore poverty areas that such areas never knew they had. . . . If those who want equality for its own sake are joined by the hypocrites who want it for the wrong reasons, [then] a convincing majority should result" (quoted in Nelson 2005, 162). According to Adam Nelson's account of the relationship between the federal government and the Boston public schools, Nixon's federal commissioner of education, James Allen, "built his commissionership around the goal of making inner-city schools more 'effective' *despite* their racial imbalance" (ibid., 94). The Equal Educational Opportunity Act of 1974 barred the use of federal funds to pay for court-ordered busing. After the U.S. Supreme Court's 1974 decision in *Milliken v. Bradley* ruled out a mandatory interdistrict desegregation remedy for segregation in Detroit, its subsequent *Milliken II* ruling (1977) said that the federal courts *could* order Michigan to spend more in Detroit and other districts where segregation could not be remedied (Nelson 2007). In all of these instances—the 1974 Equal Educational Opportunity Act, the Nixon administration priorities, and *Milliken II*—money began replacing integration as the measure of equalizing education.

The next stage of the evolution of federal policy was for the definition of equity to shift from one based on funding special programs and regulating how money was spent to one based on a common threshold of educational achievement. The first sign of change on the federal end came in the Education Consolidation and Improvement Act amendments of 1988, which for the first time included schoolwide compensatory education grants that departed from the "pull-out" model and "exchanged" (Nelson 2005, 243) regulation of allocation of funds for regulations connected with performance. There had long been tensions between the programs for special populations, such as special education and bilingual education, and the ideal of a common educational experience for all. The city of Boston, for example, faced difficulties in complying simultaneously with desegregation and bilingual education requirements (ibid.), although the Boston School Committee's steady resistance to desegregation (ibid.; and Lukas 1985) raises the questions of whether the city authorities might have exaggerated these difficulties for political effect, and whether they would have gotten any further with desegregation even if there had not been conflicting mandates. However, Nelson is right to point out that in order to decide whether equity for a particular group of students meant keeping them together and providing a bilingual or "special" (disability-related) education program for them or dispersing them into the larger system, courts had to begin to consider whether the students were deriving any educational benefit from the programs. After the Supreme Court's *Lau* decision established that the nondiscrimination provisions of the Civil Rights Act entitled language-minority students not just to places in school but to educational experiences in a language they understood, the federal definition of educational equity came to include—for some students, at least—inquiry into whether students were learning (Nelson 2005, 249–51).

Federal–State Relations

Based only on the degree to which the provisions of the ESEA changed, the 1994 IASA was arguably a more fundamental change in federal–state relations than the later NCLB. Where the 1988 reauthorization of compensatory education funding as chapter 1 of the Education, Consolidation, and Improvement Act had contained no requirements linked to state curriculum standards, and had not tried to use the funding as leverage for change in the entire education system, IASA did both (Cohen and Moffitt 2009). IASA included the first requirement that all students take tests aligned with state curriculum frameworks in math and English language arts, the first requirement that states define what would constitute "adequate yearly progress" for schools and districts, and the first requirement that states design interventions for schools or districts that did not make adequate yearly progress. However, standards-based reform had been an elite-led movement (Hochschild 2003), not an elite response to a demand by the mass public. The public still was suspicious of the federal role in education, and Republican House and Senate candidates successfully tapped into this suspicion in the 1994 midterm campaign. The charge that Democrats in Congress wanted to join President Clinton in creating a "national school board" was part of the Republicans' successful national strategy for the congressional elections. As in previous years, Republicans argued that the U.S. Department of Education should be abolished (Jennings 1998).

When the Republicans gained control of Congress after the 1994 elections, they reduced funding for IASA and Goals 2000 (see Jennings 1998). Facing congressional opposition and retaliation, the U.S. Education Department then granted waivers and did not insist on strict compliance with IASA as a condition of receiving funds. By 2001 the states had not fully implemented the IASA requirements, and the national standards and testing projects that began in the 1990s had not been completed. As late as 2002 only nineteen states had full federal approval of their accountability systems, five had entered into compliance agreements, and twenty-seven were operating under waivers (Robelen 2002, 1, 28–29). Some policy analysts viewed this low level of compliance as an equity problem that demanded solution.

Influence also ran from the states to Washington. State officials participated in congressional deliberation on NCLB. By some account, the influence of the

National Governors' Association (at the time, dominated by Republicans, who held the office in thirty-one states) exceeded that of the Democrats on the Senate Health, Education, Labor, and Pensions Committee (DeBray 2006). However, the objections of the National Council of State Legislatures to the NCLB's more extensive and prescriptive testing and accountability provisions went unheard (DeBray-Pelot 2007).

State–Local Relations

Many researchers took on the question of how the state activism of the 1980s and 1990s had affected local education authorities. Frequently, these analysts concluded that heightened state activity had spurred, rather than crowding out, local policymaking (Murphy 1982; Kirst 1988; Fuhrman, Clune, and Elmore 1988; Fuhrman and Elmore 1990). The important effect may not have come in the form of the amount of local policymaking that continued but in pressure to shift the local policymaking agenda (Malen 2003). Sometimes, state policymakers framed increases in state powers, or state interventions in local school districts, as ways of improving local control or of empowering people who were closed out of existing local political systems. For example, Pennsylvania's Act 2000-16, the Education Empowerment Act, directed the Pennsylvania state department of education to compile an annual list of school districts with histories of low test scores, titled the "Educational Empowerment List." If a district remains on this list for three consecutive years, the law states that it "shall be certified by the department as an education empowerment district and a board of control shall be established," which "except for the power to levy taxes . . . may exercise all other powers and duties conferred by law on the board of school directors" (sec. 8). School districts already classified as financially distressed under an earlier law were to go directly to the control-board stage as soon as the 2000 law took effect. Clearly this law did not exactly "empower" the local boards of education; presumably "empowerment" referred to the law's effect on the state department of education, which acted on behalf of local citizens and students. The analysis of New Jersey's state takeover policy in chapter 7 expands upon the idea that the state can empower local citizens against corrupt school officials.

A final caveat about the effect of SBR policies on the state–local relationship is that states' use of the strongest forms of sanctions remains rare. In 2004 the Education Commission of the States reported that only fifty-four school districts nationwide had ever been taken over by their states, and only eighteen of these takeovers were for primarily academic reasons (Ziebarth 2004). A 2005 study funded by the federal Institute for Education Sciences concluded that only five states had ever taken over a school (Steiner 2005). However, even the remote threat of takeover casts a long shadow over schools and districts whose test scores have begun to slip.

The No Child Left Behind Act

The 1994 reauthorization of the Elementary and Secondary Education Act had been intended to make the system more equitable for low-income students and students of color. Advocates of this and other accountability policies identified educational equity as the achievement of a particular threshold of academic knowledge and skills by all students, and as the elimination of gaps in the rates at which students in different groups attained proficiency. For this reason, some civil rights groups favored making the accountability provisions of federal law stronger in 2001 (Radin 2006). They were especially concerned about the ways in which the U.S. Department of Education had backed off from strict enforcement of IASA (DeBray 2006; McDermott and DeBray-Pelot 2009). Conversely, other civil rights groups raised concerns about the likelihood that testing would have more negative consequences for students of color than for other students. These concerns produced changes in the ESEA when it was next reauthorized as the No Child Left Behind Act of 2001 (DeBray 2006). NCLB increased federal pressure on states for uniform accountability policies, in the name of increasing educational equity. Federal authorities' pressure on states and localities to ensure educational equity had shifted from the earlier priority of desegregation to elimination of gaps among demographic groups' aggregate test scores.

NCLB expanded the state testing mandate that was already in IASA. Under the old law, states only needed to test students once in elementary school, once in middle school, and once in high school, and only in mathematics and English language arts. NCLB required annual testing in grades three through eight, and added a requirement for testing students on science. The new law also reduced states' discretion over their accountability goals and sanctions. IASA had required states to develop their own definitions of "adequate yearly progress" and of how to assess progress toward it. After several years of school or district failure to make adequate yearly progress, IASA required states to intervene or compel districts to intervene but left the choice of intervention to the states. In contrast, NCLB imposed a common definition of adequate yearly progress.

Under NCLB, the states' performance goal had to be "proficient" scores for the population as a whole and for all subgroups of students, and progress had to be defined in terms of equal increments of growth from the 2001 baseline to 100 percent proficiency. The federal law also specified a sequence of interventions for districts to take in schools and states to take in districts when AYP was not met. For states with less sanctions-oriented performance accountability policies, these changes were a significant shift in state–local relations. In the aggregate, the result of NCLB was a greater centralization of state–local relations plus a convergence on a particular set of sanctions that met NCLB requirements (McDermott and Jensen 2005).

Equity and Intergovernmental Relations in Educational Performance Accountability

The press for performance accountability in public education began in the states in the 1970s and intensified through the end of the century, eventually influencing federal policy as well. The enthusiasm for educational performance accountability among governors, state legislators, and business leaders expressed a critique of the prior forms that educational accountability had taken. They were particularly frustrated at the accumulated bureaucratic and legal forms of accountability, which they believed had crowded out attention to performance. Furthermore, they did not trust the education system to reform itself from within via professional accountability. Performance-accountability advocates succeeded in getting testing and sanctions policies enacted. These policies challenged professionals' authority over what went on in schools and made performance data the basis of accountability for schools to policymakers

Table 4.1   Educational Accountability in Standards-Based Reform

Type of Accountability	Means of Accountability
Bureaucratic	District-level bureaucratic systems persist
Professional	Standardized testing imposed by elected officials challenges professionals
Legal	Civil rights claims shift toward definition of funding "adequacy" Due process requirements
Political	Increased involvement by elected officials outside education system (mayors, legislators, governors, presidents) Requires schools to demonstrate results, via standardized tests

Source: Categories from Romzek and Dubnick 1987.

outside the education system. At the same time, however, previous forms of accountability tended to persist, even though schools and districts were indeed now more focused on "bottom line" measures of performance than they previously had been. Districts retained their bureaucratic control systems. Schools and districts still remained legally accountable for following due-process requirements and respecting student and staff civil liberties. Sometimes performance accountability became part of these other kinds of accountability, as when teachers worked together in "professional learning communities" to analyze their students' performance data, or when political authorities based their judgments about schools on student test scores. Sometimes there was tension among the various forms of accountability.

Beginning in the 1970s arguments for greater educational equity emphasized what students learned. Increasingly "equity" came to mean mastery of a common body of knowledge and skills for all students. Even lawsuits that focused on school finance often used ideas about "adequate" outputs of the system to justify increased funding for low-spending school districts. The common-threshold idea of equity also challenged the curriculum differentiation and tracking that had been accepted as good educational practice earlier in the century. This definition of equity also reinforced arguments for performance measurement and sanctions in educational accountability. By the beginning of the twenty-first century, states' performance-accountability policies had led to greater centralization of authority over curriculum and assessment at the state level, continuing the centralizing trend that had begun with school-district consolidation in the early twentieth century. The federal government continued its earlier role as guarantor of equal protection for students in vulnerable groups, such as students of color and students with disabilities, even though it deemphasized racial integration. With the IASA and NCLB, the federal government also extended its own role in performance accountability.

Federal performance-accountability policies built upon states' own performance-accountability efforts. These state policies had a common framework in the theory of performance accountability, but they also varied according to how policymakers had understood the problems they faced and the educational goals they were trying to achieve. Performance-accountability policymaking interacted with other issues on states' policy agendas to produce particular combinations of sanctions. Chapters 5–8 analyze this policymaking process in three states.

Table 4.2 Equity, Intergovernmental Relations, and Performance Accountability in Standards-Based Reform

	Equity	Accountability	Intergovernmental Relations
Prior to push for performance accountability	Desegregation Equal funding	Bureaucracy persists Political accountability increasing, to broader set of local constituents General public questioning professional competence Legal, for compliance with regulations and civil rights laws	Federal equal-protection guarantees for vulnerable populations Growing state role in funding equity Local control over curriculum and assessment (details vary among states)
Performance accountability model	Equity defined as threshold of outcomes (sometimes explicitly instead of earlier definitions) Critique of tracking and differentiation "Adequacy" of outcomes becomes basis for funding equity claims	More political accountability of education system to mayors, legislatures, etc. Pressure for performance challenges professional authority Performance (in terms of test results) becoming basis of other forms of accountability	Federal equal-protection framework continues; less emphasis on desegregation Federal role in accountability expands, via states Continued expansion of state funding role State curriculum frameworks and standardized tests for accountability—reduces local authority

Notes

1. My information on state sanctions policies came from examination of the actual legislation and regulations. I began with the legislative and regulatory citations in Ziebarth (2002), and then searched for the laws' original texts and enactment dates. Much of this information was available in the LEXIS online database related to state codes, or on the states' own legislative websites, but where I could not find information online, I found it in law libraries' state legislative collections, and in some cases, directly from the state legislative or reference library staff.

2. The ten states are Alabama, Florida, Georgia, Hawaii (since repealed), Maryland, Nevada, New Jersey, New York (the Regents' Competency Test), North Carolina, and Virginia.

3. Acts of Arkansas 1983, First Extraordinary Session, Act 54, Sec. 8.

4. Texas Education Code 21.751, 21.753, 1983.

5. Texas Education Code 21.757, 1983; and Acts of Arkansas, 1983, Regular Session, Act 445, Sec. 2.

6. Indiana Code 20-1-1.2, 1987.

7. West Virginia Statute, Section 18–2E-5(b).

8. California Laws of 1993, Ch. 455, sec. 1.

9. Massachusetts General Laws 1993, Ch. 69, sec. 1J.

10. Ibid., sec. 1K.

11. Indiana Code 20-1-1.2, 1987, sec. 7(b), and sec. 7(a)(2)(G)(iii).

12. 71st Texas Legislature 1989, Ch. 813, sec. 2.20.

13. IASA 1994, sec. 1001c–d.

14. Improving America's Schools Act, 1994, sec. 1111(b)(2)(B)(ii).

15. Ibid., sec. 1116(c)(6).

16. Texas Acts of 1995, Ch. 260.

17. *Brigham et al., v. State of Vermont*, 1997.

18. See Alabama Public Law 313 of 1995, sec. 3; California Statutes sec. 52055.5, as enacted by Public Schools Accountability Act of 1999 (First Extraordinary Session, Chapter 3X); Indiana Public Law 221-1999, sec. 3; Arkansas Act 999 of 1999, sec. 10; Georgia A+ Education Reform Act of 2000, sec. 93; Colorado Statutes 22-7-609, as enacted by Laws of 2000, Ch. 107; Pennsylvania Act 16 of 2000; and Texas Education Code, sec. 39.131, as enacted by Acts of 1995, 74th Legislature, Ch. 260.

⌒

CHAPTER FIVE

Educational Performance Accountability in Three States

Chapter 2 identified equity and intergovernmental relations as crucial issues for performance measurement and accountability. Chapters 3 and 4 surveyed how educational accountability has evolved in general, and how policymakers' understanding of educational equity came to emphasize the attainment by all students of a threshold level of knowledge and skills. This conception of equity was at the foundation of the standards-based reform movement that spread through the states and the federal government beginning in the 1980s. During this period many states enacted performance-based sanctions such as graduation tests and school or district takeovers. Many states that had begun minimum-competency testing programs in the 1970s replaced them with tests intended to measure higher-level knowledge and skills. At this point in the book I begin to focus on three states' enactment of sanctions based on test scores. This chapter introduces the three case studies, beginning by identifying the significance of the policy changes examined in them. I also provide an overview of the theories of policy change in which the case studies are grounded and information about the data and research methods.

The Cases

The three case-study states have general political and economic similarities. Overall they are among the nation's most densely populated, although some rural areas remain in all of them. Issues of educational inequality tend to be framed as urban/suburban differences, with low-income students and students of color concentrated in the cities, and more affluent, whiter populations concentrated in suburban schools. Despite these urban concentrations of poverty, the three states are all relatively wealthy with relatively high levels of education spending. In 2006–7, when the United States' average per-pupil spending was $10,041, Connecticut's average per-pupil spending was $14,165, Massachusetts' average was $13,333, and New Jersey's average was $16,762 (NCES 2010, table 185). All three states also provided a smaller share of revenue for education than many others, both at the beginning of their enactment of performance accountability policies and at present. In 2006–7 the state provided 38.8 percent of revenue for public education in Connecticut, 42.1 percent in New Jersey, and 46.8 percent in Massachusetts. For the United States as a whole, state funds accounted for 47.6 percent of educational revenue (NCES 2010, table 173).

In Romzek and Dubnick's (1987) terms, Massachusetts, New Jersey, and Connecticut all strengthened formerly unused or dormant forms of accountability and superimposed them on a system where other forms of accountability had been dominant. Policymakers' main priority in these states was to improve the performance of students in the mainstream of the education system—those who were neither disabled nor lacking academic proficiency in English. (Later federal laws would extend the performance-based accountability model to these other populations as well, but the states did not initially attempt to do so.) Politically, the enactment processes were similar across the three states in that the impetus for educational-accountability sanctions came from actors outside the education system, such as governors, legislators, and business interests, and at least some voices from within the education system objected to the reduction of local authority in education. By 2001, when the federal No Child Left Behind Act began to push states to enact accountability policies that fit a particular template, Massachusetts, New Jersey, and Connecticut had enacted policies that shared some common elements with the nationwide standards-based reform movement in education. None of them still claimed to be testing students only on "minimum competency"; all had responded to concerns about educational and economic competitiveness by instituting high or "world class" standards for students.

At the same time, the sanctions elements (graduation tests, state power to take over schools, and state power to take over districts) of the states' educational accountability policies differed considerably. Massachusetts and New Jersey both had graduation tests; Connecticut's legislature had voted down a graduation test proposal in 1990. Massachusetts and New Jersey both had a general law empowering the state to take control of a local school district. New Jersey had taken over three urban school districts; Massachusetts had not yet done so. Connecticut had used special legislation to authorize taking over the Hartford public schools but did not have a general takeover power. At the school level, Connecticut identified underperforming schools and directed school districts to intervene, subject to state approval of the intervention plan. Massachusetts had the power to replace the principal of an underperforming school. New Jersey did not have the power to intervene in individual schools.

Table 5.1   Variation in State Accountability Policies

State	Graduation Test	School/District Accountability
Connecticut	No	No general power to take over schools or districts Special legislation enabled Hartford takeover
Massachusetts	Yes	Has power to replace principals and put districts in receivership
New Jersey	Yes	General power to take over districts, but not schools

When the federal government began implementing the No Child Left Behind Act in 2002, Massachusetts had the least need to adjust its state policies while both New Jersey and Connecticut had policies in place that were inconsistent with the new law.

Massachusetts enacted its educational accountability policies in one omnibus law, so only one legislative process is analyzed in chapter 6. New Jersey built its sanctions policies in three separate enactments, subsequent to a 1975 law requiring the state to define the components of a "thorough and efficient" education. Connecticut, like New Jersey, acted incrementally but also declined to pass a comprehensive accountability law when one was proposed in 1994. The passage of three state laws and the failure to pass the fourth are analyzed in this book. Table 5.2 identifies the legislative debates and enactments analyzed in this book.

Massachusetts Overview

People who developed and worked for the passage of the Massachusetts Education Reform Act of 1993 (MERA) often characterize it as a "grand bargain," with local school administrators and teachers accepting greater accountability to the state for student performance in exchange for increased state funding of public education. MERA committed the state to seven years of increases in education spending, with the funds distributed according to a formula that favored resource-poor communities. The core of the MERA funding system was the "foundation budget," which sets a level below which a district's spending may not fall, based on per pupil spending allowances in eighteen categories. MERA also included a formula for calculating each community's required local contribution to education spending and promised that if the foundation budget is higher than the required local contribution, state aid would fill the gap. In the area of accountability, MERA directed the Massachusetts Board of Education

Table 5.2   Legislation and Proposals Included in Case Studies

State	Policy or Proposal	Year
Massachusetts	Massachusetts Education Reform Act (MERA) Laws of 1993, Chapter 71 (Includes graduation test, school intervention, district intervention)	1993
New Jersey	Minimum Basic Skills test (basic skills, 9th grade) Laws of 1979, Chapter 241	1979
	State-Operated School Districts Laws of 1987, Chapters 398 & 399	1986–1988*
	High-School Proficiency Test (standards-based, 11th grade) Laws of 1988, Chapter 168	1988
Connecticut	Connecticut Mastery Tests for elementary and middle school Public Act 84-293	1984
	Mastery Test for 10th grade Public Act 90-324	1990
	10th Grade Mastery Test as graduation requirement (floor amendment; not enacted)	1990
	Commission on Educational Excellence for Connecticut bill House Bill 5669 (not enacted)	1994
	State takeover of Hartford Public Schools Special Act 97-4	1997
	State identification of underperforming schools Public Act 99-288	1999

* The two laws empowering the state to take over school districts were first introduced in 1986, reintroduced in 1987, and signed by the governor in January 1988.

to produce subject-area standards and tests as the basis of accountability for students, schools, and districts.[1] MERA requires students to earn a competency determination by passing a tenth-grade level test in order to be eligible for a high school diploma. MERA also empowers the state Board of Education to identify underperforming schools and ultimately to remove the principal of a "chronically underperforming" school.[2] Lastly, MERA gave the state board the power to declare a school district to be chronically underperforming and put the district in receivership.[3]

The law addressed many other issues. It required each school to have an elected school council, replaced building tenure and collective bargaining for principals with performance-based contracts, converted lifetime teaching certificates to five-year renewable licenses, replaced tenure for teachers with "professional status," reduced local school committee (the district-level governing body called a "school board" in other states) power over personnel matters, expanded interdistrict public school choice, and created charter schools. It also reiterated a teacher-testing requirement that had been legislated in 1986 but not implemented. Overall, MERA shifted both the source of accountability demands (who was holding schools and districts accountable) and their substance (for what they were accountable). Although state authorities could not directly control schools and districts, they could use a performance-based accountability system to define and control expectations for schools (in Romzek and Dubnick's sense) and to establish incentives like the accountability sanctions and the competency determination that would, in theory, induce schools to do what state policymakers wanted them to.

New Jersey Overview

New Jersey has been both a pioneer and an exception in the field of standards-based reform and performance accountability, with testing and state-intervention policies that have been fundamentally shaped by court decisions in school finance lawsuits. In 1973 the state Supreme Court ruled in *Robinson v. Cahill* that its system of funding public schools did not meet the state constitutional requirement of "thorough and efficient" education for all children. The legislature's response to *Robinson* was the landmark Public School Education Act of 1975 (also known as the "thorough and efficient" or "T&E" act), which enlarged the state role in funding public education. The legislature also required the state to set goals for pupil proficiency, which became the focus of the Minimum Basic Skills test. Later in the decade, legislators voted to require students to pass the high school basic skills test in order to earn a regular diploma. These developments made the state among the first to employ basic skills tests to measure public schools' performance, and to require high-school students to pass the tests. During Thomas H. Kean's two terms as governor, the state also became the first in the country to take over underperforming school districts, and it was among the first to move from a basic skills graduation test to one that was intended as a measurement of higher-level skills.

Despite embodying the SBR model in some ways, New Jersey policies also diverged from the basic SBR model after the state Supreme Court's 1990 verdict in *Abbott v. Burke*, the successor case to *Robinson*. Other states' standards-based reforms in the 1990s generally applied to all schools or districts and focused on educational outcomes. In contrast, state policy in New

Jersey between *Abbott* and the No Child Left Behind Act channeled additional funds mainly to the small group of low-wealth, urban, "special needs" districts identified in the litigation. The state supreme court, via regulations issued by the state department of education, also directed those districts to spend the additional funds for specific programs such as early-childhood education, implementation of school reform models that had worked elsewhere, and school construction. Thus, a more process-based understanding of equity survived alongside the outcome-based one characteristic of SBR. Rather than specifying the educational ends to be pursued and leaving the means up to local decisions, New Jersey state authorities also specified the means that some districts had to use. From the 1970s through the 1990s, the state expanded its role in educational accountability. New Jersey ended the twentieth century with accountability policies that were a hybrid of the performance-threshold understanding of equity and the idea that equity meant using state power to control how school districts operate.

Connecticut Overview

Connecticut took a gradual approach to enacting a system of performance-based accountability for public education, which resulted in a less sanctions-oriented system than that of either Massachusetts or New Jersey and less of an expansion in the state role. The state was an early enactor of standards-based tests, but its House of Representatives rejected an amendment that would have made passing the high school level test a graduation requirement. In 1994 a MERA-like business-backed bill for comprehensive education reform failed even to get beyond the legislature's education committee. The strongest sanctions policy enacted in Connecticut was the 1997 state takeover of the Hartford public schools in the wake of a desegregation lawsuit. Two years later, the state also enacted a law empowering the state to identify underperforming schools but left decisions about corrective action up to the districts in which those schools were located. Although the state has the major authority to measure the performance of students, schools, and districts, its role as an accountability-holder is more limited than that of other states.

Theories of Policy Change

In their article on the *Challenger* accident, Romzek and Dubnick emphasize the ways in which changes in the overall set of political institutions as well as the political pressures on policymakers affect changes in accountability systems. Many scholars who have analyzed the U.S. policymaking process have similarly called attention to the ways in which change in the set of people and institutions that are trying to influence policy leads to change in the policies themselves. John Kingdon's *Agendas, Alternatives, and Public Policies* posited the existence of three independent "streams" of problems, politics, and solutions. Rather than first defining a problem and then seeking the ideal solution, Kingdon argues that policymakers respond to the arguments of "policy entrepreneurs" who advocate for particular changes (solutions, in his framework) at particularly opportune moments ("policy windows") when the solution can be attached to a problem on the public agenda, and when the political timing is right (Kingdon 1984).

Kingdon's model has been quite influential but has come under criticism for lacking a causal theory and predictive power, and for being excessively focused on legislators (Jenkins-Smith and Sabatier 1993, 3). Hank Jenkins-Smith and Paul Sabatier instead advance the Advocacy Coalition Framework for understanding policy change. In this view, policies change as a result of shifts in the set of public- and private-sector actors involved in the "subsystem" related to a particular policy area such as education, and related to the goals, perceptions, and causal theories embraced by those actors. Changes outside a policy subsystem, and changes in "stable system parameters" such as constitutional principles, may also lead to policy change (ibid.).

Frank Baumgartner and Bryan Jones's work on agenda change and "policy monopolies" is a useful addition to Sabatier and Jenkins-Smith's concepts of "subsystem" and "advocacy coalition." Baumgartner and Jones take on the question of why policy tends to change only incrementally for long stretches of time and then abruptly shifts in fundamental ways. The periods of incremental change are times when a "policy monopoly" is stable. A policy monopoly consists of a "definable institutional structure" and a "powerful supporting idea" shared by participants (1993, 7). Changes to either the institutional setting or the supporting ideas lead to larger shifts in policy. The U.S. public education system is particularly fertile ground for both kinds of change. It is institutionally complex, with authority shared (and often contested) among school-level, district level, state, and federal authorities. Americans expect many things of their schools and often set up contradictory sets of goals; for example, they want schools both to promote social equality and to permit some people to get ahead in economic competition (Labaree 1997).

As we will see in the case studies, the predominant forms of educational accountability changed when actors previously outside the education subsystem, such as business leaders, governors, and legislators, took a more active role. These shifts took place at times when schools faced challenges related to funding and to public perceptions of their effectiveness. The venue of policymaking also shifted toward state legislatures. The states had long had constitutional responsibility for public education but had not taken as large a governance role as their constitutional authority implied. The new actors in the education subsystem also emphasized different ideas about the goals of the education system, making social mobility a higher priority, defining equity in terms of academic output rather than inputs or processes, and reframing educational failure by some students as a problem to be solved rather than as an inevitable part of how the system worked.

Data and Methods

The general question underlying this book's case studies is how different definitions of education problems, especially related to the nature of educational equity and to the roles of state and local governments, affected the enactment (and, in Connecticut's case, nonenactment) of performance accountability policies. The unit of analysis is the state, and the beginning dates of the case studies were determined by when the first major policy enactment took place. The goal was analytical, not statistical, generalization (Yin 1984, 39). Case selection was driven by a desire to seek the kinds of variation that would shed most light on this issue, rather than by the goal of assembling a group of cases that somehow represented the United States as a whole. In pursuit of this goal, I sought to maximize variation in accountability sanctions policy while minimizing regional and institutional variation. All of the chosen states are in the Northeast, a region known for strong local control of public education. My assumption here was that arguments in favor of centralization would be most clearly articulated where starting points were less centralized. All three of these states were also recognized as leaders in education policy prior to the federal No Child Left Behind Act, and all had accountability policies that were quite well-developed by the time the federal government increased its pressure on states.

The evidence used for this analysis includes legislative documents, hearing and debate transcripts where available, and press coverage. Massachusetts does not produce verbatim transcripts of legislative hearings or floor debates. The sources used here include other legislative committee documents on file with the state archives, summaries of floor debate published by the State House News Service, the official papers of Rep. Mark Roosevelt on file with the state library's Special Collections, state Board of Education documents made available by former member Paul Reville, and articles from the *Boston Globe* and other state newspapers. For New Jersey, my analysis draws on secondary sources as well as gubernatorial files at the state archives, the 1977 report of the state's committee on high school graduation requirements, and legislative committee hearings. Connecticut produces verbatim transcripts of both legislative hearings and floor debates, which are available online for more recent years and in the state library for earlier ones. Sources used for this study include the hearing and debate transcripts for Public Acts 84-293, 90-324, and 99-288, House Bill 5669 of 1994, and Special Act 97-4, and other miscellaneous state government documents. I also used press coverage from the *New York Times* and the *Hartford Courant*. Where needed, I used interviews to fill in the documentary record.

The end date for all case studies is 2001, when the federal No Child Left Behind Act began imposing more uniformity on educational accountability policies, although I include general information on No Child Left Behind implementation in each chapter. The goal of the analysis is to understand why educational accountability, and in particular sanctions for poor school or district performance, evolved as it did in these three states prior to intensified federal pressure. As Baumgartner and Jones's work would suggest, new participants with new definitions of educational problems and policy solutions gained influence, thus disrupting earlier policy monopolies. Further, because existing institutions are important shapers of policy and debate, I assumed that the definitions of problems and solutions would be affected by the set of other educational policies in place and under debate at the times when legislatures considered enacting performance-based accountability. Examples include education finance reform in Massachusetts and New Jersey, and cross-district desegregation in Connecticut.

In all three states, consistent with national trends, advocates of performance-based sanctions argued that equity should be understood in terms of a common threshold of student performance. Even in Connecticut, which did not enact a state high school graduation test, supporters of performance measurement policies spoke of the need to "restore the value of the high school diploma" by connecting it to mastery of a particular body of knowledge and skills. Defining equity in terms of performance responded to concerns about whether increased spending on public education was leading to any real improvements. It was also politically appealing in the wake of desegregation controversies because it promised to be a means of improving schools even if their student populations remained predominantly low-income and African American or Latino. Connecticut, New Jersey, and Massachusetts policymakers expanded the state's role in curriculum and assessment. Advocates of state tests, and of sanctions based on test scores, presented the expanded powers as consistent with the states' constitutional guarantees of equal educational opportunity. The case studies begin with Massachusetts, which enacted the most extensive set of performance sanctions; then move to New Jersey, whose system of accountability emerged as a hybrid of performance-based and process-based criteria; and conclude with Connecticut, where policymakers actually rejected most sanctions-based accountability policies.

Notes

1. Massachusetts General Laws, Ch. 69, sec. 1I.
2. Ibid., Ch. 69, sec. 1J.
3. Ibid., Ch. 69, sec. 1K.

CHAPTER SIX

Education Finance and Accountability in Massachusetts

The "Grand Bargain"

On June 18, 1993, Gov. William Weld signed into law the Massachusetts Education Reform Act of 1993 (MERA). The signing ceremony marked the end of two years of debate over how to improve the finance and governance of public schools. A few days earlier, the Massachusetts Supreme Judicial Court had declared the state's education finance system unconstitutional, and many school districts were in financial trouble. The press and the public thus paid most attention to how MERA addressed the fiscal issues that were facing public schools across the state. However, the rest of the bill included a major departure from the state's earlier role in education policy. Previously, the state department of education had mostly concerned itself with protecting vulnerable populations of students through legal accountability while leaving matters of curriculum, school staffing, and evaluation of students and schools up to locally elected school committees. MERA greatly increased the state's role in education governance, especially on matters of curriculum and assessment, while also increasing state spending on education. MERA advocates described this trade of funding for accountability as a "grand bargain." A new definition of statewide educational problems and solutions had taken hold, emphasizing the link between more state money and increased state accountability.

With MERA the state shifted toward a more performance-based accountability role and set the performance standards to which students, schools, and districts would be held. The law committed the state to developing a "competency determination" based on state assessments as a graduation requirement. Ultimately, the state would have the power to put schools and districts into receivership for underperformance. At the same time, the prevailing definition of educational equity shifted from one that emphasized legal mandates for serving students with disabilities, providing bilingual education, and ensuring racial balance to one that emphasized students' performance on standardized tests. Political accountability at the local level decreased, with the power over almost all hiring decisions shifted from the elected school committee (the Massachusetts term for what is called a school board elsewhere) to the superintendent of schools. In theory, this shift enhanced the professional authority of the superintendents but in practice they had authority only to determine how to reach the performance goals set by the state and perhaps to add goals onto the state performance targets.

This chapter begins with a brief survey of the status quo in Massachusetts education policy before enactment of MERA and the crisis in state and local education finance during the 1980s and 1990s. I then show how change in the set of participants active in education policy led to a shift in the policy agenda and to the enactment of MERA. Because the most important elements of performance accountability were not settled until well after implementation of MERA, I also provide a brief summary of those developments and of how No Child Left Behind affected Massachusetts education policy.

Equity and Intergovernmental Relations before the Massachusetts Education Reform Act

Prior to the 1993 Massachusetts Education Reform Act, legal accountability was the state's main policy tool for educational equity. The state role was paradoxical. On one hand, the state department of education deferred to local administrators and teachers on nearly all matters of curriculum, instruction, and assessment. On the other hand, the state had long been a leader in enacting various laws intended to enhance educational quality and equity. In the nineteenth century the first Massachusetts secretary of education, Horace Mann, used his position to advance the cause of better local schools. By the late twentieth century, Massachusetts had become an innovator in policies intended to produce equity for disadvantaged populations.

Equity and Legal Accountability

Massachusetts' 1965 Racial Imbalance Law (RIL) was the first of its kind in the United States (Hawkes and Curtin 1969, 575.) It required all school districts to ensure that none of their schools had a student population that was more than 50 percent racial minorities (which, at the time, generally meant black students) or else the school would forfeit state aid. The RIL had little effect during its first four years, but then a more desegregation-oriented state commissioner of education pressed for compliance (Nelson 2005, 92).

Massachusetts was also an early enactor of policies that pursue educational equity by ensuring equal opportunity for students with disabilities or limited proficiency in English. The state's compensatory education program began in 1962, before the U.S. Congress passed the Elementary and Secondary Education Act (ibid., 39). The state enacted its Transitional Bilingual Education Act in 1971, which required school districts to provide special classes for groups of non-English-speaking students or else lose state education aid (ibid., 110). In 1972 Massachusetts passed a law requiring school districts to identify children with disabilities and to provide them with publicly funded, individually tailored programs.

In theory, MERA replaced these earlier definitions of educational equity with one that was instead grounded in a guarantee that the state would provide sufficient funding and accountability pressure to ensure that all students reached the same educational threshold. In practice, MERA layered performance accountability onto legal accountability. The specifics of legal accountability changed, deemphasizing racial balance as a goal and replacing bilingual education with "structured English immersion" (via a 2002 referendum), but the general principle remained in place.

Continuing Local Control

Although Massachusetts was an activist state in terms of educational equity, it deferred to local prerogatives in curriculum and instruction. In 1978 the Massachusetts Board of Education approved the Policy on Basic Skills Improvement, which required each school committee in the state to evaluate each student's basic skills competency beginning no later than in ninth grade. However, this policy left a great deal up to local discretion. School districts could choose whether to use a basic skills test developed by the state department of education, another commercially available test approved by the department of education, or a locally developed test approved by the department of education. Additionally, the board stated that the purpose of the policy was "not to establish a new condition for promotion or graduation" (Massachusetts Board of Education 1978, 6). On several other occasions state department of education spokespeople expressed opposition to graduation tests (ibid.; Massachusetts General Court, Education Committee 1987, 1991). A state testing program began in the 1980s but did not produce scores for individual students and did not include penalties for schools and districts with low scores. Until 1993 the only Massachusetts state requirements for a high school diploma were a year-long course in American history and civics and four years of physical education classes (Swartz and Goodson 1988).

The Educational Improvement Act of 1986 (Ch. 188) used state grants to districts as incentives for educational improvement, increased minimum teacher salaries, and improved professional development. An equal-opportunity grant program also targeted communities where education spending was less than 85 percent of the state per-pupil average. Chapter 188 required prospective teachers to pass a test in order to be granted certification, and instituted a statewide student assessment program (Massachusetts Department of Education 1986). Later, chapter 727 of 1987 emphasized teacher quality and programs that would make teaching a more attractive profession. Neither law was ever fully implemented, largely because the recession that began in the late 1980s led to cuts, not increases, in the state education budget. This lack of follow-through fed later cynicism about the durability of state-level reforms.

Fiscal Crisis, 1980–93

During the 1980s the high-technology sector of the Massachusetts economy grew rapidly, helping the state rebound from the decline of its manufacturing base. This "Massachusetts Miracle" put the state and its governor, 1988 Democratic presidential nominee Michael Dukakis, into the national spotlight. However, the state's economic recovery barely outlasted the Dukakis presidential bid. By the time Dukakis left office in 1991, the state was back in recession, with predictable consequences for state and local government. Local governments' fiscal circumstances were made even worse by the implementation of a 1980 ballot measure that limited increases in local property taxes. The constraints on local taxation, in conjunction with the recessions of the 1980s and early 1990s, produced a fiscal crisis in public education.

The central provision of Proposition 2½ (which remains in effect) restricts growth in the total amount of a municipality's tax levy to 2.5 percent per year plus growth from new development, hence its name (Massachusetts Department of Revenue, n.d., 4). Municipalities may override the levy limit by referendum with a simple majority vote needed for approval. Proposition 2½ also enacted a "levy ceiling" on total property tax revenue of 2.5 percent of the total assessed value of all property in a municipality with only a few exceptions. Municipalities whose tax rates exceeded that level when Proposition 2½ went into effect had to reduce their levies, and thus their spending, down to the 2.5 percent cap. At the time, the average property tax rate in the state was 8 percent (Nelson 2005, 212), and the rates of inflation and of increases in government costs tended to exceed 2.5 percent. Under these circumstances it was clear that compliance with Proposition 2½ would require local spending cuts because override votes proved difficult to win. Especially in communities with low property values, school finance deteriorated, and even wealthy communities strained under the Proposition 2½ limits. A lawsuit challenging the state's system of school finance, first filed in 1978 as *Webby v. Dukakis*, was consolidated with another case in 1989 and retitled *McDuffy v. Secretary of the Executive Office of Education*.

Change in the Education Policy Subsystem

Politically, the story of MERA began during the late 1980s, when a group of business people concerned about education formed the Massachusetts Business Alliance for Education (MBAE). The chairman of MBAE was John Rennie, the chief executive officer of an electronics firm. Its executive director, Paul Reville, was an education activist. MBAE said that its mission was "to participate in shaping the future of education in the Commonwealth and restoring its preeminent position of educational leadership, by bringing about statewide, systemic improvement in public elementary and secondary education" (MBAE 1991, 2). In the spring of 1991, MBAE released a detailed school-reform proposal titled "Every Child a Winner," whose very title hints at the possibility of achieving both democratic equality ("every child") and social mobility ("a winner").

In "Every Child a Winner" MBAE stated that reform must include "the expectation, indeed the requirement, that those involved in Massachusetts' system of public education accept thoughtful changes which must occur in how the system is guided, operated, and managed" (MBAE, 1991, 5). MBAE's proposal sought to achieve greater accountability through changes to principals' and teachers' terms of employment, including making it easier to dismiss teachers for poor performance and putting principals on performance-based contracts rather than collectively bargained ones. These changes would lessen bureaucratic controls at the local level and increase local superintendents' ability to use professional judgment in holding staff accountable for performance. For the state, MBAE also advocated the power to declare a school "educationally bankrupt," which would trigger choice for students in the school and open the door to privatization of some school functions (ibid., 2–3). The core idea in MBAE's theory of educational management was that state authorities should be "tight" with respect to setting clear goals for the system but "loose" in monitoring what schools and districts actually do in pursuit of those goals (McDermott 2006). This theory of management clearly shows the influence of ideas popular at the time among private-sector managers, in particular the notion that management should set objectives but then leave decisions about how to meet those objectives up to work teams (see, e.g., Peters and Waterman 1982, 318). This idea about business management was clearly consistent with the push for performance-based accountability and greater managerial control in public administration. MBAE's proposals included a much more active state role in testing and monitoring of school and student progress than had previously been the case. MBAE's proposed model intended that sanctions based on performance would act as incentives or inducements to change in schools.

The second important political shift in the early 1990s was a convergence of leadership changes. The 1990 election brought a new Republican governor, William Weld, into office and shook up the legislature. Election of sixteen new Republican senators ended the Democratic majority's ability to override vetoes, although it did not produce a change in party control. Leadership within the Democratic majority changed. The House had a new Speaker, Charles Flaherty. The legislature's joint education committee gained new cochairs, Sen. Thomas Birmingham and Rep. Mark Roosevelt. All of these people wanted to advance an education reform agenda. Roosevelt remembered later, "The Speaker named me education chair and basically said to me, look, the schools are in trouble. Go out there and figure out what you think we ought to do, and I'll support you."[1]

Leadership also shifted within the executive branch. In 1991 Weld appointed two state Board of Education members, MBAE executive director Paul Reville and attorney Martin Kaplan, who joined with returning members to push the board in a reformist direction. In 1991, while the *McDuffy* case was still pending, the state Board of Education asked the legislature to approve an emergency spending bill intended to bail out the four cities (Holyoke, Lawrence, Brockton, and Chelsea) whose schools were in the most financial trouble. At the same time, the board appointed a subcommittee to study distressed school districts and school reform. Governor Weld created a new executive office of educational affairs, which was intended to bring together governance of public K–12 and higher education, and he appointed Piedad Robertson as secretary of education. Finally, the state Board of Education also appointed a new commissioner of education, Robert Antonucci, in 1992.

These new participants in the education policy network were not obvious allies. Weld, a Republican, was a fiscal conservative and a social moderate. Birmingham and Roosevelt were both Harvard-educated liberal Democrats, but they came from very different backgrounds and represented very different districts. Roosevelt, a great-grandson of President Theodore Roosevelt, had been educated in private schools and represented Boston's elite Beacon Hill. Birmingham, a labor lawyer who was more receptive to union interests than

Roosevelt, represented his hometown, working-class Chelsea. Despite the new participants' differences in background and occasional disagreements on details, they generally shared a commitment to standards-based reform and a basic understanding of what that reform ought to entail. Perhaps more importantly, none had previously been part of the state's education policymaking system.

New state Board of Education members Reville and Kaplan wanted to improve the education system and saw education reform as an opportunity to demonstrate their independence from Weld. Their first opportunity to take a proreform position was as members of the subcommittee on distressed school districts, created to investigate conditions in four school districts that had requested an emergency spending package from the state. In a letter to Kaplan about a draft of the subcommittee report, Reville stated, "I believe that the Board of Education can be of greatest service by dramatizing the inequities and inadequacies of the current system and keeping the pressure on the key players, i.e., the Governor and the legislature, to make the urgently needed changes."[2] In addition to supporting emergency funding legislation for the four cities, the report also recommended that the board be empowered to declare a state of emergency and intervene in a school district (MBE 1991, 13). The distressed school districts subcommittee emphasized the state's need to protect children from their cities' and towns' desire to underfund their schools.

Policymaking Institutions

Despite the ongoing *McDuffy v. Secretary of the Executive Office of Education* finance lawsuit, the legislature and the governor's office rather than the courts took the leading roles in the enactment of MERA. The court did not decide the case until the very end of the legislative process, so MERA was not the usual sort of legislative response to court action in which the legal decision is the catalyst for legislative action. Beginning in 1991 working groups drawn from the legislature, the executive branch, and outside government developed proposals in key areas. In the early stages of drafting MERA, the school governance and management working group recommended "reaffirmation of education as a state function, not a local function, as currently stipulated by our state Constitution."[3] This reaffirmation of the state role was consistent with the findings of the distressed school districts subcommittee of the state board of education. Board chair Martin Kaplan was particularly offended by the situation in Holyoke, where voters had explicitly set the public schools as a low priority in their 1991 Proposition 2½ override vote. The 1991 Holyoke override vote had been a "menu override": a set of proposed levy limit increases beyond 2.5 percent, each tied to a particular purpose. In a menu override, voters can cast any combination of "yes" and "no" votes, depending upon their opinion of the merits of the various proposals. In their November, 1991, menu override, Holyoke voters passed overrides that eliminated trash disposal fees and reopened the city Council on Aging but rejected increases in school funding for 1991–92 and 1992–93 (O'Brien 1991).

The report of the subcommittee on distressed school districts and school reform detailed the effects of towns' insufficient efforts to fund their schools. For example, Holyoke had laid off 36 percent of its teaching staff (MBE 1991, 1) and then reassigned the remaining teachers according to a formula that provided one teacher per thirty-five students through grade ten, and one teacher per fifteen students in grades eleven and twelve. As a result, class sizes increased while some classrooms went unused. On September 26, 1991, Department of Education staff reported to the Board of Education: "At the Donahue elementary 20% of the classes were empty, while many classes exceed 37 students. We were told that a student in a wheelchair couldn't be mainstreamed into a regular classroom because the wheelchair wouldn't fit into a class with 37 students" (MBE 1991, 53). The department of education team also recommended that the state board of education be given the power to "place districts in educational receivership" if they failed to meet minimum standards for funding and educational conditions.[4]

Although the finance issue was most pressing in cities, suburbs did not escape the fiscal crisis of the early 1990s. During floor debate on MERA, bill sponsor Mark Roosevelt noted that his office had received calls from suburban parents complaining about cuts that included user fees for sports, near-elimination of professional development for teachers, and elimination of summer school. In response to the argument that MERA undermined local control, Roosevelt stated that rejecting MERA meant allowing "the adults . . . [to] continue to say to children, we're sorry, we don't feel like doing any better than that."[5] Greater state control of education finance would produce both more equity and higher quality.

The Roosevelt bill that became MERA passed the House and Senate for the final time in early June 1993. The Massachusetts Supreme Judicial Court (SJC) ruling in *McDuffy* that the state had a constitutional duty to provide more education funds to poor communities came a bit more than a week later. Because MERA was about to become law, the SJC did not order a remedy. Instead, it remanded the case to the Suffolk County Superior Court, where a judge retained jurisdiction "to determine whether, within a reasonable time, appropriate legislative action has been taken."[6] Three days later Governor William Weld signed MERA.

McDuffy played an ambiguous role in the process. On one hand, the litigation had been going on for years, and when the MERA legislative process began in 1991 it was not obvious either that the SJC would rule soon or that its ruling would necessarily be in the plaintiffs' favor. On the other hand, MERA advocates cited the threat of a *McDuffy* court order as a reason for legislators to support the bill. Robert Antonucci said, "The *McDuffy* decision was the driving force to say let's take control of this agenda before someone else does." The overall fiscal crisis certainly generated pressure to change education finance, regardless of what the court might order. According to Birmingham, *McDuffy* "strengthened our hand, but I don't know if I picked up a single vote [in the Senate] because of it."[7]

Although Massachusetts Department of Education (DOE) leaders and staff were deeply involved in producing the "Distressed School Districts" report, overall the DOE was not a major independent player in the MERA legislative process. Previously the agency had taken positions against high-stakes testing, but it tolerated the graduation test and the accountability sanctions in MERA. Following budget cuts in the late 1980s and early 1990s, the Massachusetts DOE of 1993 was, in staffing terms, a shadow of its earlier self. During this period, its total staff decreased by nearly two-thirds, and its regional centers closed in 1991 (Churchill et al. 2002, 116). These cuts may have limited its ability to continue playing a strong role in policymaking; they certainly hindered implementation of MERA after 1993.

Equity and Intergovernmental Relations

As we saw in chapter 4, the nationwide press for performance accountability in education accompanied a shift in how policymakers understood educational equity. Rather than just trying to equalize funding, or "opportunity" in some general sense, the new equity goal was to get all students to at least a threshold level of academic knowledge and skills. The idea of a threshold called for some way of measuring this knowledge and skills. Like other understandings of educational equity, the one based on performance seemed to policymakers to require more centralization of power within the intergovernmental (in this case, state–local) system.

Performance Accountability as the Priority

The essence of MBAE's reform recommendation was for state policy to shift its focus from monitoring regulatory compliance to what Paul Reville describes as the "grand bargain": increased and more equitable funding in exchange for measuring educational performance and holding schools accountable. MBAE began its push for education reform just a bit more than a decade after the Boston busing riots, when many people had lost faith in integration as a means of achieving educational equity and were looking for some way to affect what actually happened in classrooms. MERA advocates believed that performance accountability and finance reform would accomplish what desegregation advocates had ultimately been trying to achieve: the full inclusion of students of color in education, the economy, and the polity. In Paul Reville's view, "during this time [the late 1980s and early 1990s] there was an unusual convergence of the interests of the business community—the economic elite of this country—with the civil rights community. In other words, it was suddenly in our interest as this nation and in the interest of the elite to educate all kids to a high level, not only to fulfill a moral obligation, but because otherwise they'd be a drag on the economy and they'd stunt the growth of this country."[8] The shift from targeting certain categories of students to trying to improve the experience of "all kids" is one of the key tenets of performance-based accountability in education.

Desegregation was not an issue in the debate over MERA, except as a background issue to the disagreement in the legislature about interdistrict public school choice. During the stalemate, Representative Roosevelt alluded to Senate president William Bulger's support for the antibusing movement in his South Boston district: "Imagine the incredible potential irony of Billy Bulger having passed a law that would open the state to the largest busing program in the United States, which is what it might do." Senator Tom Birmingham, the cochair with Roosevelt of the legislature's joint education committee, called Roosevelt's scenario "far-fetched" but also noted that the opposition to school choice existed because "a lot of people in the suburbs don't want city kids because of their race, because of their background" (Howe 1993a, 29). The choice issue almost kept the conference committee from producing a consensus version of the bill. At the last minute, the conferees agreed to make it mandatory for districts to permit their students to enroll elsewhere, taking their per-student state aid with them, while also permitting school committees to decide not to accept out-of-district students so long as they renewed this decision annually via a public vote.

The Link between Centralizing Funding and Centralizing Accountability

Having a business-backed organization advocate increased spending on education made an enormous difference to Massachusetts education politics in the early 1990s. However, MBAE's pro-spending position was conditional on governance reform and greater accountability. In "Every Child a Winner," MBAE declared, "The Commonwealth's school systems of the future must be adequately financed, but they must also operate differently to achieve necessary performance levels" (MBAE 1991, 9). Former MBAE executive director Paul Reville explained: "The whole system was illogical to the business mind. There were no goals, there were no measurements of progress, there were no consequences for performance, there were no incentives one way or another, there wasn't a human resource development system. . . . So business people from an organizational development perspective looked at it from the outside and said, 'we've really got to redefine this in a way that has some logic to it.'"[9] Part of this logic was the MERA provision that took local school committees essentially out of their districts' hiring processes. Before MERA, school committees approved all hiring, whether of superintendent, principals, teachers, or other staff, which created many opportunities for patronage hires. After MERA, the school committee hired only the superintendent, who had the final authority on other personnel decisions. This had been one of MBAE's recommendations in "Every Child a Winner," framed as "the installation of a strong CEO form of management at the school system level" (MBAE 1991, 32). For better or for worse, this shift also weakened local political accountability by reducing school committee ability to control staffing.

MBAE and the sponsors of MERA also believed that part of increasing accountability was to give high school diplomas a clearer educational meaning. Senate MERA sponsor Tom Birmingham claimed that the graduation requirement in the law "changed a whole culture of social promotion" in the schools.[10] Section 72 of the law followed from the standards-based reform movement's critique of tracking, requiring that school districts eliminate the "general track," often a dumping ground for unsuccessful students. In addition to backing up the idea of equity as a performance threshold, the competency determination was intended as an incentive for students to work harder. It also strengthened the pressure on schools to make sure their curricula aligned with the state frameworks on which the test was based.

The Legislative Process

The simplest answer to the question of why the Massachusetts legislature passed MERA is that the House and Senate leaders supported the bill and expected the rank and file to do the same. This top-down control is typical of the Massachusetts legislature, which analysts rate as one with unusually centralized power structures (Peirce 1972; Cammisa 2006). However, this simple answer leads to a more complicated question. Why did legislative leadership support the bill? It seems just as likely that MERA would have quickly disappeared. Legislators were not receiving pressure from their constituents to reform education governance.[11] MERA's funding formula favored property-poor urban and rural communities over the suburbs, whose populations were increasing. Furthermore, almost all of the interest groups representing various education constituencies found at least one provision of the bill that they disliked: the teachers' unions opposed replacing lifetime certification with five-year licenses, the principals' organizations were angry at the abolition of collective bargaining for school administrators, and the state organization of school committees correctly perceived that the law reduced their power. The key to getting past these obstacles was funding reform. Additionally, the state association of school superintendents supported the increase in their authority over personnel decisions.

Predictably, the legislative process was long and contentious: two years from when work began on an education reform proposal to when the bill finally passed in June 1993. Less predictably, the process ended in passage of an extraordinarily far-reaching change to state education governance. The accountability provisions of MERA (the graduation test, the state power to remove the principal of an underperforming school, and the state power to take over an underperforming school district) were not extensively debated at the time the law passed. The file of letters received by Representative Roosevelt's office includes only six that addressed testing and graduation requirements and one on accountability, far fewer than Roosevelt received on school funding, school employees' terms of employment, or school choice.[12] Neither state teachers' union took positions on the graduation test at the time of its passage, although Roosevelt did recall being visited by representatives of the Massachusetts Advocacy Center who were concerned about the possible effects of a graduation test.[13] The Massachusetts Advocacy Center was the successor organization to the Boston Task Force on Children Out of School, which had been an early advocate of laws guaranteeing that children with disabilities would be included in public education (Nelson 2005, 169). The State House News Service accounts of the House and Senate floor debates hardly mentioned accountability or the graduation test. Coverage of MERA in the *Boston Globe* emphasized the controversial finance, labor relations, and choice provisions of the bill rather than the graduation test or school and district accountability.

This very breadth, linking the governance reforms to financial reform, was one part of why consensus emerged that MERA ought to pass. Conventional wisdom about policymaking generally assumes that it is easier to enact incremental change than to wipe the slate clean and start over again. As Mark

Roosevelt remembered, "By any measure of how you put a bill like this together and get it passed, we were not doing it right. . . . The only thing we did right on that score was that there was so much in the bill that people objected to in different pieces that they were fighting multiple-pronged wars."[14] Many of the issues that mattered a great deal to different groups were in the law's details, such as the exact language of the legal standard for firing a teacher with professional status, which did not lend themselves well to issue campaigns: "so much of this stuff, you're never going to have a rally on the State House steps."[15] Mark Roosevelt recalled that the *Boston Globe* reported on school districts' funding troubles and kept the pressure on policymakers to address the problem.[16] Thomas Birmingham remembered a "bipartisan sense that the schools were on the precipice."[17] The political logic of MERA inextricably linked funding with accountability. Numerous participants agree that in order to get more state funding, education interest groups accepted provisions of the bill that would otherwise have been anathema.

MBAE's efforts were also crucial. Most legislators were interested primarily in the bill's financial effects rather than its governance and accountability reforms. According to Paul Reville, "The main lobbying work you'd have to do to get this through would be to explain to reps what this meant for them financially."[18] Mark Roosevelt credits Reville and MBAE with a central role in the legislative process: "Paul would literally be sitting in a side room. And we would send people who didn't understand things to him, and he would explain. Paul has the patience of Job."[19] The desire to solve education's financial problems seems to have overridden uncertainty about what the bill's accountability provisions meant. Reville said, "When the going really got tough on this bill, the main focus was money." For many representatives, "all this other substantive stuff was along like a sidecar on this bill and most people didn't pay much attention to it."[20] Birmingham said, "There's sort of a grand bargain here. We as a state are going to put up a lot of money, but in return this is what we expect, and it seemed a fair bargain. I think there was too much peril to rock the boat, to say 'vote against ed reform over accountability.' OK, now we're back to nothing."[21] According to this logic, changing accountability came along with fixing the finance system.

Unified advocates of performance-based accountability confronted an ambivalent and divided education community. The Massachusetts Association of School Superintendents generally supported the bill because it expanded superintendents' power over personnel matters by reducing that of school committees, who consequently tended to dislike the bill. Principals' opinions were mixed, although they generally opposed losing tenure and collective bargaining. Teachers' unions had concerns about some provisions of the bill but also supported the state finance reform. In a January 1993 legislative bulletin to its members, the Massachusetts Teachers' Association (MTA, the state NEA affiliate) reported on the positions it was taking as legislators worked on MERA. These positions included accepting the replacement of tenure for teachers with "professional status," which somewhat increased the possibility that an experienced teacher could be fired, but the union also criticized the details of the termination process as outlined in the bill. The MTA also wanted to remove the five-year recertification requirement and retain the status quo of lifetime certification. It opposed some of the law's provisions on charter schools. Intriguingly, it said nothing in the bulletin about the graduation test whose implementation it would later oppose; the only position it took on an accountability-related issue was that teachers in schools labeled "underperforming" should have the same job protections as any other teachers. The MTA was also politically vulnerable because, as one *Boston Globe* reporter noted, it had "sometimes come across as more interested in its own welfare than in guaranteeing parents quality schools" (Lehigh 1992).

The uncertainty about the meaning of the accountability provisions also probably made them less controversial. For example, the legislation called for a "system of assessments" that would "as much as practicable" include "consideration of work samples, projects, and portfolios."[22] Both supporters and opponents of standardized testing might reasonably have believed this language was consistent with their positions. Indeed, Peter Sack, a graduation-test critic and a leader of the state's association of secondary school principals, remembered that "at least in the discussions that we were involved with, it was not an exit exam."[23] Given this ambiguity, it seemed likely to the education organizations that the unappealing provisions of the law could be softened or quietly ignored. The state board of education had typically been receptive to interest groups when it developed regulations to implement legislation. For example, the teacher certification test required by the 1985 education reform law had still not been developed or implemented as of 1993. The failure to fund and implement two Dukakis-era education reform bills suggested that not everything in the legislation would actually be put into practice. As Birmingham remembers, "it was the mañana thing . . . so sometime down the road there will be a test."[24] Finally, the depth of state leaders' commitment to MERA was unclear. When Governor Weld signed the bill, he said "we can do better" than the bill he was signing, and he promised to file corrective legislation (Howe 1993b). Even the financial aspects of the bill remained worrisome. The head of the Massachusetts Municipal Association called the new law "a ticking time bomb which is going to explode in lots of communities soon" because the new funds could only be spent on education rather than other municipal priorities.

Members of the education policy subsystem could well assume from all this lack of enthusiasm that the law would go away, like its predecessors.

Implementing MERA

Some of the potential controversy over the accountability provisions of MERA was not defused but instead was postponed to the implementation process. A few years after enactment of MERA, Gov. William Weld again shook up the state's education policy subsystem. Weld was frustrated at the slow pace of MERA implementation. The Massachusetts Department of Education's first major step in MERA implementation had been to begin setting curriculum standards, as MERA required, by developing curriculum frameworks for major subjects. The board of education and department of education also decided to develop a companion document called the "Common Chapters," which identified general educational goals that cut across all subject areas, even though it was not required under the law. The department of education began its standard-setting process with the Common Chapters, rather than with the specific subject areas. The process of drafting the Common Chapters was designed to encourage public participation. During the process, the state Board of Education got input from an estimated fifty thousand people (McDermott et al. 2001). Because they articulated general goals, rather than subject-specific knowledge and skills, the Common Chapters were vulnerable to being attacked as the latest example of wooly-headed educational faddism and dumbing-down of public schools (McDermott 2004, 140).

Enter John Silber. In 1995 Governor Weld took the unusual step of appointing the man he had defeated in the 1990 gubernatorial election as chair of the state Board of Education, and thus as the person in charge of a major administration priority and one of the state's largest areas of expenditure. When Weld approached Silber, then the president of Boston University, about becoming Board of Education chair, Silber made his acceptance conditional on being given the power to reorganize the board. Weld agreed to this condition because the reason he had approached Silber in the first place was his frustration at the slow pace of MERA implementation and the department of education's priorities—particularly the Common Chapters (McDermott 2004, 140). Silber was a long-time critic of the public schools, and within days of his appointment he was proposing major shifts in education policy (Cornell 1995; Zernike 1995).

As part of the agreement with Silber, Weld dismissed most of the incumbent board members, eliminated the office of state secretary of education, and appointed a new, smaller board consisting of people who agreed with his and

Silber's priorities for implementing MERA. Among the board members who lost their seats were Marty Kaplan and Paul Reville. Under Silber, the Board of Education made controversial decisions about teacher testing and curriculum frameworks, which led many of the state's educators to believe that the state was out to get them. The rift between educators and the state government undermined implementation of the actual curriculum and instructional reform that accountability advocates had been trying to produce. Silber's successor as chair, James Peyser, was less of a lightning rod, though no less an outsider to the public education establishment. Peyser was director of the Pioneer Institute, a Boston think tank dedicated to finding market-based solutions to public problems. Thus, not only MERA enactment but also the course of its implementation depended on a reduction of public education specialists' power at the state level.

This change, compounded with the realization that the state really was serious about implementing accountability, undermined trust between the Massachusetts DOE and school districts, and made the process still more conflictual (McDermott 2006). By this point, the Massachusetts DOE was beginning to regain some staffing strength as the need for more resources to implement MERA became clear (McDermott et al. 2001) and the state's economic recovery permitted adding some staff (Churchill et al. 2002, 116–17). This was a very different DOE from the one that had opposed high-stakes testing in the 1980s. During MERA implementation, many of the DOE staff seen as most friendly to educators in the field had left the department in dismay over the shift in state policy.

Implementation of the Competency Determination

Despite the ambiguity discussed earlier, the language in MERA that describes the competency determination required for the high school diploma suggests a rigorous standard:

> The "competency determination" shall be based on the academic standards and curriculum frameworks for tenth graders in the areas of mathematics, science, technology, history, social science, and English, and shall represent a determination that a particular student has demonstrated mastery of a common core of skills, competencies, and knowledge in these areas, as measured by the assessment instruments . . . Satisfaction of the requirements of the competency determination shall be a condition for high school graduation.[25]

The state board of education later had to decide what this language meant, in particular what the "assessment instruments" would be and what would constitute passing scores. The furor in the late 1990s over state tests as graduation requirements shows how an issue that was not controversial in 1993 became so later.

First, the board decided that the assessment should include only the Massachusetts Comprehensive Assessment System (MCAS) tests rather than also incorporating portfolios of work or demonstrations as some educators wanted. (The MCAS does include questions that require students to write.) When the board set the passing scores for the competency determination in 1999, it included only the mathematics and English language arts MCAS, because the tests in the other subject areas were still in development. The next challenge facing the board was to set the passing standard. In 1999, when the Board considered this question, only about a quarter of tenth-graders were scoring at or above "proficient" on the math test, and a bit more than a third met that standard in English language arts (Churchill et al. 2002). In response to this pattern, the state board of education voted to require only that students score above "failing" in the "needs improvement" category, rather than actually meeting the proficiency standard before they could earn a diploma. The state board also approved a set of retests for students who failed the first time, designed only to distinguish between the "needs improvement" and "failing" levels of achievement, and an appeals process for students whose scores did not reflect their classroom performance. Even so, many educators and parents worried that the competency determination requirement would produce an increased dropout rate by discouraging students who failed the test the first time they took it (McDermott 2004, 141–42).

If the MTA's position on testing and accountability had been equivocal in 1993, it was loud and clear in 2000. Many teachers found the MCAS intolerable. As the first group of tenth-graders for whom the MCAS competency determination would be a graduation requirement prepared for the tests, the MTA filed a bill that would have replaced MCAS in the competency determination with an assessment of student work and presentations (Coleman 2000). Around the same time, the MTA also paid for TV advertisements in which it charged that learning, which "used to be about a lot of things: imagination, creativity, discovery, and dreams," had been redefined in terms of "a flawed and unfair test. The one-size-fits-all, high-stakes, do-or-die MCAS test" (Hayward 2000). The MTA's bill did not pass the state legislature.

Although there is still controversy over how the MCAS has affected dropout and graduation rates (Darling-Hammond 2010, 94–96), on the whole the effect of the test requirement has been smaller than many originally feared, in part because the requirement as implemented is less extensive than the requirement as legislated. Once it became clear that the initial definition of the competency determination had not produced a dramatically worse drop-out crisis, the graduation requirement's major supporters in state government began to move toward a more demanding standard. This move reflected the assumption that a test can produce educational equity by pushing all students toward a high level of achievement. In 2006 Board of Education chairman James Peyser declared that when the board had adopted its competency determination standard in 1999, "we did so knowing full well that it was far below the level of knowledge and skill our students would need to succeed in higher education and today's workplace" (MBE 2006). In 2005 the board voted to add a requirement that students pass at least one MCAS examination in a science field or the MCAS technology/engineering examination, effective with the class of 2010 (MBE 2005). Changes made to the competency determination standard in 2006 will eventually require that students earn a "proficient" score in mathematics and English language arts, and add a requirement for a "needs improvement" in history and social science (McDermott 2007, 100).

School and District Accountability

Like other states, Massachusetts has used its powers to intervene in schools and districts only sparingly. The state board of education has identified several "chronically underperforming" schools but has worked with their districts on improving them rather than invoking its powers under MERA. The board has not rated any school districts as "chronically underperforming," but the state department of education has intervened in five districts declared to be underperforming. The state board and department of education frequently revised the accountability system for schools and districts, both to implement NCLB and to respond to concerns about the system's effectiveness. Early in 2010 Gov. Deval Patrick signed legislation that more fundamentally revamped school accountability, giving districts a larger role in "turnaround" plans for underperforming schools and requiring that the plans address students' and families' social service and health needs in addition to school-specific issues. The state board of education may place a school in receivership if it fails to improve after being designated underperforming and is thus labeled chronically underperforming. The 2010 law also created new procedures for designating districts as chronically underperforming and limited the total number of districts and schools that can be in this category at the same time.[26]

Education Finance Reform: What Is "Adequate?"

Although in 1993 the *McDuffy* decision and MERA advocates' logic had connected the educational-threshold definition of equity with increases in education funding, a decade later the Massachusetts Supreme Judicial Court declined to support a broader reading of how education spending and "adequate" outcomes were related. State spending on education had indeed increased, as promised, during the seven years after MERA, but many school administrators and teachers questioned whether the increases had provided them with the resources they needed to get all students to the MCAS proficiency standard. This question was asked most intensely in low-income, high-need school districts whose MCAS scores were low and often not increasing. Another issue was that special education costs had continued to rise so that much of the increased spending was concentrated on students with disabilities rather than reaching the broader population of students (Churchill et al. 2002). The Foundation Budget Review Commission reported to the legislature in June 2001 that there was a need to increase the foundation budget in several areas, including special education (Massachusetts Foundation Budget Review Commission 2001), but the recession that began in the fall of that year ended the seven-year trend of real increases in state funding of K–12 education.

Since the 1993 *McDuffy* decision, one of the justices on the Massachusetts Supreme Judicial Court (SJC) had retained jurisdiction over the case. In 1999 a new set of plaintiffs asked the SJC to declare that the funding provisions of MERA had not met the state's constitutional obligations as articulated in the *McDuffy* decision. The justice who had jurisdiction referred the case to the superior court. From June 2003 until January 2004, Judge Margaret Botsford presided over a trial in the new case, *Hancock v. Driscoll*. The plaintiffs argued that although MERA had increased the state share of education finance in their communities and the overall level of resources for the schools, the accountability provisions of MERA and their students' low scores on MCAS were evidence that the state needed to put even more money into education aid. In effect, the *Hancock* plaintiffs' argument inverted the MBAE position that had carried the day in 1993. Rather than saying that heightened accountability was the quid pro quo for increased funds, the *Hancock* plaintiffs claimed that heightened accountability created, and provided evidence of, the need for still more funding.

Judge Botsford issued her report in April 2004. She concluded that the state had indeed not met its obligations under *McDuffy*, with specific reference to four school districts: Brockton, Lowell, Springfield, and Winchendon. She also issued a book-length finding of facts report to the Supreme Judicial Court.[27] Given Judge Botsford's conclusions about the case, it came as a surprise to many policy-watchers when the SJC ruled *against* the plaintiffs in early 2005. In the opinion of a majority of the justices, the state's financial support for public education was adequate to satisfy its constitutional obligations. Thus, whether to spend more state funds in response to the conditions detailed in the findings of fact was a political question better left to the elected branches of state government than settled by unelected judges.[28]

The SJC's *Hancock* ruling may turn out to have been a turning point in the evolution of school funding lawsuits nationwide, marking the end of the advantage that plaintiffs had gained by making adequacy arguments. Until *Hancock*, the fusion of financial redistribution with educational standards, embodied in the idea that funding of public schools needed to produce "adequate" results to satisfy constitutional guarantees, had produced a trend in favor of school-finance plaintiffs (West and Peterson 2007). Critics of the trend argued that it was nearly impossible to produce an estimate of the cost of "adequacy" that did not smuggle in policy preferences disguised as constitutional rights (Springer and Guthrie 2007). In its *Hancock* ruling, the SJC acknowledged the progress made by Massachusetts public schools since MERA and rejected the plaintiffs' claim that the constitutional guarantee required the state to increase spending on public education until all students actually met the threshold of performance established in MERA. Robert Costrell, the state's chief economist and an expert witness in *Hancock*, claimed that the main lesson of the case is that "good policy is the best defense against lawsuits" (Costrell 2007, 300). The policy that Costrell had in mind was the MERA framework, especially its standards, tests, and accountability provisions.

MERA and the Federal Government

Massachusetts enacted MERA the year before the U.S. Congress passed the Improving America's Schools Act of 1994, which began the federal push for state standards and tests. Despite the state's reputation for having unusually good standards and tests, Massachusetts was not one of the models on which the Bush administration based its NCLB framework. As it turned out, however, implementation of NCLB in Massachusetts required only regulatory changes because the overall legislative frameworks of NCLB and MERA were congruent. The main difference was the frequency of testing in math and English. Massachusetts was one of the states to earn early approval of its state NCLB implementation plan (McDermott 2007, 137).

Equity, State–Local Relations, and Accountability in Massachusetts

Performance accountability came to Massachusetts public education with a single legislative enactment, the Massachusetts Education Reform Act of 1993. MERA required all of the state's public school students to take tests based on state curriculum frameworks. The law empowered the state to evaluate school and district performance on the basis of the test scores and to declare a school or district "chronically underperforming." The state could then replace the principal of an underperforming school, or could appoint a receiver to take on the powers of the superintendent and school committee of an underperforming district. MERA also requires high school students to earn a competency determination by passing state examinations before they can receive a high school diploma. This requirement puts direct pressure on students but also puts indirect pressure on their schools, even if the schools as a whole are not at risk of state intervention.

Clearly, MERA made performance data the basis of new forms of political accountability of schools and districts to the state. This represented a shift both in the source of accountability demands and in their substance. Although state authorities could not directly control schools and districts, they used a performance-based accountability system to define and control expectations for schools (in Romzek and Dubnick's sense) and to establish incentives such as the accountability sanctions and the competency determination. These incentives would in theory induce schools to do what state policymakers wanted them to. The state added these new accountability requirements to the prior system in which the state ensured regulatory compliance but did not take much of a role in curriculum or assessment of students. MERA also weakened political accountability at the local level by imposing state-defined performance goals, with which local electorates might or might not agree, and by reducing the role of elected school committees in hiring school staff.

MERA embodied new understandings of educational equity and the appropriate relationship between state and local authority. Table 6.1 summarizes the shift. Prior to MERA, the prevailing definitions of educational equity emphasized following appropriate procedures, including racial-balance requirements, intended to protect students who were members of vulnerable groups. There was broad awareness of inequality of educational funding across school districts but not much done about it by the state. The state emphasized enforcement of the procedural requirements for equity. At the same time, the state mostly left local school districts to make decisions about what to teach, how to teach it, and how to determine whether students were learning.

MERA introduced a new emphasis on threshold levels of student performance as the basis of defining educational equity, and in principle redesigned the state–local relationship around student performance. In practice, the state continued enforcing other equity-related mandates, except for the racial-imbalance law whose importance had already begun to decline by that time. Crucially, the state also tackled the finance-equity problem by using state funds to fill gaps between what districts could raise locally and what they needed to

Table 6.1   Changing Conceptions of Equity and State–Local Relations in Massachusetts

	Pre-MERA	*Post-MERA (1993)*
Equity	Defined mainly in terms of equal treatment for students of different races, students with disabilities Some efforts to equalize funding among districts	Foundation budget Threshold level of educational achievement (esp. high school competency determination) Deemphasize RIL (not in MERA, but occurring at same time)
State–Local Relations	State enforces mandates related to equity State defers to localities on matters of curriculum, assessment, and instruction	State aid guarantees foundation spending State power to intervene in under-performing schools/districts Many other state mandates continue

spend to reach a state-defined foundation level of spending. Both before and after MERA, the prevailing assumption about state–local relations and equity was that the state should use its authority to ensure that local school districts provide educational equity. What changed was the theory of action according to which the state–local relationship was supposed to work. MERA gave the state a more active role in funding public education, in order to reduce financial inequities. More crucially for education governance, it also committed the state to a performance-based definition of educational equity and to intervening when school districts or schools were failing to achieve it. Improved performance for all students was the rationale—and the quid pro quo—for increased state funding. The essence of the MERA approach was for the state to increase funding while taking on a "tight–loose" accountability role: "tight" in terms of ensuring that all students mastered a common core of material but "loose" in terms of school and district autonomy to choose how to teach.

Table 6.2 summarizes the changes in the prevailing understanding of the relationship between equity and intergovernmental relations, the dominant forms of accountability in education, and the role of performance in educational accountability. As discussed earlier, the state–local relationship around issues of educational equity shifted from one in which the state enforced procedural requirements while leaving curriculum, instruction, and assessment issues up to local districts to one in which the state specified goals for what all students should learn and held districts and schools accountable for their students' performance. Performance became the key element in accountability.

Table 6.2 Changing Educational Accountability in Massachusetts

	Pre–MERA	Post–MERA (1993)
Prevailing understanding of connection between equity and state–local relations	State ensures that districts follow regulations embodying procedural definition of equity State deference to localities on curriculum, instruction, assessment	State provides additional funds where needed and also guarantees that schools and districts are using the funds to produce performance-threshold equity State curriculum frameworks, test, and sanctions
Role of performance in accountability	Minimal	Central
Dominant form(s) of accountability	Legal (in state–local relationship) Political (relationship between local school committees and educators)	Political (of local school districts to state, due to increased state funding role) In principle, greater role of professional accountability in management of local school districts—but problematic in practice Earlier legal and bureaucratic accountability continued

In particular, the state increased political accountability of schools and districts to the state for their students' performance as a trade-off for increased state funding. At the same time, earlier layers of accountability mandates remained in place. For example, the increased degree of control that superintendents and principals had over staffing decisions was still subject to ongoing collective bargaining agreements, so what looked on paper like heightened local professional accountability was not borne out in practice. Overall, MERA strengthened political accountability at the state level and based it on performance data as part of a "grand bargain" that also increased the state share of education finance.

Notes

1. Mark Roosevelt interview with Kathryn A. McDermott, October 1, 2004, Boston MA.

2. Letter from Paul Reville to Martin Kaplan, November 4, 1991. In author's files.

3. Working group report, p. 10, in Roosevelt papers box 2 folder 33, Special Collections of the Massachusetts State Library, Boston, MA.

4. Robert H. Blumenthal, Daniel French, Pamela Kaufman, Beverly Miyares, and John Sullivan, Memorandum to Acting Commissioner Rhoda Schneider, October 23, 1991, p. 4. Copy on file with author.

5. State House News Service, House Proceedings, January 28, 1993, 14.

6. *McDuffy v. Secretary of the Executive Office of Education*, 415 Mass. 545; 615 N.E.2d 516; 1993 Mass. LEXIS 372 (1993), p. 621.

7. Thomas Birmingham interview with Kathryn A. McDermott, October 1, 2004, Boston, MA.

8. Paul Reville interview with Kathryn A. McDermott, September 18, 2004, Worcester, MA.

9. Ibid.

10. Birmingham interview.

11. State House News Service, House Proceedings, June 2, 1993.

12. Roosevelt papers, n.d., folders 35, 36, 37, 38, 39, 40, 41, 42.

13. Roosevelt interview.

14. Ibid.

15. Ibid.

16. Ibid.

17. Birmingham interview.

18. Reville interview.

19. Roosevelt interview.

20. Reville interview.

21. Birmingham interview.

22. Massachusetts General Laws, ch. 69, sec. 1I.

23. Peter Sack phone interview with Kathryn A. McDermott, October 29, 2004.

24. Birmingham interview.

25. Commonwealth of Massachusetts, Acts and Resolves of 1993, Ch. 71, sec. 68.

26. Massachusetts Acts and Resolves of 2010, Ch. 12, sec. 3, http://www.malegis lature.gov/Laws/SessionLaws/Acts/2010/Chapter12.

27. *Hancock v. Driscoll*, 2004 Mass. Super. LEXIS 118 (Suffolk County Superior Court, 2004).

28. *Hancock v. Commissioner of Education*, 43 Mass. 428; 822 N.E.2d 1134; 2005 Mass. LEXIS 78 (Mass. Supreme Judicial Court, 2005).

CHAPTER SEVEN

Accountability and Equity in New Jersey

"Where Home Rule Hasn't Worked, the Legislature Must Do What Home Rule Has Not Done"

In 1986 the New Jersey legislature began considering a set of bills that would make it the first state in the United States to be able to seize control of local school districts in cases of poor academic performance and bad management. Opponents of the bills claimed that they flew in the face of the state's tradition of home rule. State board of education president John Klagholz countered this view with the assertion in the subtitle of this chapter, expressing state officials' frustration at some local governments' failure to operate effective school districts (New Jersey Senate, Committee on Education 1986a, 33). The state-takeover proposal became law in early 1988, and soon thereafter the state took control of three urban school districts. New Jersey was also one of the earliest states to require that high school students pass a test to earn a diploma. These two policies make the state appear to be a fairly straightforward example of performance-based accountability in education. However, the New Jersey story is more complicated. While the state was relatively early to embrace the idea of state performance standards and state intervention in cases of poor performance, its system was never entirely performance based. The New Jersey Department of Education, in response to state supreme court decisions on education finance, maintained a parallel system of legal accountability, monitoring whether school districts were doing the sorts of things that would satisfy the constitutional requirement of a "thorough and efficient" education for all students.

This chapter provides accounts of several of the decisive episodes in the history of New Jersey's educational accountability policies. Beginning in the late 1970s, the state legislature and governors took on more power with respect to the state department of education and the state government itself took on more power with respect to local school districts. Over this period the state expanded its role in educational accountability. What the state held localities accountable for also changed, with the idea of educational adequacy added to the original "thorough and efficient" policy. After the *Abbott v. Burke V* decision, the state had a hybrid system of accountability that combined accountability for results and the threat of state takeover with accountability for spending new state funds in the ways specified in *Abbott V*. The major episodes covered in this chapter are (1) the enactment of the 1979 graduation-test law, which built on the legislative response to the landmark *Robinson v. Cahill* school finance case; (2) the long controversy over the 1988 law that empowered the state to take over school districts; (3) the 1988 replacement of the original Minimum Basic Skills graduation test with a test based on higher standards; and (4) the reshaping of educational accountability following the *Abbott v. Burke* finance decisions of the 1990s.

The Minimum Basic Skills Test

Prior to the enactment of performance-based educational accountability, New Jersey state law emphasized protection of vulnerable populations, such as students with disabilities and African American students. New Jersey was an early adopter of statewide special education laws, requiring districts to identify, classify, and serve students with disabilities as of 1966 (Palmer 1969, 829). The state was also earlier than many states in bringing its power to bear to end local segregation. The state constitution that New Jersey ratified in 1947 guarantees that no person shall be "segregated in the militia or in the public schools, because of religious principles, race, color, ancestry, or national origin." In 1962 the state commissioner of education ordered the Orange Board of Education to desegregate its schools.[1] Following civil rights protests, the commissioner also ordered Englewood's 98 percent black Lincoln School to be integrated in 1963 (Sugrue 2008, 455–56). In 1965 the state supreme court ruled that de facto segregation in school districts violated the state constitution.[2] Gov. Richard Hughes followed the court ruling with an executive order that expressed his commitment to ending segregation. As in other states, New Jersey's commitment to integration was ambivalent; Hughes's order also stated a commitment to maintain neighborhood schools so long as they did not conflict with the goal of integration (Hughes 1965). When local districts resisted integrating, the state was not aggressive in enforcing desegregation mandates (Onishi 1995).

Robinson v. Cahill and Chapter 212

General accounts of New Jersey politics cite the state supreme court's unusual level of activism and innovation (Segers 2006; Salmore and Salmore 1998). The 1973 *Robinson v. Cahill* decision was one of the key moments that contributed to that reputation. Attorney Harold Ruvoldt Jr. filed the case in 1970 on behalf of Kenneth Robinson, a sixth-grader in Jersey City, and Jersey City municipal and school officials. The case challenged the state's education finance laws on the grounds that heavy reliance on local property taxes forced residents of property-poor communities to tax themselves at higher rates in order to spend less on schools than residents of property-rich communities. The New Jersey Supreme Court's ruling in *Robinson* declared that "thorough and efficient" education as guaranteed in the state constitution implied equal educational opportunity and greater equality of funding (Yaffe 2007).

To comply with the *Robinson* decision, the New Jersey legislature enacted the Public School Education Act of 1975, better known as Chapter 212 or as the "T&E" (for "thorough and efficient") law. The legislative battle around Chapter 212 was epic because to increase state equalization aid to school districts, the legislature also had to enact the state's first income tax (Lehne 1978; Yaffe 2007). Chapter 212 altered the state's education finance system to bring more money to property-poor school districts, and it directed the state to identify the components of the "thorough and efficient" education guaranteed to all students by the state constitution. The legislature "accept[ed] the responsibility" to delegate to "appropriate State and local agencies" the authority "to establish goals and objectives consistent with legislative guidelines" and to "define standards of performance necessary to indicate achievement of the goals and objectives."[3] Under Chapter 212, the state commissioner of education also had the responsibility for monitoring school districts' progress toward the goals and objectives and the power to require districts to adhere to remedial plans when they failed to make progress.[4]

New Jersey's post-*Robinson* mix of performance-based and process-based accountability was largely the work of officials at the state department of education responding to Chapter 212. Although some reformers insisted that students' attainment of basic skills should be the basis of the T&E definition, the state department of education feared that "public support for education is really quite fragile, and the documentation of educational failure in New Jersey's cities would not generate more money for Newark, but less money for everyone in the system" (Lehne 1978, 106). The state's teachers' unions also opposed the output approach because they believed that it would lead to teachers being punished for poor student results that were due to factors beyond the teachers' control (Yaffe 2007, 42–43). In her account of New Jersey's education finance struggles, Deborah Yaffe explains how the participants in the T&E debate arrived at a compromise between the idea that the thoroughness and efficiency of the education system should be measured in terms of inputs such as student-to-teacher ratios, books, and classroom space, and an opposing idea that emphasized outcomes like test scores and dropout rates. William Shine, an influential member of the department of education staff, believed that emphasizing processes would avoid the pitfalls of both input-only and output-only models (Yaffe 2007, 43).

The eventual compromise emphasized districts' processes—essentially, according to Yaffe, whether a district "had set goals for improving its programs and outcomes, devised appropriate steps toward meeting those goals, and begun carrying out those steps and assessing process" (Yaffe 2007, 43). However, the outcomes-based definition also persisted in the 1976 amendment to the T&E law that required the state department of education to establish statewide goals for "pupil proficiency in basic communications and computational skills."[5] This amendment was part of a compromise with Republican legislators who were otherwise reluctant to support the income tax needed to pay for additional state education spending (Goertz and Hannigan 1978). In his remarks upon signing of the bill that established minimum statewide performance standards as part of the definition of "thorough and efficient" education, Gov. Brendan Byrne asked the state board of education to "establish minimum performance standards for high school graduation" because "we must restore meaning to the high school diploma" (Byrne 1976).

Education Insiders and Outsiders

Consistent with Frank Baumgartner and Bryan Jones's model of policy change, shifts in educational accountability in New Jersey happened when new people moved into positions of authority in the state and challenged prevailing policy monopolies. The *Robinson v. Cahill* decision and the legislative and administrative response to it opened the education policy subsystem to new actors. These included the state legislature's Joint Education Committee, which had the task of monitoring implementation of Chapter 212, as well as organizations that monitored progress toward equity. One such organization, the Education Law Center (ELC), continued to press the state government on finance issues for decades.

Margaret Goertz and Janet Hannigan wrote in 1978 that the *Robinson* finance decision had expanded the circle of influence in state education policymaking. Indeed, Governor Byrne and his allies saw themselves as critics of the education establishment, attempting to disrupt settled but ineffective practices. A member of the state board of education, Katherine K. Neuberger, sent one of Byrne's staff members a letter thanking him for sending a copy of Byrne's signing message on the 1979 graduation-test bill, and stating, "I agree with the Governor when he says that he is concerned that 1154 does not go far enough. . . . It is not the Board members who are fighting this thing. You must know that the people who are fighting it are the entrenched bureaucracy, both teachers, administrators, and school boards, who for some reason think of themselves before they think of the students' welfare" (Neuberger 1980). In particular, the legislature was more active than previously in the move to create minimum statewide standards and tests (Goertz and Hannigan 1978). Governors Byrne and Kean also took on large roles in pushing for more focus on results in the educational accountability system. The tension that had emerged after *Robinson* about how to define "thorough and efficient" continued, with pressure for results coming from outside the education system and with support for process regulations from among education interest groups and the state department of education. A bit more than a decade later, Goertz and Susan Fuhrman wrote that on the whole, governors and the state department of education tended to have more influence than the legislature in education policy (Goertz and Fuhrman 1991, 2).

The 1979 Graduation Test

Seen in hindsight, the 1976 amendment to T&E was the beginning of the process that led to the enactment of the state's first graduation test requirement. One of its cosponsors was Republican assemblyman Thomas Kean, who as governor in the 1980s would successfully push for the state-takeover law and a more demanding graduation test. In the late 1970s a state panel considered the pros and cons of a graduation test, and the legislature considered a graduation-test bill in 1979. Advocates of the bill presented it not just as part of an accountability system but also as a way of making the system more equitable by linking diplomas to particular skills. In theory, this linkage would reduce the disadvantages to students who had graduated from high schools with weak academic reputations. Administrators of disadvantaged districts seemed to agree with this proposition. The New Jersey committee that reviewed the pros and cons of graduation tests in the late 1970s surveyed school district administrators and found the highest level of support for the tests in the urban districts whose students would presumably have had the most difficulty passing the tests.[6] At the New Jersey Senate Education Committee's hearing on the bill that became the 1979 graduation test law, Greater

Newark Urban Coalition representative Gustav Heningburg expressed the hope that "a diploma that certifies a student has achieved minimum competency would at the very least require prospective employers, educational institutions, and post-secondary training programs to individualize to the specific student rather than make judgments based on a school district's or community's reputation."[7]

At a hearing on the 1979 graduation-test bill, a representative of the New Jersey School Boards Association likened the diploma's loss of meaning to the price inflation with which Americans were struggling at the time: "The diploma, which has shrunk in value as surely as the dollar, will once again be a symbol of learning" (New Jersey Assembly 1979, 31). The sponsor of the 1979 graduation-test bill stated, "State intervention in our local school system should be restrained. . . . In critical areas, statewide minimums are legitimate, and, indeed, necessary. Interference beyond this minimal level would violate the very principles on which our system of public education is based" (ibid., 2). State education commissioner Fred G. Burke said that because the graduation test results would be available to the public, the tests would be "one of the most powerful weapons we have" for improving school quality (ibid., 9–10). The performance-threshold definition of equity was visible during the debate. Supporters of the test insisted that these more meaningful diplomas would also be more egalitarian than the ones they replaced. At a 1978 hearing on the original minimum-competency test legislation, Gustav Heningburg, from the Greater Newark Urban Coalition, said,

> the position that argues against standardized tests because many minorities are bound to fail may in fact be more firmly rooted in racism than the position that champions standards. . . . The real issue is whether school systems will continue to be rewarded for failing to educate by being allowed to award diplomas that bear no relationship whatsoever to competence or proficiency and whether students have the right to a document that relates their effort and achievement as well as the quality of their educational system, to a uniform statewide standard. (New Jersey Senate 1978, 2)

Graduation-test advocates also claimed that the test requirement would not affect most of the state. The "Commissioner's Narrative" from state education commissioner Fred Burke, who supported the test, was reassuring: "The issue of local autonomy has been raised repeatedly. However, I do not believe that local autonomy would be undermined by the establishment of curricular or proficiency requirements at the state level, since most districts would be able to meet such requirements without major difficulties" (Burke 1979).

For their part, opponents of the proposal positioned themselves as defenders of local control. The idea of a state graduation test implied that local school districts could not be trusted to maintain standards on their own, and this implication was clear to representatives of local educators. For example, at a February 1979 hearing, a representative of the New Jersey Association of School Administrators complained about the symbolism of a state graduation test: "The disturbing aspect of state mandated minimum proficiency requirements is the assumption that local districts are unwilling or unable to establish minimum basic skills standards. We do not agree with this assumption" (New Jersey Assembly 1979, 24). Another legislator pointed out that local boards had not in fact set such benchmarks, and that "had we had this kind of reaction by local boards of education over the years, we wouldn't be sitting here this morning" (ibid., 26). This statement expresses the idea that state-level political accountability was preferable to local political accountability in cases where local politicians had the wrong priorities.

Performance Accountability in the 1980s

During the 1980s New Jersey enacted a wide range of changes to education policy and governance that departed somewhat from the previous decade's focus on responding to *Robinson* and working out the meaning of "thorough and efficient" education. These included a statewide minimum teacher salary and changes to teacher certification laws intended to improve the quality of the state's teacher workforce. My focus here is on the performance-accountability innovations during the decade. The most famous of these was the 1988 law empowering the state to take over school districts, which led immediately to three takeovers. The state legislature also authorized shifting from a Minimum Basic Skills graduation test to one based on higher-level standards.

The Kean Agenda

Gov. Tom Kean, elected in 1981 by the smallest margin in New Jersey gubernatorial history, became one of the 1980s generation of "education governors," discussed in chapter 4. According to Kean's 1988 political memoir, he decided to make education a priority in 1983 after the release of *A Nation at Risk*. He says that he called a special 1983 legislative session focused on education to "provoke a crisis atmosphere to get the legislators to think about education and nothing else" (Kean 1988a, 221). Kean was a cochair of the NGA's education efforts in the mid-1980s and chaired its task force on teaching ([NGA] National Governors' Association 1986). Kean also had a broader political agenda that included broadening the appeal of the Republican Party beyond "country clubs and board rooms," and education was a good issue to empha-size in order to do this. He traveled the nation making speeches about how Republicans could reach out to new constituencies and support true equality of opportunity (Sullivan 1986c). As Kean said in his memoir, "Compassion is a necessary virtue, not a luxury, in a democracy like ours, and government is the only institution that can do what is necessary." He went on to deplore the fact that many young people "do not have the chance to develop their talents and abilities," perhaps because "their local schools are nothing more than warehouses where it is impossible to learn to read and write" (Kean 1988a, 41). Kean's emphasis on inclusion and a new kind of Republicanism worked quite well in the state. In his 1985 reelection campaign, he had endorsements from Coretta Scott King, the New Jersey Education Association, and the state AFL-CIO, and he won by a wide margin.

At the base of Kean's education agenda was his belief that spending more did not necessarily lead to better schools. He had acted on this belief even before becoming governor. As the Speaker of the New Jersey Assembly, Kean voted against the T&E law (Stonecash and McGuire 2003, 138). Kean even joined the state senate president in appealing *Robinson* into the federal courts, asking the federal courts to strike down the state court decision as a violation of the separation of powers. This effort did not succeed, and afterward Kean did acknowledge that the state's elected officials now had a "clear and definite responsibility" to change the system of funding public education.[8] However, he remained skeptical about the benefits of increased spending in the absence of other changes. During his 1981 campaign, Kean asserted that the increased funds had purchased "a rapidly increasing bureaucracy which has placed self-interest ahead of the interests of the state's schoolchildren" (Stonecash and McGuire 2003, 115). Kean tended to portray urban teachers as unwilling to accept responsibility for how much their students learned, and then as quick to pin the blame either on the students themselves or on social factors beyond anybody's control: "Too many teachers complain about disruptive students, or students who are zombie-eyed from watching reruns of Johnny Carson, or who are hungry or on drugs. The truth is that every profession contends with factors that are beyond immediate control. But in return for power and prestige, teachers have got to stop making excuses and start getting kids to learn" (Kean 1988a, 225). The idea behind the state-takeover bills was that administrators in some districts had failed to get teachers to take their respon-sibilities seriously, and had abused the trust of the public by pursuing priorities other than quality education. Kean promised to end this abuse: "If anything is said of Tom Kean as governor, I hope it is that I did not sit by and watch another generation of city children treated like pawns in a political game, the resulting ignorance enslaving them just like the chains that once bound their great-grandparents" (1988a, 233).

Kean had said prior to the 1985 election that his main priority in his second term would be to complete the "educational renaissance" begun in his first term (Norman 1985). This meant questioning the assumed connection between more spending and better schools that had previously been central to education policy in the state. One analysis of Kean's policies on teacher preparation and certification says that his election "signaled a clear turning point" in terms of interest group power in education in the state (Tamir 2006, 55), in which new actors such as Kean gained power over the "orthodox" set of interests that had previously prevailed (ibid., 96–97). When Kean began his second term in 1986, he brought with him a Republican majority in both houses of the state legislature for the first time in twelve years. These circumstances fit Sabatier and Jenkins-Smith's definition of a shift in the advocacy coalition, as the election results gave the Republican party control of the state assembly for the first time in twelve years.[9]

Kean advocated a "no excuses" approach to educational issues. In his book *The Politics of Inclusion*, published in 1988, Kean describes how his experiences working in a summer camp for disadvantaged children, as a boarding-school teacher, and as a graduate student in education had led him to believe that education was crucial to producing real equality of opportunity, and that schools rather than children deserved the blame for educational failure. The state-takeover proposal arose out of tensions among the state department of education, the Trenton Public Schools, and the courts. In 1979 Commissioner of Education Fred Burke had appointed Anthony Catrambone to serve as "monitor general" of the Trenton public schools following a review that identified serious problems with finances, personnel policies, and regulatory compliance. The Trenton Board of Education remained in place, and it challenged the legitimacy of Catrambone's authority in the state superior court (Winans 1980). Ultimately, the New Jersey Supreme Court upheld the intervention: "We are satisfied that the powers exercised by the Commissioner and State Board were invoked in highly unusual, virtually unprecedented circumstances and that the power to intervene may be reasonably implied in the Public School Education Act of 1975" (New Jersey Senate, Committee on Education 1986c, 35X, 36X).

Although the courts had upheld the Trenton intervention, the Kean administration still sought a broader and clearer legal mandate for taking control of school districts with low test scores and poor management. The Trenton Board of Education had remained in place while the monitor general was overseeing the district, and it had continuously resisted his efforts (Goertz and Fuhrman 1991, 27). According to Assistant Education Commissioner Walter McCarroll, if the state appointed somebody to oversee a school district but left its Board of Education in place, the lines of authority were unclear, making the situation "inefficient, confusing, and costly." McCarroll pointed out that the state wanted to respond to poor provision of education by the district as a whole, not just the misdeeds of individual board members: "A failure to provide a thorough and efficient system of education is the responsibility of the board of education as an entity, not of individuals on that board of education" (New Jersey Senate, Committee on Education 1986c, 3). A letter from the state's attorney general and assistant attorney general to Commissioner Saul Cooperman, dated May 4, 1987, indicated that it was very difficult to predict whether courts would, in the absence of a new state law, sustain a more comprehensive state intervention that had occurred in Trenton (Edwards and Harla 1987). Yaffe's account of the New Jersey school funding controversy quotes Education Commissioner Cooperman as remembering that he had begun his time in office with an "idealistic naïve phase" in which he agreed with the urban school leaders' claims that more money was the key to solving their problems. Later, though, he decided that "some of these school districts were beyond hope, and the state had to find a way to clean them up" (Yaffe 2007, 173), and he drafted the bills that would enable the state to take control of districts.

The legislative process on the state-takeover proposal lasted for more than a year, and at one point Kean vetoed a pair of takeover bills that he believed had been unacceptably altered by the Democratic-controlled senate (at the time, Kean's Republican party controlled the assembly). Following the veto, Kean and his allies in the assembly introduced a similar pair of bills later in 1987, for which they were able to gain the support of the state's education interest groups because of compromises on the provisions pertaining to employment of district and school staff. As the education associations wanted, principals would receive tenure hearings before being terminated, but any evaluations of their work conducted before the district came under state management would not be admissible at the hearings. Dismissed central office staff would be permitted to retain some of their contractual rights, such as accrued vacation time (Cole, Herrmann, and LaVecchia 1988, 1–2). At the last minute, it seemed as if this bill would also die, when senate president John F. Russo added an amendment favored by the mayor of Jersey City, which would have shifted the entire financial burden of intervention from the district to the state level (Sullivan 1987), but ultimately the governor's office and the senate Democrats agreed on a compromise that allowed districts to draw on state aid earlier but did not require the state to fund the entire process (Cole, Hermann, and LaVecchia 1988, 1–2).[10]

Targeting Cities

A distinctive feature of educational accountability politics in New Jersey was the connection that Kean and other policymakers made between poor school performance and urban corruption. This led to the performance issue being framed as an issue that was specific to cities, rather than statewide. Deborah Yaffe, who interviewed both Kean and his education commissioner, Saul Cooperman, for her book on the New Jersey school-finance controversy, said, "both Kean and Cooperman were convinced that money shortages were not the fundamental cause of educational devastation in the cities. They blamed politics, and the culture of self-interest fostered by the political appointees who controlled and staffed urban districts" (2007, 105–6). In his memoir, which went to press during debate on the state-operated school district laws, Kean detailed his account of the problem in cities like Newark. He implied that some of these political appointees owed their original hiring to misguided good intentions, and that they had used political clout to hold onto their positions even though they were not doing their jobs:

> In Newark after the riots, for example, a great hue and cry went up that the children were somehow being cheated because schools had few minority administrators. The response was to immediately hire a number of minority administrators, many of whom had no qualifications; these people have stayed in the school system for two decades. Change is now their enemy and a threat to their jobs. In other words, Newark's children suffer because the school system contains too many people who care more about protecting their jobs than educating kids. (Kean 1988a, 215)

When Kean signed the bills, he quoted Winston Churchill ("This is not the end. It is not the beginning of the end. But it is perhaps the end of the beginning") and declared, "We don't want to use the authority we are being given today. But make no mistake, we will use these powers if no other means can be found to save our children from the educational cul-de-sacs that block their lives" (Kean 1988b, 2).

Intergovernmental Relations

At legislative hearings in 1986, opponents of the state-takeover bills claimed that takeovers would destroy local control and even undermine democracy. An officer of the New Jersey School Boards Association complained that a state-appointed local superintendent of schools would be a "bureaucrat" and a "czar." He also invoked "individuals such as Franco in Spain, Marcos in the Philippines, Duvalier in Haiti, Pinochet in Chile, and others [who] have all said it was necessary to consolidate power to themselves, to do for the people what they cannot do for themselves" (New Jersey Senate, Committee on Education 1986b). He went on to clarify that although he did not actually think state officials were the same as third-world dictators, he also believed it was important to separate the principle of home rule from the high levels of trust in the particular individual who happened at that time to be the state commissioner, because later commissioners might abuse expanded powers (Van Tassel 1986a). Similarly, according to a Newark principal who testified at one of the hearings on the takeover bill, for the state to appoint a superintendent would be "reminiscent [of] a period in our history when we were governed by a king" (New Jersey Senate, Committee on Education 1986b, 41). A representative of the Association for Children of New Jersey argued that takeover power would give the state "unprecedented and nearly unlimited power in what has been a traditional and strong area of local control" (New Jersey Senate, Committee on Education 1986c, 36).

In response to these claims, takeover supporters argued that the increased state powers were consistent with local control, and that they even strengthened it. Chancellor of Higher Education T. Edward Hollander claimed that the state's history of local control actually made it better able to implement state takeovers constructively: "Only in a State where home rule is so highly valued would I expect to see a plan this comprehensive, this cautious, this protective of a local district's rights in which State takeover is truly a last resort" (New Jersey Senate, Committee on Education 1986b, 5). The essence of the case for the takeover bill was that sometimes local political accountability failed to serve the interests of students. In these instances, political accountability to the state would be an improvement. In response to a legislator whose question suggested that he believed the takeover power would end home rule, Commissioner Cooperman said, "We see now that there has not been responsible home rule. We want to get in, try like heck to make it better, load the odds in the kids' favor, and then turn it back to responsible rule" (New Jersey Senate, Committee on Education 1986a, 23). John Klagholz, the president of the state Board of Education, similarly insisted that "when home rule hasn't worked," the state "must step in and recreate strong school districts so that the community and the students can make a fresh start" (ibid., 34). In effect, the state's power could be a counterweight against the influence of corrupt officials, to ensure that the right local voices were heard. As Governor Kean put it, "The rulers at home are no longer ruling, and we will not let our children be jeopardized by a faulty education system" (Sullivan 1986a). Here again, Kean asserted that state political accountability, focused on results, was better than local political accountability in some communities.

Advocates of the takeover bills frequently reminded other participants that ultimate authority over public education lay with the state, not local school districts. When he first made the proposal Governor Kean insisted, "The Constitution requires that we provide a thorough and efficient education . . . and if the education is not efficient we cannot philosophically, or legally, allow it to continue" (ibid.). In one of the legislative hearings, a member of the state board of education claimed, "You can read the Constitution from the beginning to the end, and I have never found the two buzz words in there that say 'local control' of education" (New Jersey Senate, Committee on Education 1986c, 117). In the legislature's hearings on the bill, supporters of the measure from outside state government made similar points. The superintendent of schools in South Orange-Maplewood noted, "The education of our children is a State responsibility; therefore, I believe that the State Legislature has an obligation to see to it that the laws are enacted to assure the education necessary for all children" (New Jersey Senate, Committee on Education 1986a, 58). A Jersey City teacher argued, "The Constitution does not guarantee this thorough and efficient educational opportunity to only . . . children whose districts are committed to providing an excellent quality thorough and efficient educational opportunity for their children" (ibid., 162). The Paramus superintendent of schools said, "Education is the State's responsibility and delegating its responsibility to local communities does not permit the Commissioner or the Legislature to ignore the negative consequences . . . that the worship of home rule can produce" (New Jersey Senate, Committee on Education 1986b, 127). State-takeover advocates also argued that a statewide responsibility followed logically from the state's statutory and constitutional power. State Assembly Speaker Chuck Hardwick made a speech to the New Jersey Education Association, in which he said, "In some cases the system that *we* have set up and the system *we* in the Legislature are responsible for isn't working. It's not the teachers who have failed, it's not the students who have failed, or is it the taxpayers. The system itself has failed, and it is our responsibility to fix it." (Hardwick 1987)

As with the 1979 graduation-test bill, state-takeover advocates emphasized the ways in which state takeovers could be understood as building incrementally on existing state powers. Technically, the state-takeover legislation was an amendment to the T&E law of 1975 and another related statute. As senate education committee chair Matthew Feldman said at the first takeover-bill hearing, "In many ways, these hearings grow directly out of that Public Education Act of 1975. We are now called upon to determine what must be done if, after 11 years, and despite the best efforts of the State, there are school districts in New Jersey which are still failing the children" (New Jersey Senate, Committee on Education 1986a, 1). Supporters of the takeover power also emphasized that it would affect only a few districts. The *New York Times* quoted Assistant Commissioner of Education Walter McCarroll as saying that only about 3 percent of the state's school districts would ever move into the third phase of state monitoring, the last step before a potential intervention (Van Tassel 1986b). Governor Kean and Commissioner Cooperman later told the *Times* that they expected only a few districts would ever be taken over, and that the threat would produce push for improvement in others (Sullivan 1986a).

State education officials described the principle or institution of home rule as subordinate to the state responsibility to ensure that all school districts were providing the constitutionally mandated thorough and efficient education. Along with the statement quoted in the subtitle of this chapter, state board of education president John Klagholz told the members of the assembly and senate education committees, "These bills do not seek to protect and preserve an institution; they seek to protect and preserve the rights and opportunities of the children and young adults of our State" (New Jersey Senate, Committee on Education 1986a, 33). A resident of East Orange said at one of the 1986 hearings on state-operated school districts, "whenever intervention is mentioned, someone invariably mentions home rule, the concept that local communities should be able to administer their own educational system without State control. This privilege is given to our local communities by the State, and should be withdrawn whenever school districts become ineffective" (ibid., 85).

Finally, supporters of the state accountability proposals invoked the need to protect the interests of the state's taxpayers. In one of the hearings on the takeover bills, Commissioner Cooperman stated, "Some have said [state takeovers are] taxation without representation. Every district in this state gets money. And, in fact, some of the districts that are having most of the problems receive large amounts of money from the State. Therefore, every taxpayer has an interest in every district doing well" (ibid., 8). Commissioner Cooperman also used the accountability argument in advocating passage of the more difficult eleventh grade test that replaced the original minimum-competency test: "we're given a lot of money—and I'm not reluctant to ask for money—But I think ask for money to do the job, but also be accountable for results to say that that money has gone somewhere" (New Jersey Assembly, Education Committee 1988, 21).

Race, Money, and Civil Rights

Although liberals and conservatives in New Jersey had united in support of
state testing in the 1970s, by the time of the state-takeover debate in the late
1980s, some liberals believed that the Kean administration was trying to use
takeovers as a way of avoiding increasing state funding of education. In 1981
the Education Law Center had filed a lawsuit known as *Abbott v. Burke* on
behalf of Camden student Raymond Abbott and other urban students. Commissioner Cooperman repeatedly argued that urban school districts needed
better management, and Kean's critique of urban mismanagement was well
known (Stonecash and McGuire 2003, 138). At hearings on the takeover bills,
several speakers from urban areas explicitly made the connection between the
state-operated district proposal and the ongoing *Abbott v. Burke* litigation.
Crosby Copeland, superintendent of schools in Trenton, said,

> The Governor and the Commissioner have used the phrase 'educational bank-
> ruptcy' to refer to urban districts that should be taken over by the State. Of
> greater concern to me as an educator and citizen of this great State is the
> concept of moral bankruptcy, and I suggest to you that those State leaders who
> have used a ploy to stall the resolution of *Abbott vs. Burke*, and who have further
> obfuscated the provision of equal educational opportunity and delivery of a
> thorough and efficient education for all children through the State interven-
> tion smoke screen, are morally bankrupt and devoid of the compassion we as
> Americans have always demonstrated for our fellow citizens (New Jersey Senate,
> Committee on Education 1986a, 141).

Harold Ruvoldt, who had been the plaintiffs' attorney in the *Robinson*
litigation, also appeared at one of the hearings and declared, "the bills before
you are not at all a remedy" for the state's education problems, and that "the
reasons that students have not been achieving is because we, as a State, have
not given local people the tools and the means to correct these problems—I
don't mean money alone, but certainly money is a significant part" (New Jersey
Senate, Committee on Education 1986d, 18–19). Ivette Alfonso, a member
of the Newark Board of Education, stated, "I think the state needs to lose
Abbott v. Burke. Let's get on with actually funding the T&E formula" (ibid.,
96). Trenton Superintendent of Schools Crosby Copeland suggested that
the state-operated school district proposal was "a ploy to stall the resolution
of *Abbott v. Burke*" and a "smoke screen" (New Jersey Senate, Committee on
Education 1986a, 141). Even one state senator said that regardless of what
Kean was claiming, "his actions seem to reflect the suggestion that there is

really not a problem of resources in these poor districts. It is more a matter of just, 'get your act together'" (ibid., 149).

Some critics of the state-takeover proposal also claimed that the idea of empowering the mostly white-led state government to take control of cities whose leaders were black or Latino was inherently racist. They even likened the state-takeover idea to the British dominion over the thirteen American colonies and to the "states' rights" defense of legally mandated racial segregation in the South. Newark's executive superintendent of schools likened state takeover to "taxation without representation" (ibid., 50). Carol Graves from the Newark Teachers' Union argued, "The main argument of [the takeover bill's] proponents is that state rights takes precedence over home rule. That scares me. State rights to me is a cold word, which translate into separate but equal" (ibid., 88). State-takeover opponents also equated local control with voter enfranchisement and participation. The president of the New Jersey Association for Black Educators pointed out that if state intervention were to be prolonged, a child who began school when his or her district entered the last stage of monitoring before takeover "may never have the experience of being educated in the very sacred tradition of home rule. The State will have attempted to educate this child within an environment that totally or partially disenfranchises his or her parents" (ibid., 123). Dadisi Sanyika, a Newark resident, stated that "a methodology that abolishes the principle of home rule—a well-established practice in New Jersey—is a denial of democratic rights and demonstrates an impatience with democracy" (New Jersey Senate, Committee on Education 1986d, 91). The hearing records do not include the race of the speakers, but if some of them were people of color (as seems likely from the urban location of the hearings, and the surnames of a few of the people who spoke), the use of terms that evoked the civil rights movement and voting rights struggles would take on extra meaning.

The High School Performance Test

In 1983 Kean initially proposed replacing the Minimum Basic Skills test with one that would be "tougher than its flabby predecessor." The department of education began development of the test, which was first administered in 1986 (Sullivan 1986b). In 1988 the legislature passed a Kean administration–backed bill that moved the graduation test to eleventh grade and increased its level of difficulty. The sponsor of the bill who moved the state graduation test to eleventh grade quoted an editor of *Fortune* magazine as saying that "as many as 30% of the nation's working age people will be unemployable by the turn of the century, because they won't have enough education to perform competently in the workplace" (New Jersey Assembly, Education Committee 1988, 1:2).

As in 1979 opponents claimed that the more difficult tests would harm disadvantaged students. At one of the hearings on the bill, Assemblyman William Pascrell heard a representative of the New Jersey Education Association argue that the tests would be unfair. Pascrell replied, "The way to move to equal opportunity is not egalitarianism. It's to understand that we want to get people to work to the optimum of their skills and their talents. . . . We want the same equal expectations and the same equal opportunity for everyone" (ibid., 1:59). This was the same basic argument about equity as a threshold of achievement that had prevailed in 1979, with the additional assumption that raising the threshold would boost achievement.

The state-takeover laws and the shift toward a higher-level graduation test during the 1980s contributed to New Jersey's reputation as an innovator in education policy. The state takeovers of three urban districts were the first ever in the United States, and other states' policymakers used the New Jersey laws as a model. Although New Jersey was one of the first states to enact performance-based sanctions, it also retained regulation of processes. Another round of education finance litigation in the 1990s strengthened the process regulations.

Accountability after *Abbott*

A new set of plaintiffs challenged the state's education finance system in the late 1980s with the *Abbott v. Burke* case. The New Jersey Supreme Court first ruled on *Abbott* in 1990, with many other decisions to follow. The 1990 decision, *Abbott II*, declared the state's finance system unconstitutional because of the way in which the system affected twenty-eight low-wealth urban school districts. At the time of this decision, Governor Jim Florio was already attempting to maneuver a controversial and complex set of fiscal changes, the Quality Education Act (QEA), through the state legislature. QEA, enacted in response to the first state Supreme Court ruling in *Abbott*, increased funds to the plaintiff districts but also required them to develop and implement education improvement plans. The state department of education, its staff reduced by budget cuts, reorganized to include a large and activist Division of Urban Education (DUE) charged with helping the cities carry out these plans (Goertz and Fuhrman 1991, 51). Each district had a DUE liaison. Other QEA measures intended to prevent waste included limits on the rate at which district budgets could increase and a requirement that any district increasing its budget by more than 10 percent must spend the increased funds on demonstrably effective programs (Firestone, Goertz, and Natriello 1997, 38–39).

QEA aroused intense opposition from voters, angry about tax increases, and from the New Jersey Education Association, which objected to a provision in the law that would shift the cost of teacher pensions from the state to local school districts (Yaffe 2007, ch. 7). In *Abbott III*, the New Jersey Supreme Court ruled that QEA also did not do enough to produce equitable education funding (ibid., 211). Inspired by the continuing national movement for standards-based reform, the administration of Governor Christine Todd Whitman proposed that the state produce curriculum standards, determine what it would cost for school districts to teach the material in the standards, and base its new education finance system on those cost estimates (ibid., 257), but this system also failed to win the approval of the state supreme court because its funding formula did not guarantee that low-resource districts would have sufficient funds (ibid., 265). This decision, *Abbott IV*, also ordered appeals court hearings to determine what programs low-income children would need in order to overcome the disadvantages of poverty (ibid., 268).

The appeals court judge made recommendations about programs and spending to the supreme court. The next ruling, *Abbott V* in 1998, ordered the education commissioner to submit proposals on spending in key areas for review; after the review, the court ordered the commissioner to implement them. The court also accepted jurisdiction to resolve implementation issues (Rebell 2009, 75). Each school in the affected districts had to adopt a state-approved whole-school reform method. The state also required these schools to implement school-level, zero-based budgets appropriate to their chosen reform model, but in practice these budgets were prepared using a standardized form, with fairly standardized results (Erlichson, Goertz, and Turnbull 1999, 54–55). The *Abbott V* mandates layered procedural requirements, overseen by the courts, to the performance-based sanctions already included in state policy.

No Child Left Behind in New Jersey

When New Jersey began implementing the No Child Left Behind Act in 2002, it had a set of state policies that fit awkwardly with the new federal push for a standards-based approach to reducing achievement gaps. Many of the schools identified as underperforming were in the districts receiving extra funding under *Abbott*, and were complying with the process requirements for spending the money under the oversight of the state's Division of Urban Education. However, NCLB implementation, like the rest of the state's Title I program, was supervised by a different part of the state department of education (McGuinn 2007, 155). New Jersey state officials were among the few in the United States who had ever actually been involved in a takeover of a school district, but their years of experience with running the state-operated districts authorized in the 1988 law made them less rather than more likely to want to intervene elsewhere (ibid., 172).

During the implementation of NCLB, New Jersey fundamentally revised the funding and accountability framework of the *Abbott V* mandates. Overall, it stopped treating the *Abbott* districts differently from other districts facing economic and performance challenges. The state department of education appointed Collaborative Assessment and Planning for Achievement teams for all low-performing *Abbott* and Title I schools (ibid.). The ELC, still involved in the continuing *Abbott* litigation, trusted the state's new Democratic governor, Jim McGreevey, more than it had trusted his Republican predecessor, Christine Todd Whitman. With the consent of the ELC, McGreevey's "*Abbott* czar," Gordon MacInnes, adopted a more standards-based reform–like approach to performance in the districts receiving extra funds. MacInnes believed his goal should be to eliminate the achievement gap in the state's schools, not to enforce whole-school reform and other similar mandates. Instead, he began pushing schools in the *Abbott* districts to adopt practices that seemed to be working in low-income districts with strong test scores, in particular, a focus on early literacy (MacInnes 2009). A 2008 state law replaced the *Abbott* funding remedies, which had applied only to the plaintiff districts, with a new statewide formula. In 2009 the New Jersey Supreme Court's twentieth ruling in *Abbott* declared this law to be constitutional (Goertz and Weiss 2009, 5–6).

Equity, State–Local Relations, and Accountability in New Jersey

New Jersey policymakers added performance accountability to their education policies in two stages. The first stage began with Chapter 212 in 1975, which defined the state's commitment to "thorough and efficient" education after the *Robinson* decision, and which included state monitoring of district test scores along with a more process-based definition of "thorough and efficient." This stage ended in 1979 when a new law required students to pass the Minimum Basic Skills test in order to graduate from high school. The second stage occurred in the late 1980s and included both the lengthy, conflictual process of enacting the state-takeover law and the much shorter process of replacing the Minimum Basic Skills test with a more difficult High School Proficiency test. Later, after the *Abbott V* ruling by the New Jersey Supreme Court, the *Abbott* plaintiff districts had additional process requirements placed on them to govern how they were to spend their increased state aid.

These policies increased the state's role in accountability. In addition to the conventional state education agency role of ensuring compliance with regulations, the state now required schools to administer tests and tracked school and district performance. Students had to pass a state examination to earn a diploma. These were all forms of political accountability in that they were efforts by actors relatively remote from the schools to impose expectations on students and schools and enforce them by tracking performance. In extreme cases of poor performance coupled with administrative dysfunction and corruption, the state even displaced local political accountability by taking control of the school district.

Educational accountability in New Jersey has been based on a mixture of performance and, for the *Abbott* districts, requirements concerning how state aid is to be spent. This mixture reflects the prevailing understandings of equity and state–local relations, as summarized in table 7.1. Chapter 212, the law that defined the state's responsibility to ensure that local school districts were providing "thorough and efficient" schooling after the *Robinson* decision, emphasized equity of funding but also identified the components of a thorough and efficient education in terms of how the state expected local districts to operate. The state added a performance threshold idea of equity to its education policies with the 1979 law that required students to pass the Minimum Basic Skills test before they could earn a high school diploma. It is clear from testimony offered to the legislature in 1979, and again in 1988 when a new law replaced the Minimum Basic Skills test with a more challenging High School Proficiency test, that state officials viewed the performance threshold as way of pushing students and schools to improve their performance, thus improving the situation of the worst-off students. Similarly, the law that authorized the state to take over school districts was intended to improve the lot of the students in the worst-performing school districts. State policymakers assumed that local political accountability was not serving students well in those districts, and that the state would be able to improve schools while also preparing the way for a more constructive form of local politics. In its first *Abbott v. Burke* decision, the New Jersey Supreme Court identified educational adequacy, not strict equality of spending, as the new goal of education finance policy. Eight years later, in *Abbott V*, the court identified the ways in which districts receiving increased funding needed to spend the money in order to meet the adequacy standard, and the New Jersey Department of Education produced regulations for implementing the court order.

Table 7.1 Changing Conceptions of Equity and State–Local Relations in New Jersey

	Chapter 212 (1975)	Graduation Tests (1979; amended 1988)	State–Operated School District Law (1988)	After Abbott V (1998)
Equity	Equal funding	Performance threshold	Ensure that worst-performing school districts improve	Educational adequacy
State– Local Relations	State defines "thorough and efficient" in terms of processes	State sets the threshold that students and schools must meet Threshold as leverage for improvement	Sometimes local political accountability does not work State can shift local balance of power in favor of students and families	Supreme Court and Department of Education set requirements for local use of increased funds

Table 7.2 Changing Educational Accountability in New Jersey

	Chapter 212 (1975)	Graduation Tests (1979; amended 1988)	State-Operated School District Law (1988)	After Abbott V (1998)
Prevailing understanding of connection between equity and state-local relations	State equalizes funds and defines "thorough and efficient"	State sets performance threshold (minimum basic skills, then high school proficiency)	Some communities' politics are so dysfunctional that state needs to intervene to produce thorough and efficient education	State provides funds needed for adequate education and determines how localities should spend them
Role of performance in accountability	Not central	Students must meet standard to earn diploma. Test scores can trigger scrutiny	Performance failure plus lack of capacity to improve triggers intervention	Not central
Dominant form(s) of accountability	Legal (in state-local relationship) Bureaucratic (state definition of what thorough and efficient districts do) Political (local school boards)	Political and legal (of local school districts to state education department and legislature)	Political (shifts from local to state if state determines that local accountability is not working) Legal (analogy to bankruptcy)	Legal (state legislature to Supreme Court) Bureaucratic (Abbott districts to state department of education)

New Jersey ended the twentieth century with a complicated version of how relations between state and local authorities contribute to educational equity. It was a hybrid of the performance-threshold understanding of equity and the idea that equity meant using state power to control how school districts (at least the ones with performance problems) operated.

Table 7.2 summarizes the changes in the prevailing understanding of the relationship between equity and intergovernmental relations, the role of performance in educational accountability, and the dominant forms of accountability in education, combining different visions of the relationship between equity and state authority with different understandings of how performance should fit into educational accountability led to an unusually complicated accumulation of accountability policies. School districts that did not receive *Abbott* funds, and districts whose students generally had little trouble with the High School Proficiency test, would have a very different experience with state accountability policies than would *Abbott* plaintiff districts with performance problems, to say nothing of the three cities whose schools the state took over. In New Jersey, the ongoing legal saga of school finance reform led to an accountability system that layered procedural requirements, overseen by the courts, onto performance-based accountability through the political system.

Notes

1. "Orange Board Rebuffed," *New York Times*, July 11, 1963.

2. *Booker v. Board of Education of Plainfield*, 45 N.J. 161 (1965).

3. New Jersey Laws of 1975, Ch. 212, Article I.

4. Ibid., Article II.

5. New Jersey Laws of 1976, Ch. 97, sec. 5.

6. "Report of the New Jersey State Committee on High School Graduation Requirements," 1977, p. 26, New Jersey State Library, Trenton, NJ.

7. New Jersey Senate, Committee on Education. 1978. "Public Hearing before Senate Education Committee on S-1154 (provides for high school graduation standards)." Trenton, NJ: Office of Legislative Services, Public Information Office, Hearing Unit, 2–3.

8. The U.S. Supreme Court denied certiorari. *Dickey v. Robinson*, 414 U.S. 976, 94 S. Ct. 292, 38 L. Ed. 2d. 219, 1973 U.S. LEXIS 1128 (1973).

9. "Local Landslides, National Lessons: Governor Kean Shatters an 'Article of Faith.'" *New York Times*, November 7, 1985.

10. See also "Kean and the Senate Agree Financing on School Takeover." *New York Times*, December 17, 1987.

Incrementalism and Local Control in Connecticut

"I'm Not Out Looking for Your Keys"

In the spring of 1997 a bill that would place the Hartford Public Schools under direct state control sped through the Connecticut legislature. The original version of the bill would have given the state the power to intervene in any district that met a set of criteria for underperformance, but what reached the floor of the house and senate applied only to Hartford. At the time Connecticut Education Commissioner Ted Sergi said to the state's school districts, "I'm not out looking for your keys" (Frahm 1997). This statement nicely summarizes the view of performance-based accountability that has prevailed at the state level in Connecticut. The state has a highly regarded set of mastery tests for students, which it put in place at a time when most other states were still testing only basic skills. State authorities intervened in Hartford after Connecticut lost a legal challenge to racial segregation between the city and its suburbs. At the same time, though, Connecticut policymakers have not embraced performance sanctions as much as their peers elsewhere. Like other states, Connecticut has shifted the item at the center of its accountability system to include student performance, but it has not expanded its accountability-holder role as much as others have.

Compared with Massachusetts and New Jersey, Connecticut developed accountability policies in gradual stages and adopted a less sanctions-oriented model. Unlike their Massachusetts or New Jersey counterparts, Connecticut legislators voted against a graduation test and declined to bring a comprehensive standards-based reform bill up for a floor vote. The Connecticut State Department of Education (CSDE) had a consistently large role in policymaking, which produced greater continuity of priorities than in New Jersey or Massachusetts. The policies Connecticut enacted reflected the lack of a connection on the policy agenda between accountability and funding, the sense that educational problems were confined to only a few of the state's school districts, and the influence of *Sheff v. O'Neill*, the Hartford desegregation case, in state courts.

Policymakers in Connecticut took an incrementalist approach to performance measurement and accountability. In 1984 the state became one of the first in the country to create an elementary and middle school testing program that targeted high standards rather than minimum competency. The legislature added a high school test to the program in 1990, although it does not have a state graduation test. In the area of school and district accountability, a 1997 special act of the legislature put the Hartford public schools under state control. A 1999 law empowers the state to identify underperforming schools and requires districts to intervene in them, subject to state approval of the district's intervention plans.

Development of accountability policy in Connecticut provides an interesting comparison to Massachusetts and New Jersey because on several occasions the Connecticut legislature considered, but declined to enact, policies that other states adopted. For example, Republicans in the Connecticut House of Representatives unsuccessfully attempted to amend the 1990 high school testing bill to include a requirement that students pass the test in order to earn a diploma. In 1994 a comprehensive education reform bill backed by the state Commission on Educational Excellence failed even to get out of committee. This bill included a general district-takeover provision like those of Massachusetts and New Jersey, as well as a school-takeover power. The special legislation to put Hartford's public schools under state control was originally drafted as a general state-takeover power, but the legislature chose to focus only on Hartford.

Performance-based sanctions proposals interacted differently with the rest of the education policy agenda in Connecticut than in the other two states. The *Sheff* case, which heightened fear of increased state power eroding local control, also led to a regional planning process that took priority over the 1994 comprehensive reform bill for the governor and the department of education. Unlike in Massachusetts and New Jersey, proposals to expand the Connecticut state accountability role were not coupled with increased state funding. The 1994 reform bill did not include finance reform, which greatly reduced legislators' interest in supporting it when teacher unions and a vocal parent group opposed it. Another major difference was the CSDE's large role in policymaking. Leaders at the department convinced legislators that "high stakes" such as graduation requirements or general threats of state takeover were not necessary, and that a test based on high standards would generate sufficient pressure for improved performance on its own.

In this chapter I analyze several key moments in the evolution of performance accountability policies in Connecticut, including both the policy enactments and the unsuccessful attempts to make policy. I begin with a brief examination of the finance equalization and racial balance policies that began before the state's standards-based reform policies. Then I move to the beginnings of the state's mastery testing program. The key part of the mastery test story is the great extent to which the state department of education was able to shape the testing program and resist pressure to make the high school–level test a graduation requirement. I then discuss a nonenactment: the intense controversy over a 1994 proposal for statewide reform based on "world-class standards," which caused legislators not to bring the proposal up for a floor vote. By 1994 the state's education community was also involved in *Sheff v. O'Neill*, a desegregation suit brought under the state constitution. In the fourth section of this chapter I explain how a state takeover of the Hartford public schools resulted from the *Sheff* case. I describe the 1999 enactment of a school accountability policy and the tensions between Connecticut's relatively low-stakes system of performance accountability and the federal government's high-stakes No Child Left Behind law in the last section.

Educational Equity before Standards-Based Reform

Prior to the beginnings of standards-based reform, education policy in Connecticut included efforts to reduce racial imbalance within school districts, and to equalize funding among districts. Connecticut's experience differed from other states' in two ways that would later affect the standards-based reform debate: The racial imbalance issue inspired a lawsuit targeting interdistrict school segregation. The successful finance lawsuit was earlier than, and separate from, the push for standards-based reform.

Racial Imbalance

Connecticut's constitution, adopted in 1965 to comply with federal voting rights laws, includes a provision stating that "no person shall be denied the equal protection of law nor be subjected to segregation or discrimination in the exercise or enjoyment of his civil or political rights because of religion, race, color, ancestry, or national origin" (Art. 1, sec. 1). In 1967 the state board of education called on school districts to "overcome the disadvantages of racial isolation" (Collier 2009, 629). Two years later the legislature followed up with its Racial Imbalance Law, which empowered the state to identify when a district's public schools had become imbalanced and to direct a solution (ibid., 630).

This apparently bold beginning lapsed into inaction. The regulations implementing the Racial Imbalance Law (RIL) were not approved until 1980, largely due to turf battles between the department of education and the state human rights commission (ibid., 633). By then, however, the state's three largest cities had public-school populations that were more than 70 percent students of color, and still increasing. Under these circumstances, it was not especially meaningful for them to adhere to the RIL requirement that no school have a substantially larger or smaller population of students of color than the district as a whole. State Commissioner of Education Gerald Tirozzi, a former superintendent of schools in the city of New Haven, attempted to build support for the idea of cross-district cooperation to achieve integration. A state department of education report issued in 1988 recommended that the state embrace "collective responsibility" for desegregation, meaning that if a city's schools could not be meaningfully integrated, its "contiguous and adjacent" districts should become involved, even if mandatory measures were necessary (CSDE Committee on Racial Equity 1988, 11). Later, in 1989, a team of attorneys led by the Connecticut American Civil Liberties Union chapter filed a lawsuit challenging the isolation of students of color in the inner cities while suburbs remained white. The suit, *Sheff v. O'Neill*, referred to the state constitution's education guarantee and to its ban on racial segregation. *Sheff* had a major effect on state education policy in the 1990s, which will be discussed later in this chapter.

Education Finance in the 1970s

The Connecticut Supreme Court threw out the state's system of education finance during the 1970s. Attorney Wes Horton filed suit on behalf of his son Barnaby, a student in the Canton public schools. Canton is a town outside Hartford, which at the time of the case had a declining tax base but low levels of poverty. The Horton family, like nearly everybody else in Canton, was white. These facts made the *Horton v. Meskill* case different from many other finance suits, in which the plaintiffs were low-income urban students of color such as Kenneth Robinson in New Jersey. Attorney Horton said that he wanted first to establish that education funding was a state constitutional issue before taking on the more complex situation of urban municipal finance and adding a racial dimension to the claims about inequity (Wetzler 2004). In 1977 the Connecticut Supreme Court ruled in favor of the *Horton* plaintiffs, declaring that even though the state's constitutional guarantee of education does not include the word "equal," it requires greater equality of funding than was the case in the state at the time (Collier 2009, 591).

The *Horton* decision led to the legislature's enactment of a new guaranteed tax base (GTB) for education funding. However, rising inflation and the recession of 1981–82 made the program a strain on the state's finances, and the legislature amended the GTB in ways that made it less egalitarian. The *Horton* plaintiffs returned to court, but the Connecticut Supreme Court upheld the amendments to the GTB (Reed 2001, 79–80). Another piece of legislation with lasting effects on education finance was the 1986 Education Enhancement Act (EEA). The EEA raised the standards for teacher certification in the state and made state funds available for school districts to use in raising teacher salaries. In its recommendations for the legislative response to *Horton*, the CSDE claimed that money alone would not solve the state's educational problems and that "standards, resources, and capacity at the local district level were equally necessary" (Fisk 1999, 100). The state enacted a minimum-competency test, which did not have any consequences attached to it, in 1978. The test was first administered to ninth graders, shifted to eighth grade in 1983, and discontinued entirely a few years later. Connecticut went on to be one of the first states to enact a testing program that was intended to measure whether students were meeting higher academic standards.

State Mastery Tests

A Nation at Risk inspired Connecticut policymakers to enact a package of education reform laws. In 1984 the state board of education issued a report titled "Connecticut's Challenge: An Agenda for Educational Equity and Excellence." This report included wide-ranging recommendations for reform, including increased course requirements for high school graduation and implementation of a set of mastery tests pegged to high academic standards. The report's recommendations also included changes to teacher preparation and certification that, when implemented, made the state a model for numerous others. Later that year the state legislature acted on these recommendations. Among other pieces of legislation, they passed a law authorizing the Connecticut Mastery Tests for grades four, six, and eight (Fisk 1999). Scores on these tests were reported in terms of whether students had met a "remedial" level and then whether they had met a higher "mastery" level, so in effect these tests included two different thresholds of performance according to which equity and effectiveness could be judged.

The CSDE played a major role in policy development. In large part, this role was the result of the work of Commissioner Mark Shedd, who held the office from 1974 until 1983. Shedd deliberately assembled a staff with expertise in testing, evaluation, and policy so that his department would be well positioned to use data to advocate for increased school funding and greater equity (Fisk 1999, 98). Even though Shedd himself was gone by the start of Connecticut's accountability policymaking, the staff he assembled mostly remained in place, and the pattern of legislative and gubernatorial respect for the department was set. Interviewees confirmed that through the 1980s and 1990s, the norm was for CSDE staff to work closely with legislators in preparing bills for consideration. Connecticut Association of Boards of Education executive director Robert Rader, who had also worked in New York and Massachusetts, praised the overall collegiality and continuity in the Connecticut education policymaking community: "I have never seen the type of bashing or the type of political gamesmanship that I saw certainly in New York, and people [in Connecticut] know each other and have worked together for years, so it makes for a much different atmosphere and environment."[1]

The State Department of Education and Problem Definition

One example of the way in which the CSDE set the policymaking agenda was its success in defining the purpose of Connecticut Mastery Tests (CMT) and the causal relationship between testing and school improvement. The CSDE convinced a majority in the legislature that simply reporting CMT scores constituted a valuable policy intervention, and that attaching further consequences to them would compromise the tests' high standards and rigor. In essence, the CSDE made a strong case for professional accountability at the local level, based on the information that the professionals would get from the state tests. CSDE leadership also successfully argued that a high-stakes test would tend to get easier over time because of political, and especially legal, pressure. In an interview years later, former deputy commissioner of education Lorraine Aronson recalled the state department of education's conviction that a demanding test without high stakes attached was the most desirable reform instrument. With high stakes, there would be vulnerability to legal challenges, and to "tests like many other states had, that are really meaningless." According to Aronson, "in order to make something palatable legally and practically, you would wind up having to do a test with such low standards that it would undermine the whole twenty-year effort."[2] Thus, the state would be better off with lower stakes that would permit maintenance of higher standards.

When the Connecticut legislature first authorized the CMT in 1984, the leadership of the CSDE made it clear that they regarded the mastery tests as the core of their reform agenda. These tests would be directly related to what the state education department saw as appropriate standards, or criterion-referenced, rather than designed to compare students to national average levels of performance, or norm-referenced. More strategic behavior is possible in reporting of scores on norm-referenced tests, since there is often a choice of which population's average is used. Lorraine Aronson remembers, "The urban districts were all using norm-referenced tests with urban norms. So everybody was looking great. And they didn't want a criterion-referenced test."[3] In the view of state education leaders, changing the test would help improve the system. Education Commissioner Gerald Tirozzi told the Education Committee,

> I feel this really is the essence of our total proposal. We are sending a message in this particular proposal that we definitely want to be in a position to determine the specific learning outcomes that should be mastered at each and every grade in our schools, and in turn, we should be in a position to assess the degree to which children are, in fact, mastering those skills. . . . We're not talking about minimal proficiency. We're talking hopefully about grade-level standards of excellence." (Connecticut General Assembly, Education Committee 1984, 5)

Deputy Commissioner Lorraine Aronson reiterated this point in a second hearing, saying that the older basic skills test came too late for real remediation of student problems and did not "set the kind of standards or expectations that we think [are] important for our students statewide" (ibid., 307).

Rejecting a Graduation Test

In 1990 the Connecticut legislature authorized adding a tenth-grade test (eventually named the Connecticut Academic Proficiency Test) to the existing mastery tests for fourth, sixth, and eighth graders. The Connecticut House of Representatives considered, but rejected, an amendment to the high school testing bill that would have required students to pass the test to graduate from high school. According to a senior department of education official, the idea of a graduation test appealed to many house Republicans, who tended to represent suburban areas, because they wanted to put pressure on the urban communities that were receiving the bulk of the state's education funds.[4] Representative Glenn Arthur, a suburban Republican, offered the graduation-test amendment. The representatives who spoke in favor of the amendment, all of whom were Republicans, claimed that high school graduates who were not prepared for college work were undermining the quality of the state's colleges, and that the education system needed "benchmarks." As in other states, they invoked the need to restore the meaning of the high school diploma. One advocate said, "The high school diploma, the way we have used it, has been degraded and depreciated to point that it really doesn't mean as much . . . as it did 25 years ago" (Connecticut House of Representatives 1990).

Opposing the amendment, Rep. John T. Hoye (D-East Lyme) argued that his colleagues were overstating the educational crisis in Connecticut: "Connecticut retains its number four ranking in the Scholastic Aptitude Test. . . . I'm sure that the problem of the low Mastery Test will dissipate over the time" (ibid.). Rep. Naomi K. Cohen (D-Bloomfield) reminded her colleagues that "a statewide committee, a couple of years ago, looking into the question of testing and exit testing recommended unanimously that Connecticut not have exit tests," and insisted that such a major change should not be made without more public debate (ibid., 7397). Betty Sternberg, who worked in the CSDE's assessment division before eventually becoming commissioner of education, remembers the argument against a graduation test: "The reality is, you create a high school exit exam and you're going to be creating an exam that is going to test 8th grade skills" because otherwise failure rates would be so high that the policy would be politically untenable.[5] The amendment failed by a vote of 80 to 70.[6] A majority of the Connecticut General Assembly thus accepted the argument that the pressure of a graduation test was not necessary to improve students' academic performance and that Connecticut public school students were doing far better than critics of the system were willing to admit.

The graduation-test debate shows that the politics of performance measurement and sanctions in Connecticut differed from those of other states. In many other states, legislators and other actors outside the education system prevailed in defining sanctions as a policy instrument that would lead to higher standards and reform. In Connecticut, state agency officials succeeded in making the opposite case: that sanctions would paradoxically lead to lower standards. Connecticut still does not have a graduation test, although high school transcripts indicate whether the student reached the mastery standard on the tenth grade test. Additionally, a 2001 law (Public Act 01-166) requires each school district to assess students' competency in basic skills necessary for graduation, using criteria that include tenth grade test scores.

The Politics of "Educational Excellence" in 1994

In 1994 the legislatively created Commission on Educational Excellence for Connecticut (CEEC) released its recommendations for systemic reform of the state's public school system. The legislature began to consider a bill that would have enacted the CEEC recommendations, but this bill generated so much controversy that it never came to the floor of either house for a vote. Connecticut policymakers thus rejected the idea of expanding the state's role in holding school districts and schools accountable for performance. Some of the resistance came from teacher unions who opposed how the bill would have changed the terms of teachers' employment. A parent group also organized to oppose the new education standards that the bill included. It was unclear to many legislators and others what the rationale for the bill was, especially because the state department of education did not work hard for its passage and the bill did not provide increased funding to make the proposed new sanctions politically palatable. Governor Lowell Weicker was more committed to a regional diversity planning process in response to *Sheff v. O'Neill*, which itself contributed to a sense that local control of education was under assault.

The Commission on Educational Excellence for Connecticut

As in many other states, business leaders in Connecticut responded to the national Business Roundtable's efforts by founding a group dedicated to reforming public education. When the Business Roundtable adopted its principles for education reform, the chief executive of Union Carbide organized the Connecticut Business for Education Coalition (CBEC), which brought together representatives of the state's other Business Roundtable companies and involved Connecticut Business and Industry Association member companies, such as banks, that were not connected with the roundtable. At CBEC's urging, the Connecticut legislature passed a 1992 law, Public Act 92-143, which created CEEC. In 1994 the CEEC released its report and recommendations, which became the basis for a comprehensive education reform bill.

The centerpiece of the bill was "world-class" education standards and changes to the education governance system that would have increased accountability for performance. Section 18 of the bill would have instructed local boards of education (not the state department of education) to identify "schools with a persistent pattern of low student achievement or which are mismanaged" and to take corrective action, which might include replacing school council members, dissolving the school council, or removing the school's principal. Section 23 would have permitted the state board of education to dissolve a local or regional board of education if the state board of education found that the district had failed to correct conditions that had led to a local failure to implement the "educational interests of the state."[7]

The Threat to Local Control: "Educational Quality and Diversity"

In January 1993 the *Sheff v. O'Neill* lawsuit was finally about to come to trial in superior court. In response, Gov. Lowell Weicker made regional school integration the centerpiece of his 1993 State of the State message. He called on the legislature to enact a law that would require regional school desegregation. Weicker's original proposal would have divided the state into six regions, each with a representative committee charged with developing a five-year plan to "reduce racial isolation in the region's schools and to provide students with a quality, integrated learning experience." Weicker's goal was that "within five years of the implementation of the plans, local school districts in the region will reflect the racial mixture of the region within limits to be established during the planning process."[8]

As enacted, the "Act to Improve Educational Quality and Diversity" (Public Act 93-263) had far less dramatic effects. The legislature replaced Weicker's mandate for racial balance with a far vaguer requirement that towns and school districts must participate in planning voluntary regional programs designed to achieve "educational quality and diversity." A regional plan would take effect only if it won approval from both the municipal governing body and the school board in a majority of a region's municipalities and representing a majority of its population (McDermott 1998, 49). Student participation in any programs would be voluntary.

Even though the quality and diversity planning process had been designed to arouse as little opposition as possible, it still raised fears of mandatory interdistrict programs and busing. In the summer of 1994, when the planning took place, fear ran high (among those paying attention) that either the eventual outcome of *Sheff* or the regional plans, or both, would require large-scale busing of students across school district lines. In the New Haven region, when municipal governments debated whether to accept the regional panel's recommendations, some citizens and officials raised the specter of "children of all ages, from kindergarten to grade twelve, being bused at great expense," and suggested that the voluntary regional programs were intended to lay the groundwork for later mandatory programs (McDermott 1999, 46). In the end, only two of the state's eleven planning regions actually produced plans that won enough local support to go forward (McDermott 1998).

Governors have often been key to enactment of major changes to Connecticut education policy (Fisk 1999). Unfortunately for advocates of the "educational excellence" bill, however, Governor Weicker's main priority was the regional quality and diversity planning. (He also spent a great deal of political capital supporting the unpopular enactment of the state's first-ever income tax in 1991.) Vincent Ferrandino, who was commissioner of education at the time, remembers that the regional planning program "was something that the Governor and I spent a great deal of time on," which meant that other educational initiatives "became almost backburner kind of activity for us."[9] Thus, when CBEC took up the cause of standards-based reform in the early 1990s, it could not make common cause with a governor and legislative leaders for whom it was also a priority.

Conservative Resistance to the Educational Excellence Bill

CBEC was not the only new entrant to the field of Connecticut education policymaking inspired by a larger national organization. At that point in the history of standards-based education reform, conservatives were organizing in several states to oppose "outcomes-based education," which they viewed as insufficiently rigorous, biased in favor of liberal and "New Age" thinking, and intrusive on family privacy. In Connecticut, people who shared these views formed an organization called Connecticut-Save Our Schools (CT-SOS). On the surface, it seems odd that people would perceive an education reform model based on high academic standards as an effort to "dumb down" the schools. However, the CT-SOS position made sense in the context of national education controversies. In other states the "outcomes" identified as educational goals had included student attitudes and beliefs rather than only academic knowledge. To traditionalists, many but not all of whom were evangelical Christians, these changes seemed to intrude upon parents' rights to teach their children whatever values they chose. Also, some "standards" or "outcomes" advocates also argued for pedagogical changes such as elimination of different curricular tracks within schools. The intent of these changes was to make schooling more rigorous for all students, but to skeptics and defenders of old-fashioned schooling, they seemed likelier to undermine rigor, especially for formerly high-track students. The term "outcomes-based education" (OBE) became a red flag for these activists and their allies (see Harp 1993, 1).

CT-SOS's objections to the bill focused on the first section: "On or before July 1, 1998, the state board of education, in consultation with a broad-based advisory group established by the commissioner of education, shall define the knowledge and skills which students are expected to acquire and establish state-wide student content and performance standards." Advocates of the bill insisted that these content and performance standards would include only academic subjects. CT-SOS claimed otherwise. Their evidence for this claim came not from the legislation itself but from references in the CEEC report and documents generated by the CEEC during the development of the report. The CEEC report, like outcomes-based education policies in other states, had said that Connecticut's standards must be "world-class" (CEEC 1994, viii). Although the bill before the legislature said nothing about values, or about tracking and other pedagogical practices, the CEEC working group on educational outcomes had consulted with former Maryland state superintendent David Hornbeck and New Standards Project director Marc Tucker. (Both Hornbeck and Tucker were nationally prominent standards-based reform advocates.) Hornbeck apparently told the group that tracking should be eliminated, that "all kids should be taught the same thing," and that "we must vary time and hold achievement as the constant." He also said that the desirable outcomes identified by state policy might include "academics, citizenship, personal qualities, values, community service, etc." (quoted in Wall 1994, 7). In a later meeting, Tucker reiterated that "the purpose of the mastery certificate is to hold standards constant and vary time" and recommended eliminating tracking (quoted in ibid., 9).

CT-SOS cofounder Kay Wall presented the state's own documentation of what Hornbeck and Tucker had told the working group on outcomes as part of her testimony. Based on these statements, opponents of the reform bill claimed that it would require schools to eliminate tracking, and to administer the same tests over and over again until all students passed. They also asserted that the state standards would force students to embrace particular beliefs and actions that might be different from what they learned at home. One parent at the education committee's hearing claimed that the proposal's focus on performance would mean that her son would receive a failing grade at school if he did not recycle: "I understand that they're trying to teach us the virtue for recycling, that that's a virtue. If my son doesn't do that, he goes to school and he hasn't done it, they say . . . your family hasn't done that. You can't pass. You haven't performed this" (Connecticut General Assembly, Education Committee 1994, 608).

According to CT-SOS, because standards-based reform (or outcomes-based education, to use their label) came from a national network, it would undermine Connecticut's autonomy. Kay Wall told the Education Committee,

> The bill is known as world class education. That was originally the phrase of Mark [*sic*] Tucker, Founder of [the] new standards project called NSP and some other consultants who market this [restructuring?] state to state. Connecticut is a partner in NST [*sic*] along with about 17 other states all of whom pay hundreds of thousands of dollars. Many like Connecticut try to say they are doing their own thing but that is simply not so. Student goals and assessments are always the same everywhere. Classroom practices are always the same. (Ibid., 559).[10]

Wall and others argued that if Connecticut adopted the standards-based reform agenda, it would end up with the same (in their opinion, low) standards as other "OBE states," such as Kentucky and California, despite the CEEC's claim that it wanted high standards. The CEEC recommendations did not seem compelling enough for legislators to want to take on both the conservative opponents of the bill and the state's two teachers' unions, who also opposed the bill for completely different reasons.

At least some state Republicans regarded the anti–OBE activists as a source of political support in a state election year. Parents opposed to the bill received sympathetic questions from some Republican members of the education committee. John Rowland, who ultimately won the 1994 gubernatorial election, sent a "Dear Voter" letter right before Election Day that appealed both to opponents of the failed reform bill and to people concerned about what might result from *Sheff v. O'Neill*. In the letter Rowland expressed his interest in "positive education reform for Connecticut" and his opposition to "efforts to water down the curriculum with fashionable, 'politically correct' ideology," "efforts to take away local control, including any regionalization programs which add layers of bureaucracy and taxes," and "forced busing of students." Rowland pledged that, if elected, he would seek assistance from CT-SOS leaders in preparing his education agenda.[11]

As Rowland's letter suggests, the ongoing regional quality and diversity planning process had spillover effects on the CEEC bill. The legislature considered the reform bill and held a hearing on it in the spring of 1994, when the regional planning process was beginning and the superior court judge was waiting until it was over to decide *Sheff*. Because of fears of what would come of the regional planning or the eventual *Sheff* decision, or both, legislators were inclined to be cautious. As then-commissioner Vincent Ferrandino said later, "there was a position being taken by many people of, 'well, this is going to be a big issue when it's resolved by the courts; it's going to have a potentially huge impact on the state . . . let's not do too much in any other arena now until we see what the court tells us we have to do with regard to the *Sheff-O'Neill* case.'"[12] Catherine Fisk, an administrator at CSDE, said in her analysis of the fate of the 1994 bill that outcomes-based education "may have served as a scapegoat for the fears of the public that the legislatively mandated regional and local plans for Quality and Integrated Education would result in proposals for busing" (Fisk 1999, 136). The CEEC report itself notes that there may be opportunities to make connections between their recommendations and the regional quality and diversity plans (CEEC 1994, ix).

The lack of a connection between accountability and funding was also a problem. Connecticut had enacted the mastery tests not long after undertaking its post-*Horton* reform of education finance. In contrast, and unlike MERA, the 1994 bill did not contain any large financial reforms that could have swayed legislators who were dubious about the standards and accountability provisions. Furthermore, the EEA of 1986, the most recent state foray into education finance, was backfiring politically in the early 1990s. According to Lorraine Aronson, who was deputy commissioner of education at the time, many EEA advocates had hoped that local school districts would use the higher salaries as leverage to get teachers to agree to longer school days or years. However, the law did not require that districts do so. In general, school districts used the new funds simply to raise salaries without adding to teachers' work commitments. Districts also tended to make the salary increase part of their contractual obligations to teachers, which left them in a difficult position in the early 1990s when recession and cutbacks in the state's defense industries lowered state and local tax receipts. From some communities' perspective, the state itself had caused their problems when it reduced funding for the Education Enhancement Act and left them solely responsible for paying higher teacher salaries (McDermott 1999, 72–73). In the absence of increased aid to school districts *from* the state, it was difficult to make a case for increased accountability *to* the state. This contrasts with the situation in Massachusetts, where even though there was no groundswell of public support for standards-based reform, there was a general sense that the system's finances were in crisis and that business support for increased funding was contingent on enactment of accountability policies. The need to address the financial problems overcame concerns about MERA's governance provisions.

CEEC itself had been unable to reach consensus on what to recommend because of resistance from the members representing teacher unions. Then-state education commissioner Vincent Ferrandino, a CEEC cochair, observed that CEEC "itself did not come out with a very strong, unanimous position in terms of its recommendations, and that "no one was passionate [enough] about most of the proposals that came forward to really go out there and do the kind of lobbying and . . . discussion of education that would have been necessary to get the bill passed."[13] Also, there was not a statewide sense that all public schools needed reform. According to Elizabeth Gara, who lobbied on education issues, "most people, when asked, would truly believe that the educational system in their community was doing just fine . . . and if you walked into the classrooms, they had smaller class sizes, they had more resources, better equipped teachers, so it was hard for us to convince them that there was a real problem."[14]

Although the Connecticut legislature's Education Committee favorably reported out the 1994 reform bill, house and senate leadership decided not to bring it up for a vote. It appeared unlikely to pass the house, and certain to fail in the senate (Frahm 1994). Legislators had heard so much opposition to the bill that some said they could not vote for it regardless of how it might be amended. Gara said, "I don't think leadership cared at that point whether or not there was a bill because they were hearing right and left from their constituents that absolutely did not want to see that bill."[15] Unlike MBAE in Massachusetts, which persisted into a second legislative session when the original MERA bill bogged down the first time, the Connecticut business organizations chose not to try again. Patrice McCarthy, the longtime lobbyist for the Connecticut Association of Boards of Education remembers, "Maybe two days before the end of the session, the representatives of the lobbyists for the Business Roundtable were told that it wasn't going to go that year, and they withdrew their lobbyists."[16]

Sheff v. O'Neill and the Hartford Takeover

When Connecticut did enact a law empowering the state to take over a school district, the power was limited to the Hartford Public Schools. The impetus for the Hartford takeover came from the Connecticut Supreme Court's decision in *Sheff v. O'Neill*. Legislators sought to respond to the decision in a way that would not be too controversial or disruptive politically.

The Supreme Court's *Sheff* Decision

Sheff v. O'Neill, filed in 1989 on behalf of Hartford African American student Milo Sheff and a racially mixed group of students from the city and its suburbs, challenged racial segregation across school district lines. The plaintiffs sued in the Connecticut courts rather than the federal court system as in most other well-known desegregation cases. Because they were in state court, they could base their claims on the state's constitutional guarantee of free public education for all students (as interpreted in *Horton* to require equality of opportunity) and on the state constitution's protection of Connecticut citizens from racial segregation. Although the plight of Hartford students got the most attention in the press, the plaintiffs claimed that the concentration of black and Latino students in cities and white students in the suburbs also harmed suburban students by depriving them of a diverse educational environment.

Much of the plaintiffs' testimony in *Sheff* concerned the low levels of resources; high levels of student educational, economic, and health needs; and poor student outcomes in the Hartford public schools. Political and administrative leadership in the city schools was also notoriously dysfunctional. In the mid-1990s the Hartford Board of Education had contracted with Education Alternatives, Inc. to run the schools. Far from turning around the district's performance, the result was still more political turmoil. The board of education feuded openly at meetings, and one member even threw a pitcher of water at another during an especially heated moment. In 1997 the *Hartford Courant* reported that the New England Association of Schools and Colleges was about to revoke the accreditation of Hartford Public High School, which could have jeopardized graduating students' chances of admission to college (Green and Hamilton 1997).

In April 1995 Superior Court Judge Harry Hammer ruled in favor of the state without rendering a decision on the plaintiffs' state constitutional claims, since in his view (based on federal precedent) the plaintiffs had not demonstrated that state action had caused the concentration of students of different races in different districts.[17] Several months later, at the Connecticut Supreme Court's request, Hammer also submitted a set of findings of fact in the case. The supreme court reversed Hammer's decision, ruling 4–3 for the plaintiffs in 1996. According to the majority opinion, the concentration of students of color in Hartford and the city's high level of poverty together violated the state constitution's education guarantee and its antisegregation clause. The 1996 *Sheff* majority attributed the segregation and the concentration of poverty to state action because the state had set school district boundaries at town lines and required students to attend school in their district of residence. An expansive reading of the majority opinion implied that the court had just found local control unconstitutional. However, the court itself did not order a remedy, instead calling on the legislature to address the issues it had raised.

Executive and Legislative Response

Neither the state legislature nor Gov. John Rowland was inclined to adopt the broad reading of *Sheff* and challenge local control. Shortly after the supreme court decision, Governor Rowland issued an executive order creating the Education Improvement Panel (EIP), a group of executive and legislative appointees with a broad mandate to "explore, identify, and report on a broad range of options for reducing racial isolation in our state's public schools, improving teaching and learning, enhancing a sense of community, and encouraging parental involvement," rather than a specific charge to end interdistrict segregation (Connecticut EIP 1997). The word "improvement" in the name of the panel signaled policymakers' intention of addressing the quality of students' educational experience in Hartford and other cities rather than attempting to produce racial balance.

The EIP's report to the legislature, issued in January 1997, included a wide range of recommendations for voluntary interdistrict educational programs and early-childhood education. In the spring and summer of 1997, three "*Sheff* bills" moved through the state legislature. One expanded a Hartford program that enabled city students to attend suburban public schools so that the program would operate in New Haven and Bridgeport and serve more Hartford students. This bill also added to the statute that identified the "educational interests of the state," to include a requirement that districts provide "opportunities for [their] students to interact with students and teachers from other racial, ethnic, and economic backgrounds." Districts could meet this requirement by providing "opportunities with students from other communities," ranging from interdistrict magnet school programs and recruitment of minority staff members to "distance learning through the use of technology" (ironic in the context of a desegregation suit) as well as "any other experience that increases awareness of the diversity of individuals and cultures" (McDermott 2001, 464). The second bill funded expansion of early-childhood education in Hartford, New Haven, and Bridgeport. The third was the takeover of the Hartford public schools.

The Hartford Takeover

The EIP had recommended "increased accountability for everyone involved in the education of Connecticut's students." Its accountability proposals were essentially the same as the ones that had been included in the failed 1994 bill, with districts holding schools accountable and the state board of education empowered to reorganize districts or appoint oversight boards if district did not make progress after implementation of improvement plans. The panel also recommended "that the Hartford Board of Education be placed on notice upon adoption of the [district accountability] process described above, with no more than six months to demonstrate progress" or else face intervention (Connecticut EIP 1997, 5). This targeting of Hartford followed logically from the *Sheff* litigation's Hartford focus.

The earliest version of 1997 S.B. 1200, which became the Hartford takeover bill, was titled "An Act concerning School and School District Accountability" and included all of the EIP's school and district accountability recommendations. However, the legislature rapidly narrowed its focus to Hartford. Shortly before the education committee's hearing on S.B. 1200, the *Hartford Courant* reported that Hartford's city council and board of education had reached an agreement in principle with legislative leaders on a state takeover of the city schools. Senator Eric Coleman (D-Bloomfield) said, "We're all agreed in principle that something dramatic and drastic needs to be done" (quoted in Green 1997c). Two days later, the education committee heard testimony on a different version of S.B. 1200, the bulk of which concerned the details of the state takeover in Hartford. The bill still contained the generally applicable school and district accountability policies. Robert Rader of the Connecticut Association of Boards of Education was supportive "as long as the Hartford Board goes along with it, that we will probably agree and feel strongly that a special act for Hartford, for the Hartford city school district would be appropriate. As a general belief, we believe that intervention in school districts should only occur in rare circumstances" (Connecticut General Assembly, Education Committee 1997, 101). Conversely, George Springer, president of the Connecticut State Federation of Teachers, the statewide organization of the American Federation of Teachers, pronounced his union to be "violently opposed" to the bill, because the state control board would have the power to alter the terms of the teachers' contract (Connecticut General Assembly, Education Committee, 1997, 27). Daria Plummer of the Connecticut Education Association urged the legislators to move cautiously because the bill they were considering affected not just Hartford but also the state's more than 160 other school districts (Connecticut General Assembly, Education Committee 1997, 72).

The controversy over Hartford became more intense. On March 12 the *Hartford Courant*'s editorial page called on the state to intervene. In a series of meetings in March and April 1997 legislative leaders agreed to two key changes in SB 1200. One was to drop all of the general accountability provisions so that the bill addressed only the Hartford takeover (Green 1997a). The other was to leave all existing labor agreements in place until their scheduled expiration dates (Green 1997b). Many participants say that they chose to move quickly on Hartford, leaving the more contentious general takeover power for later. This was the point at which Commissioner Sergi even reportedly told Hartford school officials, "I'm not out looking for your keys" (Frahm 1997). Another senior state department of education official remembers that the general power raised a host of issues that the Hartford-only takeover did not, such as "objective trigger points" for takeover and the number of districts in which the state could effectively intervene at the same time.[18] Lending credence to the idea that a state takeover allows the state to tip the balance of power in local politics, there was significant support for the takeover from within Hartford. The Hartford Federation of Teachers had dropped its opposition to the bill after the legislature reduced the extent to which the state-appointed board of education would be able to override previously negotiated contracts. The *Hartford Courant*'s editorial page had called on the state to intervene. The state legislative delegation from Hartford also supported the bill, which made it "a lot easier" for other legislators to support.[19]

Both the house and the senate debated and passed the bill on April 16, 1997. Some legislators were critical of the rush to approve the bill, and others argued that although it was specifically directed at Hartford, it would still threaten local control of education statewide. Sen. William Aniskovich, a

Republican from the suburbs of New Haven, pronounced the bill the "death knell of self-government in Connecticut" (Connecticut Senate 1997, 1005). Rep. Edna Garcia (D-Bridgeport) said, "All of a sudden those of us in the past who have firmly held the belief that communities themselves need to be empowered and allowed to decide what's in the best interest are willing to change years of tradition for one, I repeat, for one urban city" (Connecticut House of Representatives 1997, 1541–42). In the end, the bill passed the house by a vote of 135–7 and the senate by 27–9 (ibid., 1559; and Connecticut Senate 1997, 1082). Governor Rowland signed the bill two days later.

School Accountability and Afterward

By 2002, when Connecticut began considering how to implement the requirements of the federal No Child Left Behind Act, it had experienced multiple rounds of legislative debate about accountability and sanctions without actually expanding its accountability-holder role very much. The state took the largest role in measuring student performance, using the mastery tests. However, except for the Hartford takeover, it left the response to the performance data up to local decisions. Thus, it had retained a strong role for local political accountability and for professionals.

The 1999 School Accountability Law

The Connecticut legislature finally enacted a school accountability law in 1999. As introduced, the bill it considered that year directed local boards of education to evaluate the performance of their schools according to standards set by the state board of education.[20] What the full house and senate actually debated was a revised version that assigned the evaluation function to the state department of education but left the ultimate reconstitution of the school up to local authorities. The school accountability bill, which became Public Act 99-288, was not controversial, passing both the house and senate with only one vote against it in both houses combined.

At the end of the 1990s Connecticut had a less extensive set of state accountability sanctions than many other states: except for the Hartford takeover, there was no provision for district accountability, and school interventions were up to districts rather than the state. However, it was a system that fit Connecticut's political realities. The balance of state and local powers in the 1999 law reflected how lawmakers believed that Sergi and other state officials would make the process work. In contrast to the process in Massachusetts, where advocates of MERA believe that the bill's comprehensive nature was the key to getting it passed, incrementalism seems to have been the most effective approach to educational policymaking in Connecticut.

No Child Left Behind in Connecticut

In Massachusetts, the Education Reform Act approach was so similar to the federal No Child Left Behind Act that the state could comply with the federal law without changing its own policies much. New Jersey's hybrid system was harder to mesh with No Child Left Behind (NCLB). Connecticut's policies and the priorities of its executive and legislative leaders differed from No Child Left Behind to such a great extent that the state sued the U.S. Secretary of Education in an unsuccessful effort to make interpretation of the federal law more flexible. Although the state legislature did pass a law in 2003 that brought the state's testing policies into line with NCLB, that law additionally stipulated that only federal funds, not state money, could be used for NCLB compliance. The state senate also passed a resolution calling on the U.S. Congress to exempt high-performing states from NCLB requirements (McDermott 2007, 138).

State education commissioner Betty Sternberg asked the U.S. Department of Education to release the state from the mandate for annual testing in grades three through eight. The Connecticut Mastery Test included writing passages, which were expensive to score, but to which the state's policymakers were strongly committed. Sternberg argued that the cost of extending the CMT into more grades would exceed the additional federal funds the state was receiving, and would thus violate both the Connecticut law banning the use of nonfederal funds for NCLB compliance and the NCLB provision forbidding unfunded mandates. Sternberg also sought waivers of some provisions concerning testing of students with disabilities and students in English-language learner programs (McDermott 2007, 138). When U.S. Secretary of Education Margaret Spellings denied these requests, the state of Connecticut sued in federal court. Intriguingly, the Connecticut chapter of the NAACP entered the suit on the side of the federal authorities in order to uphold the principle that states should not be released from federal mandates (such as civil rights requirements) on grounds of expense. In April 2008 a federal district court judge dismissed the case, declaring that although Connecticut had provided estimates of what it would cost to comply with the federal requirements, "nowhere did it state that the federal funding was insufficient to cover those costs" (Dillon 2008).

Funding Equity Stalls

Since *Horton*, there have been at least two more attempts to use litigation to force change in Connecticut education finance. In 1998 twelve communities joined in a lawsuit, *Johnson v. Rowland*, claiming that the state had failed to satisfy the requirements of *Horton v. Meskill* because of the revisions to the education cost-sharing formula (McDermott 1999, 140). In 2007 the Hartford Superior Court denied claims made by plaintiffs in another finance suit, *Carroll-Hall v. Rell*. A supreme court ruling in March 2010 cleared the way for the case to move forward, but the high court had not ruled on the merits of the case as of June 2010. Most of the press for educational accountability policy in Connecticut happened after *Horton* and thus was not coupled on the policy agenda with litigation and increased state spending, as in both New Jersey and Massachusetts. Although accountability and state finance reform appear to be a potent combination when it comes to getting increased performance accountability through a legislature, the existence of accountability policies seems to be less likely to lead to further increases in state funding for education.

Equity, State–Local Relations, and Accountability in Connecticut

Connecticut policymakers moved incrementally when they added performance measurement to educational accountability. In 1984 the legislature authorized the development of mastery tests for grades four, six, and eight, expanding to grade ten in 1990. The state reported scores but did not punish students, schools, or districts that did poorly. In 1997, following the Connecticut Supreme Court's *Sheff* decision, the state took control of the Hartford public schools. In 1999 new legislation empowered the state to identify underperforming schools but left intervention to the school districts (subject to state approval). The state department of education, which was consistently central to policymaking, embraced the idea of standards-based testing early but remained quite skeptical about the benefits of attaching sanctions to test scores. For the most part, the department was able to convince legislators of the merit of this position. In 1990 the House of Representatives rejected an amendment that would have made passing the tenth grade mastery test a graduation requirement. In 1994 a comprehensive reform bill failed to reach the floor of either the house or the senate due to a combination of lukewarm support from the department of education and intense opposition from teacher unions and parents concerned about "outcomes based education." The 1997 Hartford takeover bill began as a New Jersey–style measure potentially applicable anywhere in the state, but legislators narrowed its focus to Hartford with the support of the state commissioner of education.

Because of the absence, for the most part, of sanctions, Connecticut's performance accountability policies did not constitute as large an increase in state-level political accountability for schools and districts as those of Massachusetts and New Jersey. Instead, it was up to local teachers and administrators to respond to low test scores, and the test scores could conceivably have fueled local political inquiry into school effectiveness. As in Massachusetts and New Jersey, Connecticut policymakers shifted the focus of accountability from regulatory compliance to performance but centralized less of the accountability-holder power at the state level. Hartford stands out as the exception to this rule because the state did directly displace its local board of education and take control of the system following the *Sheff* ruling, which called for some sort of state response to the city school system's failures. In doing this, the state replaced political accountability to local office-holders with political accountability to state appointees. Even in Hartford, though, the state returned control to a new local board of education in December 2002 (Gottlieb 2002).

Table 8.1 summarizes how the prevailing understandings of equity and state–local relations shifted in Connecticut at three key moments in the enactment of the state's educational accountability policies. When the legislature authorized development of the Connecticut Mastery Tests in 1984, the state was already using its funds to get closer to finance equity among school districts. With the mastery tests, the state took a step toward defining equity in terms of a threshold—or to be accurate two thresholds—of performance. The political significance of the mastery tests was that legislators could point to them as evidence that they were holding school districts accountable for how they spent state funds. Arguing for enactment of the mastery tests in 1984, Deputy Commissioner of Education Lorraine Aronson said, "with the enormous amount of state money that is going into the educational program in this state, it is fair for us to assess the success of our program" (Connecticut General Assembly, Education Committee 1984, 145). However, although the tests themselves were new, they did not change the overall relationship between state and local educational authorities because the state did not attach consequences to low scores.

Fear that high stakes would backfire was part of why the House of Representatives rejected a proposal to make the high school level mastery test a graduation requirement. When the legislature and Gov. John Rowland responded to the *Sheff v. O'Neill* decision in 1997, they decided to emphasize ways in which the state could help improve urban schools, rather than to

Table 8.1 Changing Conceptions of Equity and State–Local Relations in Connecticut

	Connecticut Mastery Tests (1984; 1990 for high school test)	*Hartford takeover as part of Sheff v. O'Neill legislative response (1997)*	*School Accountability Law (1999)*
Equity	Funding equity already a legislative goal "Remedial" and "mastery" performance thresholds State policymaker belief that high stakes for students leads to lowering of standards	Legislature shifts goal from integration to educational improvement	Based on performance levels
State–Local Relations	Tests were means of determining extent to which school districts were spending increased state funds effectively Local control: State develops tests; local officials and educators decide how to respond to scores	Legislature did not confront implications of *Sheff* case for local control Hartford as temporary exception to general principle of local control	State identifies schools Districts determine response subject to state approval

Table 8.2 Changing Educational Accountability in Connecticut

	Connecticut Mastery Tests (1984; 1990 for high school test)	Hartford takeover as part of Sheff v. O'Neill legislative response (1997)	School Accountability Law (1999)
Prevailing understanding of connection between equity and state–local relations	State funds used to make local funding more equal; state sets mastery and remedial thresholds; local educators respond	State policymakers seek ways of improving schools in cities to make the system more equitable despite segregation In the case of Hartford, improvement required state intervention	State identifies underperforming schools; district determines response; state approves response
Role of performance in accountability	Performance measured, but no sanctions attached	Test scores were large part, but not all, of evidence that Hartford takeover was warranted	Underperformance defined in terms of state test scores
Dominant form(s) of accountability	Weak political accountability at state level connected to tests Local political and professional accountability	As a general rule, local political and professional accountability State political accountability for Hartford	Local professional accountability to state Possibility that underperforming school could also become a local political issue

pursue interdistrict racial integration. The state took control of the Hartford public schools but clearly identified the takeover as an exception to the general rule of local control of education. This general rule continued in place after 1999, when a state law required the state department of education to identify schools with low levels of performance but to leave the details of intervention up to the school districts, subject to state approval. In general, Connecticut policymakers have sought ways of improving the performance of the state's lowest-ranked schools without actually strengthening the state very much with respect to local education authorities. State policymakers have implicitly defined equity in terms of improved performance on state tests but have accepted the state department of education's hypothesis that attaching sanctions to test scores will lead to lowering of standards and other unintended consequences.

Table 8.2 summarizes the changing understandings of the relationship between equity and intergovernmental relations, the dominant forms of accountability in education, and the role of performance in educational accountability. Performance, as measured by the state's mastery tests, remained important in all three phases of developing accountability policy. Legislators and other officials (including some in the city itself) also cited ongoing disarray in the management of the Hartford public schools and dysfunctional politics in the school system as reasons why the state should take control of the school district. Performance accountability in Connecticut did not expand state power as much as other states' policies did, in large part because the principles of professional accountability (both state and local) and local control remained central to the process.

Notes

1. Robert Rader interview with Kathryn A. McDermott, October 7, 2004, Wethersfield, CT.

2. Lorraine Aronson interview with Kathryn A. McDermott, October 7, 2004, Storrs, CT.

3. Ibid.

4. Anonymous interview with Kathryn A. McDermott, December 15, 2004, Hartford, CT.

5. Betty Sternberg interview with Kathryn A. McDermott, November 5, 2004, Hartford, CT.

6. Connecticut General Assembly, House, *Roll Call Votes 1990*, part 2, p. 1348.

7. Section 10-4a of the Connecticut General Statutes identifies the "educational interests of the state," which local school districts must implement. Under Section 10-4b, a resident of a school district may initiate a claim against the district with the state board of education if she or he believes the district is not meeting the requirements of Section 10-4a.

8. Lowell Weicker. 1993. State of the State Address, January 6, 1993, p. 10–12. Connecticut State Archives, Papers of Governor Lowell P. Weicker, Series 2, Box 3, Folder 39.

9. Vincent Ferrandino phone intereview with Kathryn A. McDermott, November 30, 2004.

10. The transcriber seems to have rendered the word "restructuring" as "restructure in."

11. John Rowland, "Dear Voter" letter. Undated, but clearly sent immediately before the November 1994 general election. Provided to author by People for the American Way.

12. Ferrandino interview.

13. Ibid.

14. Elizabeth Gara interview with Kathryn A. McDermott, October 7, 2004, Hartford, CT.

15. Ibid.

16. Patrice McCarthy interview with Kathryn A. McDermott, December 15, 2004.

17. *Sheff v. O'Neill,* 1995 Conn. Sup. LEXIS 1148, 1995.

18. Anonymous interview with Kathryn A. McDermott, December 15, 2004, Hartford, CT.

19. McCarthy interview.

20. Connecticut Public Act 99–288, sec. 2.

CHAPTER NINE

Assessing Performance Accountability in Education

A s the historical account in chapter 3 showed, public schools in the United States have always experienced accountability pressures, beginning when the first board of education members dropped in to observe the first one-room school. Since the 1970s education accountability policies have emphasized measurement of what students have learned and have increased state and federal governments' authority to hold schools accountable. Although this book has emphasized the reasons why policymakers have found it appealing to add performance measurement to earlier layers of educational accountability, it is also important to consider the effects of performance accountability in education, not just on schools but also on the political debate around education policy. Performance accountability policies have focused public attention on achievement gaps between more- and less-advantaged groups of students. At this point in the evolution of educational accountability, it is necessary to strike a balance between what we aspire to have students and schools achieve and what schools can reasonably accomplish. To realize Americans' aspirations for their schools, it will be necessary to identify the resources and practices that will enable schools to improve their performance, and to reconsider the extent to which schools can reduce inequality in learning without complementary social and economic policies to address the other inequalities that affect their work.

The Argument Thus Far

Earlier chapters in this book have showed how and why states added performance accountability to their systems for monitoring public schools. Policymakers began to define educational equity in terms of a common threshold of performance. Holding schools and districts accountable for their students' performance continued an overall trend toward centralization of intergovernmental relations in education policy.

Equity as a Performance Threshold

Chapters 3 and 4 showed how the dominant ideas about the goals of public education have changed over time. Beginning in the 1970s concern about school performance and effectiveness moved to the top of the political agenda. In all three of this book's case-study states (including Connecticut, which did not enact a graduation test), advocates of high school graduation tests spoke of the need to "restore the meaning of the high school diploma." The "meaning" that policymakers wanted to restore to the U.S. high school diploma beginning in the 1970s was chiefly defined in terms of academic content and in terms of signaling to employers and colleges that a graduate had mastered a body of knowledge.

The Connecticut, Massachusetts, and New Jersey case studies show that the emphasis on performance, and on defining equity in terms of performance, drove the shift toward performance accountability. Earlier understandings of equity had emphasized equal access to education. Policies based on the access definition of equity had required racial balance (in theory, if not generally in practice) and bilingual education programs, and had forbidden gender discrimination. Starting in the 1970s all three states enacted policies that made their education-finance systems more egalitarian than they had been. Later, policymakers adopted a definition of equity centered on student performance and layered policies based on this definition onto the states' existing equity-promoting policies.

Advocates of accountability based on performance measurement understood high school graduation tests as equitable because if a diploma certified that a high school graduate had mastered a common body of knowledge and skills, then graduates of all high schools would be competing with each other on a equal footing. As promised by the title of the influential Massachusetts Business Alliance for Education (MBAE) report, striving toward a higher level of learning for all students would make "every child a winner" (MBAE 1991), improving both educational equity and the potential for social mobility. Connecticut legislators' rejection of the graduation test proposal in 1990 paradoxically shows the extent to which they had accepted the idea that a demanding standard will prompt improved performance. When the Connecticut House of Representatives voted down the graduation test proposal, the main argument against making the test a prerequisite for high school graduation was that the risk of lawsuits from students who failed would push the state's standards down, presumably hindering performance improvements.

According to the standards-based reform model, setting common goals for all students, regardless of school and district demographics, creates incentives and conditions for school reform. It would be unfair to say that standards-based reform advocates approve of "separate but equal" schools, but they certainly do insist that separate schools can be equal in terms of their students' test results. It is common to hear that maintaining high standards and closing achievement gaps are civil rights issues (for examples, see Dobbs 2004; and Bruni 2001). In this view, insisting that all students meet challenging academic standards is in itself an antiracist intervention. Some standards advocates go even further and insist that calling any attention to the greater challenges that face low-income students and students of color constitutes making excuses for failure. By defining equity in terms of a common educational threshold for all students, the performance-based understanding of educational equity shifts to a universal definition of equity and away from understandings of equity that targeted specific disadvantaged groups such as low-income students, students of color, or girls.

The three state case studies show how the performance-based definition of educational equity interacted with the earlier equity definitions. A definition of equity in terms of performance fit politically with the one based on education finance because expansions of the state role in funding public education tend to enable passage of laws that also expand the state's accountability role. In Massachusetts and New Jersey, performance-based sanctions were linked with finance reform on the state education policy agenda. In Connecticut, the legislature failed to pass a Massachusetts-like bill that did not include major finance reform.

Centralizing Intergovernmental Relations

In all three of the case study states, performance accountability policies originated at the state level and increased the state's power over issues related to curriculum and student assessment. All three states adopted mandatory standardized tests to be used for performance assessment. Prior to NCLB, all of them also enacted some kind of sanctions connected to underperformance. Connecticut had the most modest state sanctions; its legislature rejected a proposal for a state graduation test in 1990, and rejected a comprehensive standards-based reform package, including school and district sanctions, in 1994. The state took control of the Hartford public schools in 1997 but limited the state role in a 1999 school-accountability law to identification of (not intervention in) underperforming schools. Massachusetts had the most extensive set of state sanctions, including a graduation test as well as state power to displace the principal of an underperforming school and to place an underperforming district in receivership. New Jersey enacted a graduation test in 1979 and the nation's first state-takeover law in 1988.

The definition of educational equity in terms of a threshold level of performance was new, but the general idea of increasing state power in the name
of equity was familiar. Although state performance-accountability policies
constituted a significant increase in state authority, advocates of the policies
presented them as fitting within the states' existing power over and responsibility for public education. All three states' constitutions declare, with differing
levels of specificity and in different centuries' language, that public schooling
is a state responsibility and that the state is the guarantor of students' right to
public education.[1] Connecticut, Massachusetts, and New Jersey all had laws
requiring services for students with disabilities before the federal government
enacted its own such requirement. They also had state laws requiring racial
balance in public schools. Particularly in issues related to race, the United
States has a historical tendency to use larger governmental entities to redress
inequities in smaller ones.

In all three states advocates of state intervention power argued that it
would not replace local control but rather would make it work better. The
state involvement could tip the local balance of power in favor of people who
supported better schools and against corrupt or incompetent local officials.
Examples of this logic include the arguments for the Hartford takeover and
for the state as a countervailing power to urban corruption in New Jersey, and
the claim in Massachusetts that the state could protect children when their
local leaders did not make public education a spending priority.

Another claim about intergovernmental relations common to arguments
for accountability in all three states was that because the state provided funds
for public education (and, in New Jersey and Massachusetts, was increasing
that funding), the state legislature had a duty to protect the interests of state
taxpayers by ensuring that corrupt or incompetent local officials did not waste
the money. In Massachusetts it was clear from the beginning that any increase
in state funding would have to be accompanied by governance reform and accountability for it to be politically palatable. In New Jersey the original state
minimum standards law was part of a compromise that permitted enactment
of the income tax to pay for increased state education aid. The argument
about taxpayers' interests was particularly important in the justification of the
New Jersey state takeover laws. Advocates of the various state testing and accountability laws in Connecticut similarly linked state testing to state funding.
Arguing for enactment of the Connecticut Mastery Tests in 1984, Deputy
Commissioner of Education Lorraine Aronson said, "With the enormous
amount of state money that is going into the educational program in this state,
it is fair for us to assess the success of our program" (Connecticut General
Assembly, Education Committee 1984, 145).

The Expanded Education Policy Subsystem

Nationally, pressure for performance-based accountability in education came from people outside the education system, such as governors and business leaders. Among the three case-study states, Connecticut, where specialists at the state department of education were most involved in policymaking, enacted the least sanctions-oriented policies. In the 1970s and 1980s New Jersey's policy agenda was set mainly by governors (especially Kean) in conjunction with state commissioners of education. After its first *Abbott* decision, the New Jersey Supreme Court also took a large role in identifying priorities for the urban plaintiff districts. The Connecticut State Department of Education played a major role in policymaking, which goes a long way toward explaining why the sanctions pieces of the standards-based reform agenda, which business leaders support but educators often criticize, did not catch on there. In contrast, MBAE was the major agenda-setter in Massachusetts education policy. In New Jersey the Kean policy agenda clearly shows the influence of the governors and business leaders who were articulating the standards-based reform agenda in the 1980s, later joined by a vision of financial equity advanced by the Education Law Center, the public-interest law firm that represented the *Abbott* plaintiffs.

Performance accountability in education generally has meant increased political accountability (in Romzek and Dubnick's sense) of schools and districts to entities outside the school system. Even in Massachusetts, where MERA reduced local superintendents' political accountability to elected school committees, the goals that superintendents were supposed to be pursuing came from state policymakers. The Massachusetts situation shows the tension between performance accountability and expertise: as Radin (2006) points out, performance accountability both targets professionals and "require[s] the active involvement of professionals in order for desired performance to occur" (84).

Effects of Performance Accountability in Education

This book has emphasized the reasons for the move toward performance accountability in education, and the ways in which policymakers understood the relationship between performance accountability and educational improvement. Before examining the implications of my analysis for education policy, I begin this section with a brief account of how performance accountability has affected students' test scores and achievement gaps among groups of students, how it has changed schools, and how it has influenced political debate about public education. It is hard to generalize about the effects of performance accountability on schools because the exact form of the policies has varied among states. Even within states, the effects of performance-based account-ability generally have not been uniform because schools with patterns of low performance experience more pressure from accountability policies than schools whose students have typically scored well on tests.

Effects on Test Scores and Achievement Gaps

The extent to which accountability policies have led to increased test scores and narrowed achievement gaps is one of the most controversial issues among educational researchers. One well-known study found that states with the strongest systems of accountability had the largest gains in National Assess-ment of Educational Progress (NAEP) math scores during the 1990s (Carnoy and Loeb 2002). Another study drew more skeptical conclusions about the effects of accountability policy (Marchant, Paulson, and Shunk 2006). The strongest conclusion that can confidently be drawn from existing research is that accountability policies have been accompanied by narrowing achievement gaps, according to some measures, in some places. Nationally, according to a 2009 U.S. Department of Education report, fourth and eighth graders' scores on the 2007 NAEP were higher than they had been in prior years for which there was data (going back to 1990). Although white students outscored blacks, the gap between the races had narrowed (Vannemann et al. 2009, 1). The study did not include analysis or speculation on the extent to which accountability policies might have contributing to this narrowing.

In this book's three case-study states, students as a whole continue to do well on NAEP compared with their peers nationwide. However, gaps among demographic groups persist in all three. According to the Education Trust's analyses of NAEP data from the 1990s, Connecticut's black students outscored those of all other states, but the state nonetheless had the nation's seventh-largest gap between white and black students on the fourth-grade reading test (Education Trust 2003b, 4). Connecticut also had the largest white–black gap in the country on the eighth-grade mathematics test (ibid., 5). Comparing white with Latino students, Massachusetts had the fifteenth-largest gap in fourth-grade reading scores and the sixteenth-largest in eighth-grade mathematics, with the state's Latino students ranked toward the middle of states nationally (Education Trust 2003a, 4–5). Looking at the most recent available data for all three states, all continue to have gaps between white and black, white and Latino, higher-income and lower-income, and regular educa-tion and special education students.

Effects on Schools

The most common criticism of how performance accountability has affected schools is that it has led to "teaching to the test," which emphasizes preparing students for the tests rather than more general kinds of learning. Countless examples of this phenomenon exist in scholarly and popular accounts. There is also evidence that focusing on the tested "bottom line" has crowded out the subjects that are not included in states' accountability determinations, such as social studies, physical education, and the arts (Center on Education Policy 2007), and anecdotes abound about schools that have eliminated recess to make more time for academics. To the extent that low-income students have experienced more narrowing of curriculum and instruction than their more-advantaged peers (because their schools are likelier to be under pressure to raise test scores), these tendencies are especially troubling.

The positive counterpart to emphasizing test preparation and focusing narrowly on test scores is the use of data by teachers to examine their practice and consider how they might better serve students. Some schools, many of them charter schools, have had encouraging results with this approach (Raudenbush 2009). Although teachers in these schools are generally using state test results as one source of data, these results are not always the most useful tools for instructional improvement because the tests generally are given toward the end of the school year, and student-level results are often not available until the summer or fall. Additionally, how teachers use test results depends at least as much on issues internal to their schools as on whether their state has high-stakes accountability. Richard Elmore, who has spent several decades examining policy implementation in schools and considering the effects of accountability, points out the need to understand both the "external" accountability required by public policy and the professional accountability within schools. Elmore defines this "internal" accountability as "agreement and coherence around expectations for student learning" and "the means to influence instructional practice in classrooms in ways that affect student learning" (2004, 234). Elmore concludes that without internal accountability, external accountability does not produce improvement (2004, 114). It follows from this insight that people who believe accountability and sanctions have had positive effects and people who believe the effects have been destructive could both be right, albeit about different schools.

Effects on Politics

In addition to affecting what goes on in schools, accountability policies have affected the larger political debate about education policy. As the case studies in this book have shown, enactment of accountability policies sometimes has been a prerequisite, or a corequisite, for changes in education finance that increase school funding or redistribute it to communities with lower wealth. Advocates of accountability policies are probably also right when they say that data on student performance has helped increase public awareness of achievement gaps, and of the difficulties faced by schools that educate low-income students.

The crucial next question is what happens after the achievement gaps are shown to persist. One possibility is a general drop in public perceptions of school success, and perhaps an increase in support for alternatives such as charter schools and vouchers for private education. This dynamic seems to be strengthening in large urban systems such as Chicago, New York, and Washington, DC. Another possible political consequence of performance data could be increased attention to the social and economic reasons why low-income students do less well in school than others, perhaps leading to changes in health and economic policy that might address these challenges. President Obama's public support for the Harlem Children's Zone, which combines an extensive network of social services with educational innovation, is an example of what this increased attention might look like. However, of late we have heard more from the federal government about teacher evaluation and school turnarounds than about social services, and the fiscal crises at all levels of U.S. government make this a politically unpropitious moment for expanding social programs.

Challenges to Performance Accountability in Education Policy

The push for standards-based reform in education came from a concern that schools were under so many competing pressures that they were no longer able to attend effectively to whether students were learning. However, the emphasis on measurable results in core academic subjects has shortcomings. The first is that schooling has valuable outcomes other than what tests in core subjects measure. These outcomes include social and emotional development as well as learning in nontested subjects such as physical education, art, and music, which some children only experience in school. This is especially likely to be the case for children whose families cannot afford to enroll them in extra activities and children who live in places where these activities are not available. The second problem is that some of the bureaucratic constraints are themselves related to valuable goals. For example, students with disabilities are protected by an elaborate system of legal accountability designed to ensure that school districts are using appropriate processes to develop students' individualized education programs and meeting federal and state requirements to serve students with

Figure 9.1 Challenges to Performance Accountability in Education Policy

1. Students' ability to score well on tests in mathematics and English is important, but so are other educational goals:
   Less-measurable outcomes of schooling
   Learning in subjects that are not included on state tests
   Due process for students with disabilities, and other contextual goals
2. Setting performance thresholds that are attainable, without being trivial, requires both technical expertise and decisions about public values.
3. Increased performance demands call attention to gaps in schools' capacity to improve.
4. Centralization may not always produce more egalitarian systems.

disabilities in the "least restrictive environment." These guarantees protect students with disabilities, who are a minority of any district's students, from spending cuts that might seem acceptable to the majority in their communities. Other challenges in educational performance accountability include identifying performance thresholds that are generally attainable without being trivial, deciding how to include students with disabilities, and distinguishing between performance differences that schools can and cannot control. Additionally, performance accountability highlights the differences in schools' and districts' capacity to improve without addressing these differences. Finally, although more centralized policymaking has often contributed to equity in education, this connection is contingent on politics, not intrinsic to centralization.

Setting Thresholds

As we have seen in the state case studies, legislators tend to accept the idea that specifying performance thresholds will lead to greater equity in terms of performance. They tend not to debate what the threshold should be; the actual performance thresholds come instead from the regulatory process and from technical analyses undertaken by the companies that develop standardized tests in response to state policies. However, threshold-setting requires decisions about goals and values, not just technical expertise. The first challenge is where to set the "proficiency" threshold. Currently, the states' proficiency thresholds are at many different levels (Reed 2009), a situation that gives rise to the criticism that standards are still too low in some states. A low proficiency standard can make achievement gaps between affluent and poor students or among racial groups seem to disappear. For example, assume that a particular state has set its cut score for proficiency at a level that corresponds to the twentieth percentile on a nationally normed test. Under these circumstances, this state could have one subgroup at the twenty-fifth percentile nationally and another at the eightieth, but still show 100 percent proficiency across subgroups (this insight, though not this particular example, is drawn from Rothstein 2004).

Another question that demands more than a simple technical answer is how to hold schools accountable for their work with students who have disabilities. In the history of education for children with disabilities, what looks from one perspective like excusing students from having to meet inappropriate performance demands can look from another perspective like excluding students with disabilities from the mainstream curriculum, or permitting schools to escape accountability for their work with certain students by classifying them as disabled. At first, states exempted disabled students from their testing programs, and as the three state case studies show, special education was not a prominent issue in debate over performance-based accountability. No Child Left Behind and current state laws require that students with disabilities take mainstream tests but also permit alternate assessments for the small proportion of students in special education who have severe cognitive disabilities. Even with alternate assessments for students with cognitive disabilities, the inclusion of disabled students in accountability testing still poses a logical problem for the much larger population of students diagnosed with learning disabilities. The process of diagnosing a student as having a learning disability or attention-deficit disorder generally begins when the student has trouble learning grade-level material, so for teachers it can seem illogical to base accountability judgments on whether these students reach grade-level performance thresholds. At the same time, advocates for students with disabilities insist that their scores must count in measurements of school performance so teachers will continue to set high standards for them.

Finally, to set thresholds for performance it is necessary to decide whether it is legitimate to hold schools accountable for all differences in educational outcomes. Setting a single threshold for all students, regardless of poverty or other conditions of their home lives, blurs the distinction between two kinds of reasons why low-income students might not learn as much in school as others. One set of reasons, including teachers' low expectations or lack of effort, is clearly within the schools' power to change. Other factors that might impede students' academic progress, such as hunger, unstable housing situations, and poor health care, are outside schools' control (Rothstein 2004). One option would be to hold schools accountable for the extent to which their teachers use instructional practices that have been demonstrated to work well (see Raudenbush 2009), but that would produce a very different kind of accountability system from one focused only on results.

Capacity Challenges

The problem of setting thresholds leads directly to the issue of the extent to which schools and districts have the capacity to improve. Advocates of performance-based accountability in education tend to believe that measurement coupled with sanctions is itself an intervention in schools and districts. Some of the differences among educational accountability policies in Massachusetts, New Jersey, and Connecticut can be traced to different interpretations of the connection between performance measurement and school (or student) improvement. Policymakers in Massachusetts and New Jersey saw sanctions as crucial. Senator Thomas Birmingham, reflecting on MERA, said, "I'm not sure the graduation requirement was needed for the teachers to make the effort, but I think it was for the kids."[2] In New Jersey, the arguments for replacing the Minimum Basic Skills test with the High School Proficiency test emphasized the positive effects of raising standards. Chancellor of Higher Education T. Edward Hollander argued that a more difficult test would benefit urban students because "their schools will be required to increase the performance of their high school graduates" (New Jersey Assembly, Education Committee 1988, 32), stating flatly at one point that although "this sounds harsh, . . . it's better to teach to the test than not to teach" (ibid., 40). In contrast, Connecticut policymakers accepted the argument that sanctions, especially high school graduation tests, would have the perverse effect of actually lowering performance standards.

In their history of federal ESEA Title I programs, Cohen and Moffitt point out that whether capacity is adequate depends on how high policymakers' aspirations are, or "whether the policies' instruments and capability in practice and its environments could enable the changes that the policies envisioned" (2009, 144). A relatively weak system may have sufficient capacity if the demands on it are modest. However, standards-based reform makes far more than modest demands. It specifies a completely novel and large goal for public schools: bringing all students up to high levels of achievement. To get the benefits of standards-based reform as Smith and O'Day (1991) outlined it, teachers need to do their jobs not just better but differently, so that students master challenging material rather than just practicing "basic skills." Doing a complex job such as teaching differently from how one has done it in the past requires learning on the part of adults. In the absence of sufficient training and support, teachers may decide that the reforms do not make sense, or, as James Spillane's work has convincingly shown, they may "buy in" to the reform and think they are doing what reformers intend while actually misinterpreting the new policy (Spillane 2004).

There probably are no "silver bullet" interventions for underperforming schools and districts. State departments of education are only beginning to identify what they can do to support local improvement efforts. Making this process more difficult, state education departments are generally not well staffed for leading improvement, either in terms of numbers of employees or in terms of those employees' substantive expertise. In the late 1990s this situation began to change for the better in Massachusetts, given increased state revenue and increased visibility of the department of education's capacity issues (McDermott et al. 2001; and Rennie Center for Education Research and Policy 2005), but the 2001–3 and 2008–9 fiscal crises in most states threaten to erode those gains.

As we have seen in the state-level case studies, legislators tended not to concentrate much effort on how to increase the education system's capacity to improve. All three states did enact policies intended to improve the education and skill levels of teachers, which are an important part of the system's capacity, but they did not focus on other parts of the "educational infrastructure" such as curriculum development (Cohen and Moffitt 2009). Schools and districts did not necessarily have slack capacity that they could apply to the tasks of curriculum redesign and instructional improvement, and if they did, they did not necessarily know how to deploy it.

Is Educational Centralization Egalitarian?

E. E. Schattschneider, cited earlier in this book, identified one set of "ideas concerning individualism, free private enterprise, localism, privacy and economy in government" as seemingly "designed to privatize conflict or to restrict its scope or to limit the use of public authority to enlarge the scope of conflict" (1960, 7). A corresponding set of ideas "concerning equality, consistency, equal protection of the laws, justice, liberty, freedom of movement, freedom of speech and association and civil rights" tend to broaden or "socialize" conflict (ibid.). Shifting the venue of policymaking to the state or federal level by socializing conflict can help groups that are disadvantaged in local politics. Schattschneider's insight was that shifting political debate to a larger or more inclusive community advantages some kinds of political positions and disadvantages others. In U.S. education policymaking, expanding the scope of conflict has generally been a move made by people seeking greater equity in the system, as in the federal and state policies discussed in chapter 3. These efforts activated powers that the state and federal governments already had, as matters of constitutional law, but were not fully exercising. For example, when the federal government pressed for desegregation, its legal warrant was its Fourteenth Amendment power to ensure that state governments did not deprive U.S. citizens of "equal protection" and "due process" under law. When state courts ordered legislatures to enact redistributive systems of public school finance, despite histories of local control and local funding of public education, they were asserting the states' responsibilities under their own constitutions to ensure that students in different local jurisdictions enjoyed equal educational opportunities. Wealthier communities could not legally opt out of sharing their wealth just because it was local wealth. Advocates of state performance-based educational accountability argued that state power was also needed to improve local performance and make the system more equitable.

Standards-based reformers aspire toward an educational system in which students' educational opportunities and levels of educational attainment will not vary according to where in a state they live, and achievement gaps between advantaged and disadvantaged groups will disappear. Chapters 6, 7, and 8 showed how advocates of standards-based reform (SBR), or performance-based accountability, in education presented it as the continuation by other means of the general movement toward educational equity that began with *Brown v. Board of Education* and continued through the state education finance suits. According to the SBR model, state graduation tests and state intervention ensure that localities cannot decide to set low standards for their students or tolerate ineffective schools. Centralized, objective judgments about what children have learned will push local communities to increase their attention to equity (Scheurich and Skrla 2001).

However, in the context of crime policy, Lisa Miller (2007) has pointed out that, contra Schattschneider, expanding the scope of conflict (making policy at the state or federal rather than the local level) may actually reshape the political agenda in ways that oversimplify and distort issues, harming rather than advancing the interests of localized, vulnerable populations. Despite the egalitarian intent of standards-based reform advocates, the state-level politics of educational performance accountability show this distorting tendency in addition to the egalitarian one. In all three of the states included in this study, performance-based accountability policies shifted the terms of political debate about education in ways that directed increased attention to the problems faced by certain school districts. However, legislators tended to emphasize the idea that the problems facing schools with low-income students and students of color are due to insufficient will or ability to use resources effectively, rather than the idea that such problems result from mismatches between locally available capacity and local needs. It has been difficult to find a balance between insisting on high expectations for all students and recognizing the challenges of educating children in schools where poverty is concentrated.

The underlying problem with counting on states to make policies that challenge the inequalities produced by local control is that state legislatures are politically responsive to voters who believe strongly in localism (Reed 2001). This book's case studies show the results of this responsiveness. The New Jersey legislature resisted changing education finance as much as the state supreme court was pushing it to do in the *Abbott* decisions. Governor Weicker's proposal for regional school integration had become a regional planning process for voluntary "educational quality and diversity" programs by the time it emerged from the Connecticut legislature. The Massachusetts Racial Imbalance Law, which had been easy for state legislators to support when it applied mainly to Boston, became weaker as more legislators faced integration challenges in their hometowns (Levy 1971). Sometimes, legislators manage to overcome these centrifugal forces; often they do not. Thus, although Schattschneider was right that an expanded scope of conflict can work to the advantage of people who are disadvantaged in local disputes, Miller is also right that the connection between scope and equity is not automatic but rather contingent on politics.

These politics are complicated. Consider Connecticut's lawsuit against the U.S. Department of Education. The state charged that the U.S. Department of Education had overstepped the bounds of its authority by not approving the way in which state policymakers wanted to comply with the NCLB requirement for annual testing in grades three through eight. The U.S. Department of Education disagreed, and the state chapter of the NAACP joined the suit on the side of the federal authorities. Would the federal or the state government be the better guarantor of Connecticut children's right to equal educational opportunity? The tepid response to *Sheff* seems to call for skepticism about the state's willingness and ability to play this role. However, some policy analysts believe that Connecticut's education policies are a more productive mix of capacity-building and performance pressure than the federal NCLB model (Darling-Hammond, 2010), so perhaps Connecticut children would be better served by the state than by the federal government. Neither the states nor the federal government has an entirely consistent record of promoting equity in education.

Most people who follow education policy developments believe that standards and testing are not going away any time soon. They are probably right, but even if they are wrong, the more fundamental truth is that pressure for accountability in education, in some form, will always be with us. The standards-based reform movement changed what schools and districts were held accountable for and shifted that accountability further away from the classroom. It did not, however, invent educational accountability. As long as there have been public schools in the United States, somebody has been holding somebody else accountable for some aspect or aspects of schooling. What has changed since the 1970s is the specifics of this accountability relationship, not its existence.

Americans should push their public schools to educate students to higher standards while also closing gaps in achievement between racial and socioeconomic groups. The relatively demanding definitions of proficiency in states such as Massachusetts are a good start. However, there is enough uncertainty about what schools can do in the absence of supportive changes elsewhere in society and the economy that we should avoid punishing schools or districts for failing to do what may not be possible. Americans have such high expectations for what public schools can do that these expectations often backfire. Historians Norton Grubb and Marvin Lazerson (2004) have identified the components of an "Education Gospel" and an accompanying cycle of high expectations and blame for public schools. This cycle begins when advocates for reform in public education claim that public schools, if they just adopt certain reforms, can overcome educational disadvantage as well as deeper socioeconomic and racial inequalities. The problem is that the schools cannot fulfill such high expectations, and when they fall short, critics use the failure as evidence that public schools are fundamentally flawed. Paradoxically, Grubb and Lazerson suggest, we would be less inclined to harsh criticism of schools if we began with more modest expectations of what they can accomplish. Accountability policies embody public expectations for public schools. The politics of educational accountability is thus an inescapably high stakes contest, especially for the children whose fates are intertwined with the success of their schools.

Notes

1. Massachusetts Constitution, Ch. 5, Sec. 2; New Jersey Constitution, Art. 8, Sec. 4(1) and 4(2); and Connecticut Constitution, Art. 8, Sec. 1.

2. Thomas Birmingham interview with Kathryn A. McDermott, October 1, 2004, Boston, MA.

CHAPTER TEN

Lessons for Performance Measurement Research and Practice

Performance measurement has been established longer in public education than in most other policy areas, and sanctions based on performance are especially extensive in public education. Thus, study of performance measurement in education can produce insights applicable to other policy areas. This chapter begins with a review of the main points from the review of performance accountability research in chapter 2. It then considers how public education compares with other policy areas and draws general conclusions about performance accountability. Analyzing educational performance accountability highlights several general challenges for performance accountability: the identification of goals, the setting of thresholds, the role of experts, and the question of organizational capacity. These challenges could be confronted at the federal, state, or local levels. Deciding where in the intergovernmental system authority over them should rest is a question with political and value components, not just technical ones. Finally, politics matters; performance accountability generates political feedback and may lead to shifts in the policy agenda.

Equity and Intergovernmental Relations in Performance Accountability

Performance accountability has been one of the dominant ideas in public administration for the past several decades. Part of its appeal is that it seems to overcome the problem of how to influence agency behavior that is difficult to observe and control directly. According to the performance accountability theory of action discussed in chapter 2, imposing (or threatening) sanctions on an agency whose measured performance fails to reach a particular benchmark will cause the agency to improve its performance.

Research on performance accountability has identified numerous ways in which this theory can fall short in reality. In the first place, not everything agencies do is equally amenable to measurement, and attention to the measured functions could lead to insufficient attention to what is less measurable. If the measured activities are more important than the less-measurable ones, there is not a serious problem, but in general, the unmeasurable or less-measurable realm includes many important things that agencies do. A related problem is that the agency may respond to pressure to improve its measured indicators in ways that are inconsistent with what it needs to do to improve the less-measurable outcomes of its work. Performance accountability can only lead to improvement if the agency that it targets actually has the knowledge, staffing, and funding to improve its performance. To the extent that these three kinds of capacity are insufficient, performance accountability may have perverse effects. The "cream-skimming" problem is an example of this phenomenon. A job-training program under pressure to increase the percentage of its clients who are employed at the end of their training could meet its placement target simply by enrolling clients who are more employable to begin with, but because these people might have gotten jobs even without the training, the improved indicator does not actually mean that the program is performing better.

Although performance measurement could be part of any of the four types of accountability identified by Romzek and Dubnick, it is especially consistent with "political" accountability as they have defined it. Recall from table 2.1 that in political accountability the power to define expectations is external to an agency, and there is little potential for direct control of the agency's operations. Performance accountability is attractive under these circumstances because it promises to use incentives to do what cannot be done via direct intervention. The expectations and priorities can be embodied in benchmarks, and the sanctions ensure that the benchmarks will inspire action. Chapters 3 and 4 of this book and the three state case studies show how actors outside of public schools have increased their involvement in setting goals and expectations for education, with performance-based accountability as the means of ensuring that schools met these goals.

Chapter 2 concluded with discussion of equity and intergovernmental relations, two areas that have often been problematic in performance measurement and accountability. As the rest of the book shows, a shift in how policymakers understood the goal of equity in education was actually a main reason for adoption of performance accountability in education. When economic change in the 1970s and 1980s intensified public concern over whether students were learning enough, equity defined in terms of a threshold level of academic performance for all students became more appealing than earlier goals defined in terms of increasing access to school, equalizing funds, or ensuring due process. Framing performance accountability as a means of achieving equity enhanced its appeal. The history of state and federal intervention in pursuit of educational equity also made the resulting shifts in authority toward state and federal government seem consistent with earlier equity-promoting policies and thus less like a departure from prior norms.

How Public Education Is Distinctive

Public education is a prime example of a policy area in which the problem of control looms large because the relative autonomy of principals in their schools and of teachers in their classrooms makes bureaucratic management difficult (even though it has frequently been tried). Compared with other policy areas, public education is distinctive in four ways. First, Americans have an unusually broad range of goals for their education system, compared with the goals of other policy areas. Contextual goals (in Wilson's sense) are part of this wide range, but so are multiple primary goals. Americans want their public schools to prepare all students for productive adult lives, to reward hard work and punish laziness, to contribute to social mobility, and to compensate for the lack of a safety net elsewhere in U.S. social policy. Second, the "street-level bureaucrats" in schools face a particularly acute version of the dilemma facing public servants that Michael Lipsky identified in his 1980 book. Teachers know that they cannot actually meet all of the public's goals, and that they may not even be able to teach in the ways their professional training teaches them to value, so they instead concentrate on doing what they perceive to be the best that they can do within the constraints that they face. Third, public education operates under an unusual degree of political scrutiny because it is important to so many constituencies, including parents, legislators, and business leaders, for different reasons. Finally, education is unusual in its intergovernmental complexity. The origins of the U.S. public education system, and much of political legitimacy, are local. However, the constitutional guarantees of equal educational opportunity come from the states. The federal government is a relatively late addition to the system but has a growing role. Because of the ways in which education is distinctive, examination of performance account- ability in education can generate insights for the practice of public management and for general inquiry into performance accountability.

Performance Measurements and Political Accountability

In public education, policymakers turned to performance accountability in re- sponse to shortcomings they perceived in other types of accountability. Elected officials, business leaders, and sometimes the public had come to believe that schooling was too important to leave to the educators. People outside the education system believed that bureaucratic procedures failed to provide adequate checks on the power of educational administrators, who often seemed both disconnected from the realities of social and economic change and unresponsive to legitimate community demands. As a profession, education has never enjoyed much public deference in the United States, so professional accountability in public education is not a strong tradition except to the extent that Progressive Era administrators linked professionalism with bureaucracy and scientific management. Legal accountability in public education grew during the second half of the twentieth century and remains strong except for the rollback of racial desegregation mandates. Legal protections for students with disabilities remain extensive, and even the states that have cut back on bilingual education must still be mindful that federal law protects the educational rights of students who do not yet have academic proficiency in English.

As discussed in chapter 2, accountability based on performance measures fits particularly well into policies or systems of political accountability in which people outside an agency are attempting to influence agency behavior that is not amenable to direct control. When performance accountability comes from outside an agency, it constitutes a challenge to both bureaucratic and professional accountability. The case of performance accountability in public education demonstrates both the appeal of political accountability and the ways in which it adds to, rather than replacing, other kinds of accountability. As summarized in table 10.1, the challenges to bureaucratic accountability and professional accountability operate in tandem because they share a general critique of control by insiders. Analysis of the development of education policy makes this connection particularly evident because bureaucracy and experts' faith in their own expertise have been mutually reinforcing since the progressive era, when public school districts took their modern form. Legal accountability, like bureaucratic accountability, can readily be attacked as a set of obstacles to "getting the job done" effectively. However, to the extent that legal accountability creates interests that become the focus of constituency demands, it persists, like the procedural requirements for special education students' individualized education programs. Against the backdrop of legal mandates, policymakers enacted performance accountability in education as a way of showing the extent to which schools were actually getting students to learn, thereby justifying increased state expenditures on public schools. Thus, the shift toward performance-based political accountability in public education suggests that there is general tendency for political accountability to strengthen when the public (especially organized business interests) seeks

Table 10.1   **Intensified Political Accountability**

Degree of Control over Agency	*Source of Control over Agency*	
	Internal	*External*
High	Bureaucratic accountability	Legal accountability
	Challenged by greater public participation or demands for participation	Challenged as constraints on agencies' ability to meet goals
		Persists when backed by organized constituency
Low	Professional accountability	Political accountability
	Challenged by skepticism about extent, content, or relevance of expertise	Expands when demanded by elites or the public, or both
		Expands when pressure for resources increases

Source: Adapted from Romzek and Dubnick 1987.

evidence that the system is working and legislators feel pressure to justify public expenditures.

The Practice of Performance Accountability

The challenges in educational accountability underscore some of the issues that may arise for performance-accountability policies in any field. First, although the "bottom line" of agency performance clearly matters (assuming that the agency is charged with doing something worthwhile), performance accountability does not eliminate other legitimate public expectations, such as the "contextual goals" identified by Wilson (1989). Goals such as due process and nondiscrimination are especially important in government agencies. Second, the history of state testing and accountability policies and of the controversy over the 100 percent proficiency goal in No Child Left Behind raises the general question of how to distinguish between the levels of government agency performance to which the public ought to aspire and the levels of performance that agencies should be punished for failing to achieve. Experts in particular fields of public policy could help set performance targets, but this leads to a third general issue: even though performance accountability requires the cooperation of agency professionals to have positive effects, policymakers' skepticism about those same experts' intentions and abilities is generally one of their main motivations for enacting performance-accountability policies in the first place. Experts know this, which is part of why they often resist performance accountability. Finally, the lack of attention to capacity-building in educational accountability reflects a general tendency in performance accountability over-all. Performance-accountability policies assume that agency staff already have the skills and resources they need to improve their performance when in fact they may not (Lipsky 1980). All four of these issues affect the likelihood that performance accountability policies will have perverse effects. Measuring the wrong indicators or leaving out other important elements of performance may lead to system-gaming or distortions (Smith 1995; DeBruijn 2002; Dahler-Larsen 2007; Ebrahim 2007). Sanctions create pressure that can exacerbate this tendency (Hatry 1999; Grizzle 2002; DeBruijn 2002).

In general, performance accountability in education provides a good ex-ample of how these policies raise complicated political issues in intergovern-mental relations but respond insufficiently to them. The question of which level of government should have authority over which issues of means and ends is not purely technical. Federal, state, and local definitions of goals may conflict. Sometimes, as when federal authorities forced the elimination of state and local laws requiring racial segregation in public facilities, there are obvi-ous constitutional and normative reasons why one level's goals should prevail. In other cases, the appropriate resolution of an intergovernmental conflict is less clear.

Broader Questions about Performance Measurement

What we know about the politics that surround educational accountability policies suggests that they have three general implications for public-sector performance measurement. The first issue is the connection between capacity and positive or perverse outcomes from performance measurement policies. Scholars agree that sanctions for performance can increase the likelihood of perverse outcomes (Hatry 1999; Grizzle 2002; Dahler-Larsen 2007; DeBruijn 2002). Kelman and Friedman argue that constructive rather than perverse outcomes are likeliest where the measured outcomes are consistent with the less-measurable goals (Kelman and Friedman 2009).

The public education example does not contradict either of these two find-ings. It does, however, add two additional dimensions. The first is the need to pay attention to how accountability sanctions interact with the capacity of agencies and organizations. This is Elmore's point, referred to in chapter 9, about the need for internal accountability if external accountability is to lead to improved performance. This point is related to "professional accountability" in Romzek and Dubnick's sense of the term. One way of summarizing the story

Figure 10.1   General Implications for Public Administration

---

1. Challenges for performance accountability:
   Goals other than performance remain important.
   The level of performance to which an agency ought to aspire is not necessarily the same as the level of performance it should be punished for failing to achieve.
   Performance accountability reflects skepticism about experts, but improving agency performance requires experts' participation.
   Performance accountability advocates pay insufficient attention to organizational capacity.
2. Which level of government should have authority over which questions of means and ends is not purely a technical question.
3. Analysis of a performance-based accountability policy's effects should include consideration of the political feedback it generates.
4. Accountability policies that shift authority within the intergovernmental system may also change the political agenda in the affected policy area.

---

that Romzek and Dubnick tell in their account of the *Challenger* disaster is that NASA had well-functioning professional accountability, but the political accountability system layered on top of it impeded its functioning. The relationship between accountability and capacity is thus a complex and reciprocal one. External accountability for performance works best and is least likely to have perverse consequences when the institutions on which it is imposed actually have the capacity in terms of knowledge, human resources, and money to improve their performance. (Sadly, these institutions are probably least likely to be the ones where performance is problematic in the first place.) At the same time, the politics that surround accountability policy themselves affect institutional capacity.

In education, the politics of performance accountability enactment often emphasized the idea that local authorities and school staff could not be trusted to do a good job or, put more positively, that they needed a new system of incentives that would make it likelier that they would do a good job. However, given Lipsky's insight about the gap between capacity and demands that is a predictable part of life in human service agencies, it is equally plausible that teachers already know they could improve but simply do not see a way of doing so within existing resource constraints. The line between effectively pushing schools to improve and hammering them so much that teachers become demoralized is thin.

The second area that deserves greater attention in public administration research is the political effects of performance accountability policies. The general idea of performance measurement recognizes and explicitly includes one kind of political feedback—use of performance data by citizens to hold elected officials accountable for the performance of the institutions they oversee. However, where the stated aspirations of the performance measurement policy are high ("no child left behind") and its performance targets are demanding, the political feedback may become a political backlash. The people who work in institutions hear the same messages as the public, and a constant drumbeat of bad performance news may undercut their morale, thus lowering the system's capacity for improvement. The state policy debates reviewed in this book demonstrate how high the expectations for the policies were as well as how intense the pressure was that policymakers hoped to put on schools.

The third general insight that should be taken away from a study of performance accountability policies in education is that shifts in the distribution of authority among levels of government should be expected to lead to change in the political agenda surrounding a particular policy issue. This expectation was explicit in educational performance accountability; the whole point of the enterprise was to get schools and school districts more focused on producing better performance in the academic areas that state education agencies had identified as important. This sort of shift had happened in earlier periods, as when state agencies pushed consolidation of local school districts over local objections in the early twentieth century, or when state and federal pressure ended legally mandated school segregation in the late twentieth century. Since the civil rights movement, American political scientists have tended to assume that centralization leads to more equitable policies by mobilizing more resources on the side of whoever is disadvantaged in local politics. However, future research on centralized performance accountability should consider the extent to which shifts in the venue of politics lead to shifts in problem definition, and consider the consequences of these shifts if they occur.

Accountability policies such as No Child Left Behind and the state policies that NCLB was intended to change conflate aspirations with enforceable performance requirements. Eugene Bardach addressed the problem of impossible goals in his book *The Implementation Game*:

> If Congress were to establish an agency charged with squaring the circle with compass and straight edge—a task mathematicians have long ago shown is impossible—we could envision an agency coming into being, hiring a vast number of consultants, commissioning studies, and reporting that progress

was being made. . . . After five years, much more would have been spent in vain, congressional sponsors would have dissociated themselves from the whole enterprise, and scholars would gravely cluck over the program's problems of implementation. (1978, 250–51)

Bardach's example of the circle-squaring agency dramatizes the importance of how policymakers define goals. There has been a tendency in performance-based educational accountability to choose goals based on what works well as a slogan. "No child left behind" is the strongest example here, since any questioning of this goal leads its defenders to ask the questioners what number of children they are willing to accept leaving behind.

Right after the circle-squaring metaphor Bardach goes on to say, "Any social program worth having a governmental policy about at all is likely to be a serious and complicated problem and therefore not amenable to easy solution or even amelioration" (1978, 251). We can hope to transcend history rather than to discover that we have been trying to square a circle, but we also need to resist pressure to oversimplify and reach for all-purpose carrot-and-stick combinations. The answer to the problems with performance-based accountability in education, and in other policy domains, is not to stop measuring performance but rather to admit the complexity of what we have undertaken and acknowledge that deeply rooted, centuries-old inequalities will not yield to a simple model, however much we might want them to.

References

Bardach, Eugene. 1978. *The Implementation Game: What Happens after a Bill Becomes a Law*. Cambridge: Massachusetts Institute of Technology Press.

———. 1986. "Educational Paperwork." In *School Days, Rule Days: The Legalization and Regulation of Education*, edited by David L. Kirp and Donald L. Jensen, 124–44. Philadelphia: Falmer Press.

Bardach, Eugene, and Cara Lesser. 1996. "Accountability in Human Services Collaboratives: For What? And to Whom?" *Journal of Public Administration Research and Theory* 6 (2): 197–224.

Barnow, Burt S., and Carolyn J. Heinrich. 2010. "One Standard Fits All? The Pros and Cons of Performance Standard Adjustments." *Public Administration Review* 70 (January–February): 60–71. doi: 10.1111/j.1540-6210.2009.02111.x.

Baumgartner, Frank R., and Bryan D. Jones. 1993. *Agendas and Instability in American Politics*. Chicago: University of Chicago Press.

Behn, Robert. 2001. *Rethinking Democratic Accountability*. Washington, DC: Brookings Institution.

Bestor, Arthur. 1985. *Educational Wastelands: The Retreat from Learning in Our Public Schools*, 2nd ed. Urbana: University of Illinois Press.

Blalock, Ann B., and Burt S. Barnow. 2001. "Is the New Obsession with Performance Management Masking the Truth about Social Problems?" In *Quicker, Better, Cheaper? Managing Performance in American Government*, edited by Dall W. Forsythe, 485–518. Albany, NY: Rockefeller Institute Press.

Borman, Kathryn, Louis Castenell, and Karen Gallagher. 1993. "Business Involvement in School Reform: The Rise of the Business Roundtable." In *The New Politics of Race and Gender: The 1992 Yearbook of the Politics of Education Association*, edited by Catherine Marshall, 69–84. Washington, DC: Falmer.

Boyer, L. Kate, Catherine Lawrence, and Miriam Wilson. 2001. "Performance Management: Does It Matter in the New World of Welfare?" In *Quicker, Better, Cheaper? Managing Performance in American Government*, edited by Dall W. Forsythe, 179–206. Albany, NY: Rockefeller Institute Press.

Bruni, Frank. 2001. "Bush Promotes Education, and in a Calculated Forum." *New York Times*, August 2.

Bumgardner, John, and Chad B. Newswander. 2009. "The Irony of NPM: The

Inevitable Extension of the Role of the American State." *American Review of Public Administration* 39 (2): 189–207.

Burke, Fred. 1979. "Commissioner's Narrative, Bill S-1154." Trenton: New Jersey State Archives, Papers of Governor Brendan T. Byrne, Counsel's Office, Bill Files 1979–1980, Bill S1154.

Bushaw, William J., and Alec M. Gallup. 2008. "The 40th Phi Delta Kappan Poll on the Public's Attitudes toward the Public Schools." *Phi Delta Kappan* 90 (September), www.pdkintl.org/kappan/k_v90/k0809toc.htm.

Byrne, Brendan T. 1976. "Signing Message," Laws of 1976, Chapter 97. Trenton, NJ: State Library Legislative History Collection.

Callahan, Raymond E. 1962. *Education and the Cult of Efficiency: A Study of the Social Forces That Have Shaped the Administration of the Public Schools.* Chicago: University of Chicago Press.

Cammisa, Anne Marie. 2006. "Massachusetts Political and Religious Culture." In *Representing God at the Statehouse: Religion and Politics in the American States,* edited by Edward L. Cleary and Allen D. Hertzke, 27–54. Lanham, MD: Rowman & Littlefield.

Carnoy, Martin, and Susanna Loeb. 2002. "Does External Accountability Affect Student Outcomes: A Cross-State Analysis." *Educational Evaluation and Policy Analysis* 24 (4): 305–31. doi: 10.3102/01623737024004305.

CEEC (Commission on Educational Excellence for Connecticut). 1994. "Report of the Commission for Educational Excellence in Connecticut." Hartford, CT: CEEC.

Center on Education Policy. 2007. *Choices, Changes, and Challenges: Curriculum and Instruction in the NCLB Era.* Washington, DC: Center on Education Policy.

Churchill, Andrew M., Kathryn A. McDermott, Susan Bowles, Carolyn Lee-Davis, Andrew Effrat, Joseph B. Berger, John C. Carey, Catherine C. Brooks, and Rebecca Klock. 2002. *Annual Report on the Progress of Education Reform in Massachusetts.* Boston: Massachusetts Education Reform Review Commission.

Cohen, David K., and Susan L. Moffitt. 2009. *The Ordeal of Equality: Did Federal Regulation Fix the Schools?* Cambridge, MA: Harvard University Press.

Cole, Michael R., Arthur F. Herrmann, and Jaynee LaVecchia. 1988. Executive Office Inter-Communication to Governor Thomas H. Kean, January 9. Trenton: New Jersey State Archives, Papers of Governor Thomas H. Kean, Counsel's Office, Bill Files 1986–87, Bill A4644.

Coleman, Sandy. 2000. "Teacher Bills to Seek Aid, Exam Reform." *Boston Globe,* December 6.

Collier, Christopher. 2009. *Connecticut's Public Schools: A History 1650–2000.* Orange, CT: Clearwater Press.

Connecticut EIP (Educational Improvement Panel). 1997. "Report to the Governor and General Assembly." Hartford: Connecticut EIP.

Connecticut General Assembly, Education Committee. 1984. Hearing before the Education Committee, February 27.

————. 1994. Hearing before the Education Committee, March 11.

————. 1997. Hearing before the Education Committee on S.B. 1200, March 10.

Connecticut House of Representatives. 1990. *Connecticut House Journal*, May 3, *Proceedings* 33, part 21.

————. 1997. *Connecticut House Journal*, April 16, *Proceedings* 40, part 3.

Connecticut Senate. 1997. *Senate Journal*, April 16, *Proceedings* 40, part 3.

Cornell, Tim. 1995. "Silber Spells Out Mass. Education Reform." *Boston Herald*, November 5.

Costrell, Robert M. 2007. "The Winning Defense in Massachusetts." In *School Money Trials: The Legal Pursuit of Educational Adequacy*, edited by Martin R. West and Paul E. Peterson, 278–304. Washington, DC: Brookings Institution Press.

Cremin, Lawrence A. 1964 [1961]. *The Transformation of the School: Progressivism in American Education, 1876–1957*. New York: Vintage Books.

————. 1965. *The Wonderful World of Ellwood Patterson Cubberley: An Essay in the Historiography of American Educational History*. New York: Houghton Mifflin.

————. 1980. *American Education: The National Experience 1783–1876*. New York: Harper & Row.

CSDE (Connecticut State Department of Eduction) Committee on Racial Equity. 1988. "A Report on Racial/Ethnic Equity in Connecticut's Public Schools." Hartford: Connecticut State Department of Education.

Cuban, Larry. 1993. *How Teachers Taught: Constancy and Change in American Classrooms, 1880–1990*, 2nd ed. New York: Teachers College Press.

Cubberley, Ellwood Patterson. 1916. *Public School Administration: A Statement of the Fundamental Principles underlying the Organization and Administration of Public Education*, rev. ed. Boston: Houghton Mifflin Company.

Dahler-Larsen, Peter. 2007. "Constitutive Effects of Performance Indicator Systems." In *Dilemmas of Engagement: Evaluation and the New Public Management, Advances in Program Evaluation*, 10th ed., edited by Saville Kushner and Nigel Norris, 17–35. Oxford: Elsevier.

Darling-Hammond, Linda. 2010. *The Flat World and Education: How America's Commitment to Equity Will Determine Our Future*. New York: Teachers' College Press.

Davies, Gareth. 2007. *See Government Grow: Education Politics from Johnson to Reagan*. Lawrence: University Press of Kansas.

DeBray, Elizabeth H. 2006. *Politics, Ideology, and Education: Federal Policy during the Clinton and Bush Administrations*. New York: Teachers College Press.

DeBray-Pelot, Elizabeth. 2007 "Dismantling Education's 'Iron Triangle': Institutional Relationships in the Formation of National Education Policy between 1998 and 2001." In *To Educate a Nation: Federal and National Strategies of School Reform*, edited by Carl F. Kaestle, Alyssa E. Lodewick, 64–89. Lawrence: University Press of Kansas.

DeBruijn, Hans. 2002. *Managing Performance in the Public Sector*. London: Routledge.

DeParle, Jason. 2004. *American Dream: Three Women, Ten Kids, and a Nation's Drive to End Welfare*. New York: Viking.

Diefenbach, Thomas. 2009. "New Public Management in Public Sector Organizations: The Dark Sides of Managerialistic 'Enlightenment.'" *Public Administration* 87 (4): 892–909.

Dillon, Sam. 2008. "Judge Dismisses Connecticut's Challenge to Education Law." *New York Times*, April 30.

Dobbs, Michael. 2004. "Remembering a Segregated Childhood: Education Secretary Paige Says *Brown v. Board of Education* Helped Shape His Ideas." *Washington Post*, May 17.

Ebrahim, Alnoor. 2007. "Towards a Reflective Accountability in NGOs." In *Global Accountabilities: Participation, Pluralism, and Public Ethics*, edited by Alnoor Ebrahim and Edward Weisband, 193–221. New York: Cambridge University Press.

Education Trust. 2003a. "Education Watch: Massachusetts." Washington, DC: Education Trust.

———. 2003b. "Education Watch: Connecticut." Washington, DC: Education Trust.

Edwards, W. Cary, and William Harla. 1987. Letter to Education Commissioner Saul Cooperman, May 4. New Jersey State Archives, Papers of Governor Thomas Kean, Counsel's Office, Bill Files 1986–87, Bill A-2927.

Elmore, Richard F. 2004. *School Reform from the Inside Out: Policy, Practice, and Performance*. Cambridge, MA: Harvard Education Press.

Erlichson, Bari Anhalt, Margaret E. Goertz, and Barbara J. Turnbull. 1999. *Implementing Whole-School Reform in New Jersey: Year One in the First Cohort Schools*. New Brunswick, NJ: Rutgers University Center for Government Services.

Firestone, William A., Margaret E. Goertz, and Gary Natriello. 1997. *From Cashbox to Classroom: The Struggle for Fiscal Reform and Educational Change in New Jersey*. New York: Teachers College Press.

Fischel, William A. 2009. *Making the Grade: The Economic Evolution of American School Districts*. Chicago: University of Chicago Press.

Fischer, Louis, David Schimmel, and Leslie R. Stellman. 2007. *Teachers and the Law*, 7th ed. Boston: Pearson Education.

Fisk, Catherine W. 1999. "The Emergence of Bureaucratic Entrepreneurship in a State Education Agency: A Case Study of Connecticut's Education Reform Initiatives." PhD diss., University of Massachusetts, Amherst.

Flaharty, William H. 1969. "Connecticut Department of Education." In *Education in the States: Historical Development and Outlook*, edited by J. B. Pearson and E. Fuller, 178–203. Washington, DC: National Education Association.

Frahm, Robert A. 1994. "'Watered-Down' School Reform Bill Likely to Fail." *Hartford Courant*, April 28.

———. 1997. "Reluctant Sergi Thrust into City Schools Crisis." *Hartford Courant*, March 14.

Frankenberg, Erica, Chungmei Lee, and Gary Orfield. 2003. *A Multiracial Society with Segregated Schools: Are We Losing the Dream?* Cambridge, MA: The Civil Rights Project at Harvard University.

Frederickson, David G., and H. George Frederickson. 2006. *Measuring the Performance of the Hollow State*. Washington DC: Georgetown University Press.

Frederickson, H. George. 1996. "Comparing the Reinventing Government Movement with the New Public Administration." *Public Administration Review* 56 (3): 263–70.

Fuhrman, Susan H. 1989. State Politics and Education Reform. In *The Politics of Reforming School Administration: The 1988 Yearbook of the Politics of Education Association*, edited by Jane Hannaway and Robert Crowson. New York: Falmer.

Fuhrman, Susan H., William H. Clune, and Richard F. Elmore. 1988. "Research on Education Reform: Lessons on the Implementation of Policy." *Teachers College Record* 90:237–257.

Fuhrman, Susan H., and Richard F. Elmore. 1990. "Understanding Local Control in the Wake of State Education Reform." *Educational Evaluation and Policy Analysis* 12:82–96.

Fung, Archon, Mary Graham, and David Weil. 2007. *Full Disclosure: The Perils and Promise of Transparency*. New York: Cambridge University Press.

Fusarelli, Lance D. 2005. "Gubernatorial Reactions to No Child Left Behind: Politics, Pressure, and Education Reform." *Peabody Journal of Education* 80 (2): 120–36.

Gamson, David. 2007. "From Progressivism to Federalism: The Pursuit of Equal Educational Opportunity, 1915–1965." In *To Educate a Nation: Federal and National Strategies of School Reform*, edited by Carl F. Kaestle and Alyssa E. Lodewick, 177–201. Lawrence: University Press of Kansas.

Geisel, Theodor [Dr. Seuss, pseud.]. 1973. *Did I Ever Tell You How Lucky You Are?* New York: Random House.

Gilmour, John B., and David E. Lewis. 2006. Does Performance Budgeting Work? An Examination of the Office of Management and Budget's PART Scores. *Public Administration Review* 66 (September–October): 742–52. doi: 10.1111/j.1540-6210.2006.00639.x.

Goertz, Margaret E., and Susan Fuhrman. 1991. *Core State Policy Integration/Background, New Jersey*. Philadelphia: Consortium for Policy Research in Education.

Goertz, Margaret E., and Janet Hannigan. 1978. "Delivering a 'Thorough and Efficient' Education in New Jersey." *Journal of Education Finance* 4 (1): 46–64.

Goertz, Margaret E., and Michael Weiss. 2009. *Assessing Success in School Finance Litigation: The Case of New Jersey*. New York: Campaign for Educational Equity. http://www.equitycampaign.org/i/a/document/11775_EdEquityLawNo1.pdf.

Goldin, Claudia, and Lawrence F. Katz. 2008. *The Race between Education and Technology*. Cambridge, MA: Belknap Press of Harvard University Press.

Gormley, William T., Jr. 1998. "Assessing Health Care Report Cards." *Journal of Public Administration Research and Theory* 8 (3): 325–52.

Gormley, William T., Jr, and David L. Weimer. 1999. *Organizational Report Cards*. Cambridge, MA: Harvard University Press.

Gottlieb, Rachel. 2002. "City Schools: Goodbye Trustees; Nation Will be Watching New Board." *Hartford Courant*, December 2, p. B1.

Gould, Stephen Jay. 1981. *The Mismeasure of Man.* New York: Norton.

Grant, Gerald, and Christine E. Murray. 1999. *Teaching in America: The Slow Revolution.* Cambridge, MA: Harvard University Press.

Gray, Virginia. 1973. "Innovation in the States: A Diffusion Study," *American Political Science Review* 67: 1174–85.

Green, Rick. 1997a. "For Core Group of Activists, There's Satisfaction with Takeover." *Hartford Courant*, April 16.

———. 1997b. "Takeover of Hartford Schools on Fast Track." *Hartford Courant*, April 9.

———. 1997c. "Leaders Call for Reform Panel to Run Hartford Schools." *Hartford Courant*, March 8.

Green, Rick, and Anne Hamilton. 1997. "Hartford Public Feels the Pain." *Hartford Courant*, April 8.

Grizzle, Gloria. 2002. "Performance Measurement and Dysfunction: The Dark Side of Quantifying Work." *Public Performance & Management Review* 25:363–69.

Grubb, W. Norton, and Martin Lazerson. 2004. *The Education Gospel: The Economic Power of Schooling.* Cambridge, MA: Harvard University Press.

Hardwick, Chuck. 1987. "Speech to New Jersey Education Association." New Jersey State Archives, Papers of Governor Thomas Kean, Counsel's Office, Bill Files 1986–87, Bill A-2927, 1987.

Harp, Lonnie. 1993. "PA Parent Becomes Mother of 'Outcomes' Revolt," *Education Week*, September 22: 1.

Harvey, Gordon E. 2002. *A Question of Justice: New South Governors and Education, 1968–1976.* Tuscaloosa: University of Alabama Press.

Hatry, Harry P. 1999. *Performance Measurement: Getting Results.* Washington DC: Urban Institute Press.

Hawkes, Franklin P., and Thomas J. Curtin. 1969. "Massachusetts Department of Education." In *Education in the States: Historical Development and Outlook*, edited by J. B. Pearson and E. Fuller, 564–91. Washington, DC: National Education Association.

Hayward, Ed. 2000. "Teachers Union Blasts MCAS in TV Ad Campaign." *Boston Herald*, November 8.

Henig, Jeffrey R. 2009. "Mayors, Governors, and Presidents: The New Education Executives and the End of Educational Exceptionalism." *Peabody Journal of Education* 84 (3): 283–99.

Hochschild, Jennifer L. 2003. "Rethinking Accountability Politics." In *No Child Left Behind? The Politics and Practice of School Accountability*, edited by Paul E. Peterson and Martin R. West, 107–23. Washington, DC: Brookings Institution Press.

Hood, Christopher, and Guy Peters. 2004. "The Middle Aging of New Public Management: Into the Age of Paradox?" *Journal of Public Administration Research and Theory* 14 (3): 267–82.

Howe, Peter J. 1993a. "School Reform Spawns Concern; 'Havoc' Predicted If Bill Is Passed." *Boston Globe*, April 1.

———. 1993b. "Weld Puts Lukewarm Pen to Education Reform Bill." *Boston Globe*, June 19.

Hughes, Richard. 1965. State of New Jersey, Executive Order #21. www.state.nj.us/infobank/circular/eoh21.htm.

Iannaccone, Laurence, and Frank W. Lutz. 1970. *Politics, Power, and Policy: The Governance of Local School Districts.* Columbus, OH: Charles E. Merrill.

Ingraham, Patricia W., and Donald P. Moynihan. 2001. "Beyond Measurement: Managing for Results in State Government." In *Quicker, Better, Cheaper? Managing Performance in American Government.* edited by Dall W. Forsythe, 309–33. Albany, NY: Rockefeller Institute Press.

Jackson, Kenneth T. 1985. *Crabgrass Frontier: The Suburbanization of the United States.* New York: Oxford University Press.

Jenkins, Robert L., and William A. Person. 1991. "Educational Reform in Mississippi: A Historical Perspective." In *School Reform in the Deep South: A Critical Appraisal*, edited by D. J. Vold and J. L. DeVitis. Tuscaloosa: University of Alabama Press.

Jenkins-Smith, Hank, and Paul A. Sabatier. 1993. "The Study of Public Policy Processes." In *Policy Change and Learning: An Advocacy Coalition Approach*, edited by P. A. Sabatier and H. Jenkins-Smith, 1–12. Boulder, CO: Westview Press.

Jennings, John F. 1998. *Why National Standards and Tests? Politics and the Quest for Better Schools.* Thousand Oaks, CA: Sage Publications.

Johnson, Clifton. 1963. *Old-Time Schools and School-Books.* New York: Dover Publications.

Kaestle, Carl F. 1983. *Pillars of the Republic: Common Schools and American Society, 1780–1860.* New York: Hill and Wang.

———. 2007. "Federal Education Policy and the Changing National Polity for Education, 1957–2007." In *To Educate a Nation: Federal and National Strategies for School Reform*, edited by Carl F. Kaestle and Alyssa E. Lodewick, 17–40. Lawrence: University Press of Kansas.

Kahlenberg, Richard D. 2007. *Tough Liberal: Albert Shanker and the Battles over Schools, Unions, Race, and Democracy.* New York: Columbia University Press.

Karabel, Jerome. 2005. *The Chosen: The Hidden History of Admission and Exclusion at Harvard, Yale, and Princeton.* Boston: Houghton Mifflin.

Katz, Michael B. 1975. *Class, Bureaucracy, and Schools: The Illusion of Educational Change in America*, exp. ed. New York: Praeger.

Katznelson, Ira, and Margaret Weir. 1985. *Schooling for All: Race, Class, and the Decline of the Democratic Ideal.* New York: Basic Books.

Kean, Thomas H. 1988a. *The Politics of Inclusion.* New York: Free Press.

———. 1988b. Signing Message on Laws of 1987, Chapter 398. Trenton, NJ: State Library Legislative History Collection.

Kelman, Stephen, and John N. Friedman. 2009. "Performance Improvement and Performance Dysfunction: An Empirical Examination of Distortionary Impacts of the Emergency Room Wait-Time Target in the English National Health Service." *Journal of Public Administration Research and Theory* 19:917–46.

Kettl, Donald F. 2005. *The Global Public Management Revolution*, 2nd ed. Washington, DC: Brookings Institution Press.

———. 2007. "The *Next* Government of the United States: Challenges for Performance in the 21st Century." In *Reflections on 21st Century Government Management*. Washington, DC: IBM Center for the Business of Government.

Kingdon, John W. 1984. *Agendas, Alternatives, and Public Policies*. New York: HarperCollins.

Kirst, Michael W. 1988. "Recent State Education Reform in the United States: Looking Backward and Forward." *Educational Administration Quarterly* 24:319–28.

Kluger, Richard. 1975. *Simple Justice: The History of Brown v. Board of Education and Black America's Struggle for Equality*. New York: Vintage Books.

Koretz, Daniel. 2008. *Measuring Up: What Educational Testing Really Tells Us*. Cambridge, MA: Harvard University Press.

Labaree, David F. 1997. *How to Succeed in School without Really Learning: The Credentials Race in American Education*. New Haven, CT: Yale University Press.

Lehigh, Scot. 1992. "Pace Picks Up on School Reform." *Boston Globe*, December 3.

Lehne, Richard. 1978. *The Quest for Justice: The Politics of School Finance Reform*. New York: Longman.

Levy, Frank. 1971. *Northern Schools and Civil Rights: The Racial Imbalance Act of Massachusetts*. Chicago: Markham.

Lipsky, M. 1980. *Street-Level Bureaucracy: Dilemmas of the Individual in Public Services*. New York: Russell Sage Foundation.

Lortie, Dan C. 2002 [1975]. *Schoolteacher*, 2nd ed. Chicago: University of Chicago Press.

Lukas, J. Anthony. 1985. *Common Ground: A Turbulent Decade in the Lives of Three American Families*. New York: Vintage Books.

MacInnes, Gordon. 2009. *In Plain Sight: Simple, Difficult Lessons from New Jersey's Expensive Effort to Close the Achievement Gap*. New York: Century Foundation Press.

Malen, Betty. 2003. "Tightening the Grip? The Impact of State Activism on Local School Systems." *Educational Policy* 24:113–132.

Manna, Paul. 2006. *School's In: Federalism and the National Education Agenda*. Washington, DC: Georgetown University Press.

Manzo, Kathleen Kennedy. 2003. "Lawmakers Pursue Flexible Text Selection." *Education Week* 22 (May 21), 17, 21.

Marchant, G. J., S. E. Paulson, and A. Shunk. 2006. "Relationships between High-Stakes Testing Policies and Student Achievement after Controlling for Demographic Factors in Aggregated Data." *Education Policy Analysis Archives* 14 (30), http://epaa.asu.edu/epaa/v14n30.

Massachusetts Department of Education. 1986. *Chapter 188: The Massachusetts School Improvement Act, 1985—A Snapshot of Program Implementation as of October 1986*. Quincy: Massachusetts Department of Education.

Massachusetts Department of Elementary and Secondary Education (2009). *Spring*

2009 MCAS Tests: Summary of State Results. Malden, MA: Massachusetts Department of Elementary and Secondary Education.

Massachusetts Department of Revenue, Division of Local Services. N.d. *Everything You Always Wanted to Know about Levy Limits . . . but Were Afraid to Ask: A Primer on Proposition 2½.* Boston: Massachusetts Department of Revenue. http://www.cltg.org/primer-prop.pdf.

Massachusetts Foundation Budget Review Commission. 2001. "Report of the Foundation Budget Review Commission." Boston, MA: Massachusetts Foundation Budget Review Commission.

Massachusetts General Court, Education Committee. 1987. Hearing materials, March 5. Massachusetts State Archives, CO22/352X, Box 16.

———. 1991. Hearing materials, April 2. Massachusetts State Archives, CO22/352X, Box 25.

MBAE (Massachusetts Business Alliance for Education). 1991. "Every Child a Winner!" Boston, MA: Massachusetts Business Alliance for Education. www.mbae.org/uploads/13102003114120EveryChildAWinner.pdf.

MBE (Massachusetts Board of Education). 1978. *Policy on Basic Skills Improvement.* Boston: Massachusetts Board of Education.

———. 1991. "Report of the Subcommittee on Distressed School Districts and School Reform." Boston: Massachusetts Department of Education.

———. 2005. "Minutes of the Regular Meeting," June 28.

———. 2006. "Minutes of the Regular Meeting," May 23.

McDermott, Kathryn A. 1998. "Regionalism Forestalled: Metropolitan Fragmentation and Desegregation Planning in Greater New Haven, Connecticut." In *Changing Urban Education*, edited by Clarence N. Stone, 45–65. Lawrence: University Press of Kansas.

———. 1999. *Controlling Public Education: Localism versus Equity.* Lawrence: University Press of Kansas.

———. 2001. "Diversity or Desegregation? Implications of Arguments for Diversity in K–12 and Higher Education." *Educational Policy* 15:452–73.

———. 2004. "Systemic Reform in Massachusetts: Implementing the Massachusetts Education Reform Act, 1993–2003." In *American Education Finance Association 2004 Yearbook*, edited by Kenneth K. Wong and Karen DeMoss. Larchmont, NY: Eye on Education.

———. 2006. "Incentives, Capacity, and Implementation: Evidence from Massachusetts Education Reform." *Journal of Public Administration Research and Theory* 16 (1): 45–65.

———. 2007. "'Expanding the Moral Community' or 'Blaming the Victim?': The Politics of State Accountability Policy." *American Educational Research Journal* 44 (March): 77–111. doi: 10.3102/0002831206299010.

———. 2009. "The Expansion of State Policy Research." In *Handbook of Educational Policy Research*, edited by Gary Sykes, Barbara Schneider, and David Plank, 749–66. New York: Routledge.

McDermott, Kathryn A., Joseph B. Berger, Susan Bowles, Catherine Cunniff Brooks, Andrew M. Churchill, and Andrew Effrat. 2001. *An Analysis of State Capacity to Implement the Massachusetts Education Reform Act of 1993.* Boston: Massachusetts Education Reform Review Commission.

McDermott, Kathryn A., and Elizabeth DeBray-Pelot. 2009. "Accidental Revolution: State Policy Influences on the No Child Left Behind Act." In *The Rising State: How State Power Is Transforming Our Nation's Schools,* edited by Lance D. Fusarelli, Bonnie C. Fusarelli, and Bruce S. Cooper. Albany: State University of New York Press.

McDermott, Kathryn A., and Laura S. Jensen. 2005. "Dubious Sovereignty: Federal Conditions of Aid and the No Child Left Behind Act." *Peabody Journal of Education* 80 (2): 39–56.

McDonnell, Lorraine M. 2004. *Politics, Persuasion, and Educational Testing.* Cambridge, MA: Harvard University Press.

———. 2005. "No Child Left Behind and the Federal Role in Education: Evolution or Revolution?" *Peabody Journal of Education* 80 (2): 19–38.

McGuinn, Patrick. 2007. "New Jersey: Equity Meets Accountability." In *No Remedy Left Behind: Lessons from a Half-Decade of NCLB,* edited by Frederick M. Hess and Chester E. Finn, Jr., 153–78. Washington, DC: American Enterprise Institute.

Meier, Kenneth J., and Laurence J. O'Toole Jr.. 2009. "The Proverbs of New Public Management: Lessons from an Evidence-Based Research Agenda." *American Review of Public Administration* 39 (1): 4–22.

Meier, Kenneth J., Joseph Stewart Jr., and Robert E. England. 1989. *Race, Class, and Education: The Politics of Second-Generation Discrimination.* Madison: University of Wisconsin Press.

Miller, Lisa L. 2007. "The Representational Biases of Federalism: Scope and Bias in the Political Process, Revisited." *Perspectives on Politics* 5 (2): 305–21.

Mintrop, Heinrich. 2004. *Schools on Probation: How Accountability Works (and Doesn't).* New York: Teachers College Press.

Morris, Debra, and Ian Shapiro, eds. 1993. *John Dewey: The Political Writings.* Indianapolis: Hackett Publishing Company, Inc.

Mukamel, Dana B., William D. Spector, Jacqueline S. Zinn, Lynn Huang, David L. Weimer, and Ann Dozier. 2007. "Nursing Homes' Response to the Nursing Home Compare Report Card." *Journal of Gerontology: Social Sciences* 62B (4): S218–25.

Murphy, Jerome T. 1982. "Progress and Problems: The Paradox of State Reform." In *Policy Making in Education: Eighty-First Yearbook of the National Society for the Study of Education,* edited by A. Lieberman and M. W. McLaughlin, 195–214. Chicago: University of Chicago Press.

Murphy, Marjorie. 1990. *Blackboard Unions: The AFT and the NEA, 1900–1980.* Ithaca, NY: Cornell University Press.

NCES (National Center for Education Statistics). 2009. "Digest of Education Statistics 2008," http://nces.ed.gov/pubsearch/pubsinfo.asp?pubid=2009020.

———. 2010. "Digest of Education Statistics 2009." Washington, DC: NCES, http://nces.ed.gov/programs/digest/d09/tables_1.asp.

Nelson, Adam R. 2005. *The Elusive Ideal: Equal Educational Opportunity and the Federal Role in Boston's Public Schools, 1950–1985.* Chicago: University of Chicago Press.

———. 2007. "*Rodriguez, Keyes, Lau,* and *Milliken* Revisited: The Supreme Court and the Meaning of 'Equal Educational Opportunity,' 1973–1974." In *To Educate a Nation: Federal and National Strategies of School Reform,* edited by Carl F. Kaestle and Alyssa E. Lodewick, 202–24. Lawrence: University Press of Kansas.

Neuberger, Katherine K. 1980. Letter to Daniel O'Hern. Trenton: New Jersey State Archives, Papers of Gov. Brendan T. Byrne.

New Jersey Assembly. 1979. "Public Hearing before Assembly Education Committee on Graduation Standards (S-1154)." Trenton: New Jersey Assembly.

New Jersey Assembly, Education Committee. 1988. "Public Hearing before Assembly Education Committee, Assembly Bill 2928 (establishes an eleventh grade high school graduation test)," April 7, 1988. Trenton: Office of Legislative Services, Public Information Office, Hearing Unit.

New Jersey Senate, Committee on Education. 1986a. "First Public Hearing before Senate Education Committee and Assembly Education Committee on Senate Bills 2355, 2356 and Assembly Bills 2926, 2927 (establishment and governance of state operated school districts)," Trenton, NJ (September 16)." Trenton: Office of Legislative Services, Public Information Office, Hearing Unit.

———. 1986b. "Second Public Hearing before Senate Education Committee and Assembly Education Committee on Senate Bills 2355, 2356 and Assembly Bills 2926, 2927 (establishment and governance of state operated school districts)," Paramus, NJ (September 25)." Trenton: Office of Legislative Services, Public Information Office, Hearing Unit.

———. 1986c. "Third Public Hearing before Senate Education Committee and Assembly Education Committee on Senate Bills 2355, 2356 and Assembly Bills 2926, 2927 (establishment and governance of state operated school districts)," Camden, NJ (October 7, 1986)." Trenton: Office of Legislative Services, Public Information Office, Hearing Unit.

———. 1986d. "Fourth Public Hearing before Senate Education Committee and Assembly Education Committee on Senate Bills 2355, 2356 and Assembly Bills 2926, 2927 (establishment and governance of state operated school districts)," Jersey City, NJ (October 14, 1986)." Trenton: Office of Legislative Services, Public Information Office, Hearing Unit.

NGA (National Governors' Association). 1986. *Time for Results.* Washington, DC: NGA.

Norman, Michael. 1985. "Kean Urges a Broader GOP and Lists Goals for 2d Term." *New York Times,* November 6.

Oakes, Jeannie. 1985. *Keeping Track: How Schools Structure Inequality.* New Haven, CT: Yale University Press.

O'Brien, Meredith. 1991. "Aging and Trash Overrides Prevail." *Holyoke Transcript-Telegram*, November 6.

Onishi, N. 1995. "Imbalance Persists, Defying Courts." *New York Times*, June 11.

Orfield, Gary. 1969. *The Reconstruction of Southern Education: The Schools and the 1964 Civil Rights Act*. New York: Wiley-Interscience.

Orfield, Gary, and Susan Eaton. 1996. *Dismantling Desegregation: The Quiet Reversal of* Brown v. Board of Education. New York: Norton.

Osborne, David E. 1988. *Laboratories of Democracy*. Cambridge, MA: Harvard Business School Press.

Palmer, Robert F. 1969. "New Jersey Department of Education." In *Education in the States: Historical Development and Outlook*, edited by J. B. Pearson and E. Fuller, 812–38. Washington, DC: National Education Association.

Patterson, James T. 2005. *Restless Giant: The United States from Watergate to* Bush v. Gore. New York: Oxford University Press.

Pear, Robert. 1995. "Source of State Power Is Pulled from Ashes." *New York Times*, April 16.

Peirce, Neal R. 1972. *The Megastates of America: People, Politics, and Power in the Ten Great States*. New York: Norton.

Peters, T. J., and R. H. Waterman, 1982. *In Search of Excellence: Lessons from America's Best-Run Companies*. New York: Harper and Row.

Purkey, Stewart C., and Marshall S. Smith. 1982. "Too Soon to Cheer? Synthesis of Research on Effective Schools." *Educational Leadership* 40 (3): 64–69.

———. 1983. "Effective Schools: A Review." *Elementary School Journal* 83 (4): 426–52.

Radin, Beryl A. 1998. "The Government Performance and Results Act (GPRA): Hydra-Headed Monster or Flexible Management Tool?" *Public Administration Review* 58 (4): 307–16.

———. 2002. *The Accountable Juggler: The Art of Leadership in a Federal Agency*. Washington, DC: Congressional Quarterly Press.

———. 2006. *Challenging the Performance Movement: Complexity, Accountability, and Democratic Values*. Washington, DC: Georgetown University Press.

Raudenbush, Stephen W. 2009. "The *Brown* Legacy and the O'Connor Challenge: Transforming Schools in the Images of Children's Potential." *Educational Researcher* 38 (3): 169–80.

Ravitch, Diane. 1983. *The Troubled Crusade: American Education, 1945–1980*. New York: Basic Books.

Ray, Carol Axtell, and Roslyn Arlin Mickelson. 1990. "Business Leaders and the Politics of School Reform." In *Education Politics for the New Century: The Twentieth Anniversary Yearbook of the Politics of Education Association*, edited by Douglas E. Mitchell and Margaret E. Goertz, 119–35. New York: Falmer.

Rebell, Michael A. 2009. *Courts and Kids: Pursuing Educational Equity through the State Courts*. Chicago: University of Chicago Press.

Reed, Douglas S. 2001. *On Equal Terms: The Constitutional Politics of Equal Opportunity*. Princeton, NJ: Princeton University Press.

———. 2009. "Is There an Expectations Gap? Educational Federalism and the Demographic Distribution of Proficiency Cut Scores." *American Educational Research Journal* 46:718–42.

Reese, William J. 1986. *Power and the Promise of School Reform: Grassroots Movements during the Progressive Era*. Boston: Routledge and Kegan Paul.

———. 2005. *America's Public Schools: From the Common School to "No Child Left Behind."* Baltimore, MD: Johns Hopkins University Press.

Rennie Center for Education Research and Policy 2005. *Reaching Capacity: A Blueprint for the State Role in Improving Low Performing Schools and Districts*. Boston: Reenie Center. http://renniecenter.issuelab.org/research/listing/reaching_capacity_a_blueprint_for_the_state_role_in_improving_low_performing_schools_and_districts.

Riccucci, Norma M., and Frank J. Thompson. 2008. "The New Public Management, Homeland Security, and the Politics of Civil Service Reform." *Public Administration Review* 68 (5): 877–90.

Robelen, Erik. 2002. "States, Ed. Dept. Reach Accords on 1994 ESEA." *Education Week*, April 17.

Rogers, David L. 1968. *110 Livingston Street: Politics and Bureaucracy in the New York City Schools*. New York: Random House.

Romzek, Barbara S., and Melvin J. Dubnick. 1987. "Accountability in the Public Sector: Lessons from the *Challenger* Tragedy." *Public Administration Review* 47 (May–June): 227–38.

Rosenberg, Gerald N. 1991. *The Hollow Hope: Can Courts Bring About Social Change?* Chicago: University of Chicago Press.

Rothstein, Robert. 2004. *Class and Schools: Using Social, Economic, and Educational Reform to Close the Black-White Achievement Gap*. Washington, DC: Economic Policy Institute.

Salmore, Barbara G., and Stephen A. Salmore. 1998. *New Jersey Politics and Government: Suburban Politics Comes of Age*, 2nd ed. Lincoln: University of Nebraska Press.

Savoie, Donald J. 1995. "What Is Wrong with the New Public Management?" *Canadian Public Administration* 38 (1): 112–21.

Schattschneider, E. E. 1960. *The Semi-Sovereign People: A Realist's View of Democracy in America*. New York: Holt, Rinehart, and Winston.

Scheurich, J. J., and L. Skrla. 2001. "Continuing the Conversation on Equity and Accountability: Listening Appreciatively, Responding Responsibly." *Phi Delta Kappan* 83 (4): 322–26.

Schwartz, Robert B. 2003. "The Emerging State Leadership Role in Education Reform: Notes of a Participant-Observer." In *A Nation Reformed?*, edited by D. T. Gordon. Cambridge, MA: Harvard Education Press.

Segers, Mary C. 2006. "Religious Advocacy in New Jersey." In *Representing God at the Statehouse: Religion and Politics in the American States*, edited by Edward L. Cleary and Allen D. Hertzke, 1–25. Lanham, MD: Rowman & Littlefield.

Sipple, John W., Cecil G. Miskel, Timothy M. Matheney, and C. Philip Kearney. 1997. "The Creation and Development of an Interest Group: Life at the Intersection of Big Business and Education Reform." *Educational Administration Quarterly* 33 (October): 440–73. doi: 10.1177/0013161X97033004003.

Smith, Marshall S., and Jennifer O'Day. 1991. "Systematic School Reform." In *The Politics of Curriculum and Testing: Politics of Education Association Yearbook 1990*, edited by Susan H. Fuhrman and Betty Malen, 233–67. New York: Falmer.

Smith, Peter. 1995. "On the Unintended Consequences of Publishing Performance Data in the Public Sector." *International Journal of Public Administration* 18 (2–3): 277–310.

Spillane, James. 2004. *Standards Deviation: How Schools Misunderstand Education Policy.* Cambridge, MA: Harvard University Press.

Springer, Matthew G., and James W. Guthrie. 2007. "The Politicization of the School Finance Legal Process." In *School Money Trials: The Legal Pursuit of Educational Adequacy*, edited by Martin R. West and Paul E. Peterson, 102–30. Washington, DC: Brookings Institution Press.

Stark, Andrew. 2002. "What *Is* the New Public Management?" *Journal of Public Administration Research and Theory* 12 (1): 137–51.

Steiner, L. 2005. *State Takeovers of Individual Schools.* Naperville, IL: Learning Point Associates.

Stoker, Robert P. 1991. *Reluctant Partners: Implementing Federal Policy.* Pittsburgh: University of Pittsburgh Press.

Stone, Deborah. 2002. *Policy Paradox: The Art of Political Decision Making*, rev. ed. New York: W.W. Norton.

Stonecash, Jeffrey M., and Mary P. McGuire. 2003. *The Emergence of State Government: Parties and New Jersey Politics, 1950–2000.* Madison, NJ: Fairleigh Dickinson University Press.

Strang, David. 1987. "The Administrative Transformation of American Education: School District Consolidation, 1938–1980." *Administrative Science Quarterly* 32 (September): 352–66.

Sugrue, Thomas J. 2008. *Sweet Land of Liberty: The Forgotten Struggle for Civil Rights in the North.* New York: Random House.

Sullivan, Joseph F. 1986a. "Kean Seeks State Control of Worst School Systems." *New York Times*, June 22.

———. 1986b. "Kean Sticks by Plan for Tougher Test." *New York Times*, March 2.

———. 1986c. "Kean Takes His Message of 'Inclusion' on the Road." *New York Times*, June 1.

———. 1987. "Kean and Jersey City Mayor Clash on Schools." *New York Times*, December 16.

Swartz, Janet P., and Barbara Dillon Goodson. 1988. *Chapter 188 State Report on High School Graduation Requirements.* Boston: Abt Associates.

Tamir, Eran. 2006. "The Politics of Education Reform: State Power and the Field of Educational Policy in New Jersey." PhD diss., Michigan State University.

Taylor, Jeannette. 2009. "Strengthening the Link between Performance Measurement and Decision Making." *Public Administration* 87 (4): 853–71.

Therriault, Susan Bowles. 2005. "The Beginning of Intervention: A Study of the Working Relationship between the State Department of Education and Underperforming Schools during the Implementation of a New School Accountability Policy." EdD diss., University of Massachusetts, Amherst.

Timar, Thomas. 1997. "The Institutional Role of State Education Departments: A Historical Perspective." *American Journal of Education* 105 (May): 231–260.

Toch, Thomas. 1991. *In the Name of Excellence: The Struggle to Reform the Nation's Schools, Why It's Failing, and What Should Be Done.* New York: Oxford University Press.

Trebilcock, Michael J. 1995. "Can Government Be Reinvented?" In *The State under Contract*, edited by Jonathan Boston, 1–35. Wellington, New Zealand: Bridget Williams Books, Ltd.

Tyack, David. 1974. *The One Best System: A History of American Urban Education.* Cambridge, MA: Harvard University Press.

———. 1986. "Toward a Social History of Law and Public Education." In *School Days, Rule Days: The Legalization and Regulation of Education*, edited by David L. Kirp and Donald L. Jensen, 212–37. Philadelphia: Falmer Press.

Tyack, David, and Elizabeth Hansot. 1982. *Managers of Virtue: Public School Leadership in America, 1820–1980.* New York: Basic Books.

Tyack, David, Thomas James, and Aaron Benavot. 1987. *Law and the Shaping of Public Education, 1785–1954.* Madison: University of Wisconsin Press.

Urban, Wayne J. 1982. *Why Teachers Organized.* Detroit, MI: Wayne State University Press.

Van Tassel, Priscilla. 1986a. "School 'Takeover Plan' Criticized." *New York Times*, July 27.

———. 1986b. "State May Force Building of a School." *New York Times*, February 9.

Vannemann, Alan, Linda Hamilton, Janet Baldwin Anderson, and Taslima Rahman. 2009. *Achievement Gaps: How Black and White Students in Public Schools Perform in Mathematics and Reading on the National Assessment of Educational Progress.* Washington, DC: U.S. Department of Education.

Verstegan, Deborah A., and Terry Whitney. 1997. "From Courthouses to Schoolhouses: Emerging Judicial Theories of Adequacy and Equity." *Educational Policy* 11 (September): 330–52.

Vinovskis, Maris. 1999. *The Road to Charlottesville: The 1989 Education Summit.* Washington, DC: National Education Goals Panel.

Vlanderen, Russell B. 1980. *State Minimum Competency Testing Programs: Review and Resources.* Washington, DC: National Institute of Education.

Vold, David J., and Joseph L. DeVitis, eds. 1991. *Education Reform in the Deep South: A Critical Appraisal.* Tuscaloosa: University of Alabama Press.

Walker, J. L. 1969. "The Diffusion of Innovations among the American States," *American Political Science Review* 63: 880–99.

Wall, Kay. 1994. Presentation Materials from General Assembly Education Committee Hearing, March 11. Hartford: Connecticut State Library, Bill File for S.B. 321.

Waller, Willard. 1965 [1932]. *The Sociology of Teaching*. New York: John Wiley and Sons.

Weick, Karl E. 1976. "Educational Organizations as Loosely Coupled Systems." *Administrative Science Quarterly* 21 (March): 1–19.

West, Martin R., and Paul E. Peterson. 2007. "The Adequacy Lawsuit: A Critical Appraisal." In *School Money Trials: The Legal Pursuit of Educational Adequacy*, edited by Martin R. West and Paul E. Peterson, 1–22. Washington, DC: Brookings Institution Press.

Wetzler, Lauren A. 2004. "Buying Equality: How School Finance Reform and Desegregation Came to Compete in Connecticut." *Yale Law and Policy Review* 22:481–524.

Wilson, James Q. 1989. *Bureaucracy: What Government Agencies Do and Why They Do It*. New York: Basic Books, Inc.

Winans, R. Foster. 1980. "Trenton Schools: No Resolution Yet." *New York Times*, November 23.

Woodward, C. Vann. 1974. *The Strange Career of Jim Crow*, 3rd. rev. ed. New York: Oxford University Press.

Wright, David J. 2001. "Empowerment Zones and the Promise of Accountability." In *Quicker, Better, Cheaper? Managing Performance in American Government*, edited by Dall W. Forsythe, 245–85. Albany, NY: Rockefeller Institute Press.

Yaffe, Deborah. 2007. *Other People's Children: The Battle for Justice and Equality in New Jersey's Schools*. New Brunswick, NJ: Rivergate Books.

Yin, Robert K. 1994. *Case Study Research: Design and Methods*. 2nd ed. Thousand Oaks, CA: Sage Publications.

Zernike, Kate. 1995. "Silber Shocker; Calls for End to Busing, Bilingual Classes." *Quincy (MA) Patriot Ledger*, November 8.

Ziebarth, T. 2002. *ECS StateNote: Accountability—Rewards and Sanctions*. Denver: Education Commission of the States.

———. 2004. *State Takeovers and Reconstitutions*. Denver: Education Commission of the States.

Index

Page numbers followed by f indicate figures; those followed by t indicate tables.